Star Authors

Star Authors

Literary Celebrity in America

Joe Moran

Pluto  Press

LONDON • STERLING, VIRGINIA

First published 2000 by Pluto Press
345 Archway Road, London N6 5AA
and 22883 Quicksilver Drive, Sterling, VA 20166-2012, USA

British Library Cataloguing in Publication Data
A catalogue record for this book is available from the British Library

ISBN 0 7453 1524 0 hbk

Library of Congress Cataloging in Publication Data

Moran, Joe, 1970-
    Star authors : literary celebrity in America / Joe Moran.
        p.   cm.
    Based on the author's thesis (doctoral)-University of Sussex.
    Includes bibliographical references.
    ISBN 0-7453-1524-0 (hbk)
    1. American literature–20th century–History and criticism. 2, Authors and
readers-United States–History–20th century. 3. Popular culture–United
States–History–20th century. 4. Acker, Kathy, 1948–Appreciation–United
States. 5. DeLillo, Don–Appreciation–United States. 6. Updike, John–
Appreciation–United States. 7. Roth, Philip–Appreciation–United States. 8.
Celebrities–United States. 9. Canon (Literature) 1. Title.

PS225 .M67 2000
8l0.9′0054–dc21   99-054537

Designed and produced for Pluto Press by
Chase Production Services, Chadlington, OX7 3LN
Typeset from disk by Marina typesetting, Minsk, Belarus
Printed in the European Union by T. J. International, Padstow

Contents

Acknowledgements

This book began life as a doctoral thesis at the University of Sussex and it is a pleasure to thank my supervisor, Stephen Fender, for all his advice and encouragement. I would also like to thank Ross Dawson, Geoff Hemstedt, Michael Moran, Win Moran, Douglas Tallack and my editor, Anne Beech, for many helpful comments and suggestions. Some brief sections of this book first appeared in very different form in the *Journal of American Studies* (vol. 29, no. 3 (December 1995)), *Media, Culture and Society* (vol. 19, no. 3 (July 1997)) and the *International Journal of Cultural Studies* (vol. 1, no. 1 (April 1998)), and I am grateful to Cambridge University Press and Sage Publications for permission to republish. This book is for mum and dad, with love and thanks.

1
Introduction: The Charismatic Illusion

There is no avoiding authors in contemporary American culture. The books and arts sections of newspapers and magazines are filled with author-interviews and profiles and features about them; they crop up on talk shows and other television programmes, as well as infomercials and shopping channels; they draw audiences to readings, lectures, signings, book fairs, literary festivals, public debates and writers' conferences. Aside from these concrete appearances, they also circulate in a more nebulous sphere of gossip and rumour, as the media reproduce speculation about their private lives, peer-group rivalries and million-dollar publishing deals, run articles about where to spot the most fashionable literary celebrities around town and produce helpful charts for readers ranking writers according to their status and visibility, revealing which are 'in' and which are 'out'.[1] What is going on here, in this culture in which, as one commentator puts it, 'Nobel laureates in literature give their recipes to the New York *Times* living section'?[2] If celebrity authors hardly rival their counterparts in film, television and popular music for column inches, they are still a significant cultural phenomenon, one well worth examining critically.

This book is about this phenomenon of literary celebrity – how it is produced and disseminated, what kinds of meanings are attached to it, and how celebrity authors themselves have grappled with and added to these meanings in their work. Above all, I want to challenge the way the emergence of literary celebrity is most commonly explained – in terms of the vulgarization of literary life by commercial mass media in America. In this argument, contemporary literary fame becomes part of the overall pervasiveness of 'entertainment celebrity' (any fame linked to the sphere of popular culture) which is seen as 'an imperialist phenomenon, moving into new arenas and making them over in its own image'.[3] More specifically, it is linked to the ubiquity of media images in contemporary culture and a new emphasis on mere visibility or notoriety as a source of fame. This recalls Daniel Boorstin's seminal definition of the celebrity as being simply *well-known for his well-knowness* ... the human pseudo-event', a perniciously artificial figure produced by the influence of mass media on American culture and society. According to Boorstin, 'the star system has reached far beyond the movies. Wherever it reaches it confuses traditional forms of achievement. It focuses on the personality rather than on the work. It puts a premium on well-knowness for its own sake'. He notes, for example, the way in which 'the American publishing scene has been dominated by a few stars ... who have prospered as authors partly because they could be touted as "personalities"'.[4]

Like Boorstin's distinction between the traditional figure of the 'hero' and the contemporary 'celebrity' – the former being 'a big man' and the latter simply 'a big name'[5] – much of the existing discussion of literary celebrity is in jeremiadic vein, opposing the hype and publicity of celebrity to an earlier, purer form of deserved fame. A *Newsweek* article from the 1980s – a time of frantic buyouts of publishing firms and the introduction of sophisticated new marketing techniques into the book industry – put it in these terms:

> Open just about any magazine today, turn on any talk show, and you'll find a writer holding forth ... on where he gets his ideas, what he eats for breakfast and, of course, the state of the American novel. Imagine what Herman Melville ... would have thought of Jerzy Kosinski half-naked on the cover of the *New York Times Magazine* ... What would he have made of John Irving scantily clad in wrestler's briefs to advertise the new magazine *Vanity Fair*? ... Melville, who made an average of $1,600 a year at his writing peak and was therefore one of the best-paid authors of his day, might find it hard to credit the vast sums of money that now flow toward writers whose faces flash across the country on the covers of national magazines and whose images enter America's living rooms via cathode-ray tubes.[6]

This descension narrative, contrasting 'serious' literature with the frivolous, titillating agenda of the media and the disposability of consumer culture, is reiterated in academic cultural criticism. John Cawelti, for example, makes a clear distinction between literary 'fame' and contemporary literary 'celebrity':

The test of artistic fame is that one's words or images remain in the minds of men; the test of celebrity is being followed everywhere by a photographer ... The object of celebrity is the person; the object of fame is some accomplishment, action, or creative work.[7]

Alan Spiegel similarly agrees that the turning of contemporary authors into public curiosities serves them up as part of the meaningless ephemera of consumerism:

Celebrity watching is still one of this culture's most efficient antidotes to the poison of dead time in a leisure economy; our national pastime of converting an artist into a screen star while dragging his art along as a stand-in is the customary price serious work usually pays for permission to leave the cell of the specialist and enter the marketplace.[8]

These comments seem to tap into general anxieties in postmodern, mediatized culture about the replacement of the 'real' with surface image, and the subsequent blurring of boundaries between reality and fiction, public and private, high and low culture.

It is possible, though, to challenge this narrative from two perspectives. First, its view of mass culture can be seen as too uniformly hostile: critical discussions of mainstream celebrity have moved on from early accounts by critics like Boorstin, James Monaco and Christopher Lasch which characterized stars as uncomplicatedly shallow and superficial, distinguished from 'ordinary' people by notoriety rather than genuine achievement.[9] More recent work on celebrities in the sphere of commercial entertainment by Richard Dyer, Joshua Gamson, P. David Marshall and others has challenged these straightforward oppositions between performance and work, surface and depth, promotional packaging and content. It has shown that celebrity is an unstable, multifaceted phenomenon – the product of a complex negotiation between cultural producers and audiences, the purveyor of both dominant and resistant cultural meanings and a pivotal point of contention in debates about the relationship between cultural authority and exchange value in capitalist societies. This new emphasis is part of a larger trend within cultural studies which has challenged early attempts to dismiss popular culture as formulaic and one-dimensional, and presented it instead as heterogeneous and open to multiple readings.

Second, the complicated relationship between cultural elites and the marketplace means that literary celebrity is different in significant ways from the celebrity produced by commercial mass media. The encroachment of market values on to literary production, while clearly having a major impact on literary celebrity, has not occurred in a vacuum – it forms part of a complicated process in which various legitimating bodies compete for cultural authority and/or commercial success, and regulate the formation of a literary star system and the shifting hierarchy of stars. Literary celebrity in the US is not simply an adjunct of mainstream celebrity, but an elaborate system of representations in its own right, produced and circulated across a wide variety of media. Rather than being a straightforward effect of the commodification of culture, it raises significant questions about the relationship between literature and the marketplace, and between 'high', 'low' and 'middlebrow' culture in contemporary America.

'The Cultural Value Stock Exchange'

In order to begin to make sense of some of these questions, this book will need to examine them in relation to wider theories about the relationship between cultural and economic capital. In this connection, the work of the French sociologist, Pierre Bourdieu, is particularly useful. Bourdieu's work on culture is specifically concerned with the struggles for power and position amongst cultural producers which result when traditional systems of authority – such as those provided by ecclesiastical and aristocratic patronage – collapse. He argues that there has been a historical development since the decline of these old forms of patronage and the first emergence of a literary marketplace, by which the social sphere of writers and other cultural producers has grown larger, more sophisticated and more 'autonomized', transforming itself into 'a field of relations governed by a specific logic: competition for cultural legitimacy'.[10]

The term 'field' is a crucial concept in Bourdieu's work – it describes a semi-autonomous, structured system with its own internal logic, rules of operation and inherently hierarchical relationships created by the struggle between agents for whichever form of capital is appropriate to that field – the principal forms being symbolic, social, economic and cultural. The field of cultural production, according to Bourdieu, is specifically concerned with the creation and dissemination of cultural capital within what he refers to as 'the cultural value stock exchange'.[11] Cultural producers are relatively autonomous, gaining power within this field by the extent of their separation from other fields, by investing in cultural capital which has an ostensibly antagonistic relationship to other forms of capital – particularly economic capital. In fact, according to Bourdieu, cultural capital is only gained when directly economic interests are either absent or concealed, because they threaten the field's claim to a monopoly of influence over which cultural goods are valued. The individualization of the author or artist as a person with special gifts or qualities (what Bourdieu calls the 'charismatic illusion'[12]) is the focal point of this separation of cultural from economic capital – it is 'the ultimate basis of belief in the value of a work of art and ... is therefore the basis of functioning of the field of production and circulation of cultural commodities'.[13] Leo Braudy's more general history of fame argues in similar vein that the idea of the famous author as distanced from and superior to other kinds of public notoriety – and in particular as occupying a privileged position outside the sphere of exchange and profit – has been inscribed in the concept of literary fame since the displacement of aristocratic patronage by the rise of the author as individual entrepreneur within the literary marketplace.[14]

Although Bourdieu argues that power within the field of cultural production is gained by those who present themselves as free of outside influences, however, there are also different sectors which vary in their level of autonomy from other fields. Indeed, Bourdieu uses the relatively loose term, 'field', precisely to point to its provisional, relational and conflictual nature, the fact that it is made up of constant struggles between dominant and peripheral figures. He sees the field of cultural production as being divided roughly into two subfields: the 'pure' subfield of restricted production and the 'extended' subfield of large-scale production. The subfield of restricted production is an 'autonomous' grouping associated with elite culture and organized around the specific, self-contained interests of the field, in which commercial success is frowned upon and the myth of the individual producer as charismatic genius is most prevalent; the subfield of large-scale production, in contrast, is a 'heteronomous' sphere in which success is primarily measured by commercial gain, the satiation of a pre-existent demand, the widest popular success and other forms of capital not specific to the field, and the status of individual producers is correspondingly at its lowest.[15] (As an example of this, one could point to the ways in which popular genre and pulp fiction have traditionally been viewed as less firmly linked to an individual author than more 'literary' texts.) Bourdieu, however, emphasizes the dynamic nature of these subfields and their continual mutual interaction and conflict, so that the field of cultural production as a whole is 'a *field of forces*, but it is also a *field of struggles* tending to transform or conserve this field of forces'.[16] In other words, there is a constant battle between agents occupying different points of hierarchy within each field and correspondingly different levels of autonomy from other fields, about what Bourdieu calls 'the rules of the game' – the role and purpose of authors and artists and the work they produce. As he puts it:

The struggle between occupants of the two opposite poles of the field of cultural production has at stake the monopoly on the imposition of the legitimate definition of the writer, and it is comprehensibly organized around the opposition between autonomy and heteronomy.[17]

It must be said that, although he continually emphasizes the applicability of his ideas to other countries, much of Bourdieu's extensive ethnographic research is specific to France – and, in particular, the class stratifications in French society which inform his general notion that literature, art and culture fulfil 'a social function of legitimating social differences'.[18] However, his theory of the competition for different forms of capital within and between different fields provides a useful analytical framework for examining literary celebrity in the United States, since my argument in this book is that this phenomenon tends be mediated in such a way that the author represents both cultural capital and marketable commodity. In general, celebrity in the United States has been conferred on authors who have the potential to be commercially successful and penetrate into mainstream media, but are also perceived as in some sense culturally 'authoritative' – in other words, they occupy a contested area of cultural production between the restricted and extended subfields.

Consider, for example, some of the bestselling authors in America (and the world) today: John Grisham, Danielle Steel, Thomas Harris, Scott Turow, Michael Crichton, Tom Clancy, Stephen King – famous people certainly, but writers more read than read about. Celebrity authors, by contrast, tend to be (for example) those who are reviewed and discussed in the media at length, who win literary prizes, whose books are studied in universities and who are employed on talk shows as what one host (Merv Griffin) once called 'heavy furniture', adding 'the minor authority of the authorial' to the proceedings as a serious counterweight to the more lightweight celebrities on view.[19] They are, in short, usually 'crossover' successes who emphasize both marketability and traditional cultural hierarchies, occupying what Charles Newman describes as 'that immense and pleasurable space between belletristic coterie and mass-market hype'.[20] Bourdieu's theories will therefore be useful in working through some of the tensions involved in the production of literary celebrity between the legitimacy of culture and the less ambiguous sanction of the marketplace. Literary celebrity clearly complicates the moralistic approach of Boorstin and others – it is either an indication that celebrity is now worryingly omnipresent and that even high culture is 'dumbing down', or that the cultural pessimists have misunderstood the complex dynamics by which fame and reputation are acquired in contemporary culture.

Since they tend to straddle the divide between the restricted and extended subfields of cultural production, celebrity authors are ambiguous figures. As cultural signifiers they often contain elements of the idea of the charismatic, uniquely inspired creative artist associated with the autonomization of the cultural field, but they also gain legitimacy from the notion of celebrity as supported by broad popularity and success in the marketplace. In fact, the ambivalence with which literary celebrities are often represented itself feeds into the conflicted ideologies of celebrity in general, drawing simultaneously as it does on aristocratic notions of fame as the setting apart of a natural elite and democratic-capitalist notions of fame as inclusive and meritocratic.[21] Literary celebrities are also controversial and much-discussed figures in American cultural life because they have a contentiously intermediate position in relation to literary production as a whole. They have thus been at the centre of an ongoing debate – particularly between cultural producers in the restricted and extended subfields – about the relationship between literature and the market. A number of critics have already pointed to the historical significance of this struggle over cultural legitimation in the US between traditional highbrow standard-bearers who insist on the absolute separation of art and commerce, and proponents of popular and middlebrow culture who insist on their commensurability.[22]

Although, as Ken Worpole has suggested, those who argue that the literary world has been overtaken by commercialism often suppose that this has been 'a recent and regrettable phenomenon, evidence after all of the final collapse of cultural values in the face of relentless consumerism and the bitter exigencies of mass production',[23] this debate has actually been going on ever since the emergence of literature as a commodity within capitalism. My emphasis in this book is primarily contemporary, but I also want to show that literary celebrity has a historical context in the United States which dates back to at least the middle of the nineteenth century. The dividing line between premodern 'fame' and mediatized 'celebrity' is, as Braudy has shown, by no means clear-cut – he traces the beginnings of 'a modern international European fame culture' as far back as the eighteenth century, when the development of a market culture allowed ambitious individuals to press themselves into the cultural void created by the decline of the traditional sources of power and influence – the church, the monarchy and the aristocracy. Before the eighteenth century, for example, the author's aristocratic patron was perceived as the more likely candidate for fame as the subject of the author's work, whilst the author was compensated with the favourable judgement of posterity, but with the emergence of the modern literary marketplace the author began to achieve an independent status and became a candidate for public esteem. Questioning

Boorstin's assumption that 'heroism and its expression can ever really be fully separated', Braudy suggests that fame has always been 'enhanced by and feed[s] upon the available means of reproducing the image'.[24] This historical grounding – examining the emergence of literary celebrity in the US in relation to the development of early forms of mass media in the nineteenth century – will help to provide a context to the contemporary debates and controversies which surround celebrity authors.

The Individualization of Authorship

In *Mythologies*, his classic deconstruction of the cultural artefacts of 1950s France, Roland Barthes uses a typical example of how writers are discussed in mainstream culture – the magazine or newspaper profile – to point to this complicated relationship between cultural authority and celebrity visibility in the representation of famous authors. Barthes highlights a common feature of these profiles (both in France and elsewhere), which is the attempt to show the author in prosaic circumstances, ostensibly to highlight his or her 'ordinariness'. He argues that in this convention the writer

> concedes that he is endowed with a human existence, with an old country house, with relatives, with shorts, with a small daughter, etc.; but unlike the other workers, who change their essence, and on the beach are no longer anything but holiday-makers, the writer keeps his writer's nature everywhere. By having holidays, he displays the sign of his being human; but the god remains, one is a writer as Louis XIV was king, even on the commode. Thus the function of the man of letters is to human labour rather as ambrosia is to bread: a miraculous, eternal substance, which condescends to take a social form so that its prestigious difference is better grasped. All this prepares one for the same idea of the writer as superman, as a kind of intrinsically different being which society puts in the window so as to use to the best advantage the artificial singularity which it has granted him.[25]

In one sense, this representation of authors is a typical example of the way in which stars in general are presented in contemporary culture, the ubiquity of celebrity creating what Gamson calls a 'pull between hierarchy and equality', celebrating stars as simultaneously extraordinary and familiar.[26] But there is no doubt that this tension is particularly apparent in the case of authors, the lives and work of whom are ransacked for their human interest at the same time as they are lauded for their difference and aloofness. This paradox shows that literary celebrities cannot simply be reduced to their exchange value – they are complex cultural signifiers who are repositories for all kinds of meanings, the most significant of which is perhaps the nostalgia for some kind of transcendent, anti-economic, creative element in a secular, debased, commercialized culture. They thus reproduce a notion, popular since the Romantic era, of authors and their work as a kind of recuperated 'other', a haven for those creative values which an increasingly rationalistic, utilitarian society cannot otherwise accommodate.[27] In other words, the human impulses that cannot be expressed within the social and economic realities of a society transformed by capitalism are channelled into our representation of authors and artists, who perform the role of spiritually legitimizing society by virtue of their separateness from it.

It is important to unpack the process by which these cultural signifiers are created precisely because the whole logic of literary celebrity is based around mystifying and concealing it, by celebrating the author as an individual of superior talent or even genius, free of external determination – what Walter Benjamin calls

> the overtaxing of the productive person in the name of ... the principle of 'creativity'. This overtaxing is all the more dangerous because as it flatters the self-esteem of the productive person, it effectively guards the interests of a social order that is hostile to him.[28]

In this sense the figure of the literary celebrity conforms to Marx's definition of the fetishized commodity – it works actively to suppress the intricate network of social relations that has produced it. As Bourdieu puts it, this process of individualization 'directs attention to the *apparent producer*, the painter, writer or composer, in short, the "author," suppressing the question of what authorizes the author, what creates the authority with which authors authorize'. He suggests that this process is particularly prevalent within the fields of art and literature: 'There are in fact few other areas in which the glorification of "great individuals," unique creators irreducible to any condition or conditioning, is more common or uncontroversial'.[29] As Barthes has argued, however, it is also true of the celebrity system as a whole, which has a vested interest in disguising its own operations: 'Through star-making society imposes a strong tension which permits the fan to consume stars without however dignifying the processes which produce them'.[30] I want to interrogate this 'taken-for-granted' nature of literary fame – the way in which it helps to naturalize the visibility and authority given to certain kinds of authors and texts. At the same time, as

I have suggested, the peculiar nature of literary celebrity has led to it being the source of perpetual controversy, which provides a useful starting point in any attempt to demystify this naturalized element. This book therefore aims to unravel the cultural meanings of literary celebrity primarily by exploring these debates around it.

The first part of the book examines literary celebrity in relation to three main frameworks: the historical relationship between literature and pub- licity in America, and attempts by commercial media to market the author as public personality; the contemporary literary star system and debates surrounding it; and theoretical and institutional perspectives on author- ship. The second part of the book comprises chapters on the work and careers of four literary celebrities – John Updike, Philip Roth, Don DeLillo and Kathy Acker – which follow up on these issues and discuss how these authors position themselves and have been positioned in relation to their own fame. Celebrity seems to enforce self-reflexiveness: for those authors who experience it, it often becomes a constant preoccupation – they talk and write about it constantly, in both fictional and non-fictional forms, usually describing fame as a negative influence pervading their whole life and work. These authors have been chosen as extended examples because they have each dealt at length with the experience of literary celebrity in their work and in public statements, and because the different ways in which their celebrity has been constructed, including their own attempts to manage and control it, demonstrate the complexity and diversity of the phenomenon. Their work provides them with a unique opportunity to interrogate their feelings of unease about the machinery of celebrity – what Updike calls 'the silken mechanism whereby America reduces her writers to imbecility and cozenage'.[31]

In fact, a central argument of this study is that authors actively negotiate their own celebrity rather than having it simply imposed on them. The book therefore necessarily entails combining cultural and historical contextualization, biographical material and textual analysis. By focus- ing on a subject which demands a study of the intersection between the textual and contextual aspects of American writing, it will argue for some degree of situated agency for authors, without reverting to an uninflected intentionalist stance which risks replicating the assumptions of celebrity itself. Finally, the conclusion points to some wider contexts to the cultural phenomena I have been examining, by considering other kinds of star- dom associated with intellectual production, and literary celebrity beyond the US. The relevance of this latter development to a British readership lies in the pervasive global influence of contemporary American culture and its position at the leading edge of developments in the book industry,

mass media and marketplace culture as a whole. The increasing prominence of the mediagenic, high-profile author in the UK is certainly one of
the more apt demonstrations of the fact that, in commercially oriented
cultural production at least, 'America's present will be Britain's future'.[32]

Part One
Cultural Contexts

2
Mark Twain Absurdity: Literature and Publicity in America

Although star authors are most commonly seen as the products of a media-fixated, market-driven contemporary culture, there are interesting parallels to be drawn between literary celebrity and historical versions of fame, which also point to some of the broader conditions which make the US an especially significant site of celebrity authorship. This chapter therefore seeks to place literary celebrity within the context of the underlying connections between literature and the marketplace in America, and the broader development of a celebrity 'culture industry' from the mid-nineteenth century onwards. It begins by examining the ways in which mass media helped to individualize and promote the figure of the author in the nineteenth century; it then explores how this cult of authorship was continued in the twentieth century through the profiling of authors in massmarket magazines; and finally analyses the intense debates that this produced about the commodification of literature and culture which continue today.

The Emergence of a Star System

In America, traditional means by which writers could gain support and approval – such as aristocratic patronage – were never very strong. The individualization and professionalization of authorship in America from the early nineteenth century onwards thus coincided with the rise of literature as a commodity within a broader system of market exchange, and in particular authorship became entangled with a developing industry of advertising and publicity. A key event here was the emergence, from about 1850 onwards, of advertising as 'a radically new discursive practice ... a center of knowledge production, a determining economic site, as well as a

15

representational system comprising a vastly heterogeneous set of individual artifacts'.[1] Advertising now started to impinge crucially on the ways in which literature was produced and received: by creating a trend for books to be published as serials, either in periodicals or separately, accompanied by advertisements; by subsidizing a whole series of magazines which stimulated an interest in literary personalities; and by indirectly sponsoring other cultural activities which arose out of this new ephemeral print culture.

It may be significant that the word 'celebrity', to mean a famous person rather than the state of being famous, was first used at about the same time – the mid-nineteenth century – that advertising was assuming this new, broadly cultural significance. (The OED dates the first use of the term to 1849.) As Gamson argues, the first stirrings of the star system as mass phenomenon were seen on both sides of the Atlantic around mid-century – partly due to improvements in communications through technological innovations like the telegraph, the rotary press and photography, but mainly because of the expansion in media subsidized by advertising.[2] According to Philip Collins, writers were at the forefront of this new phenomenon, as in the 1850s there emerged, in both Europe and America, 'a new cult of literary personality which made the public eager to see as well as read their favourite authors'.[3] A Dublin newspaper commented on Charles Dickens's reading tours in 1858:

> Nowadays the public must know all about your domestic relations, your personal appearance, your age, the number of your children, the colour of your eyes and hair – must peep into the arcana of your social existence ... A photography likeness sells a book; how much more likely that it would sell when the living author stands before you?[4]

One of the reasons why authors were important at this time, as David Shumway points out, is that books, magazines and newspapers were the dominant mass media before film, radio, television and popular music began to produce other types of stars.[5] John Cawelti's comparison between Dickens's second American tour in 1867 and a more recent British invasion – that of the Beatles in the early 1960s[6] – is not as great an exaggeration as it at first seems. Certainly the kind of hysteria that authors like Mark Twain and transatlantic stars like Dickens and Oscar Wilde experienced on their lecture tours of the US – overnight queues, packed theatres, huge box-office receipts, ticket touts and the use of police reserves to control crowds – anticipated the treatment meted out to contemporary celebrities. The principal reason for these writers' popularity is that it did not just emerge out of published books, but 'operated in and on a relatively new context – the world of commercialized print and the burgeoning industry of publicity'.[7] In particular, the public personality of the author was sponsored by two lucrative areas of public activity which were closely interrelated – the lecture circuit and the popular press.

These phenomena were particularly important in an American context in which book publishers were struggling to produce books by home-grown authors, let alone promote and sell them. There was a huge appetite for reading matter in the increasingly literate population, but not the economic infrastructure to satisfy it. Inefficient printing and distribution techniques seriously hindered the early expansion of the American book industry, and a central problem persisted throughout the century – the flooding of the home market with cheap, pirated editions of English books. (It was not until the 1891 Chase international copyright act, which finally outlawed pirate editions, that American authors could function within a market in which the law fully regulated and protected their intellectual property rights.) In this difficult economic climate, authors often gravitated towards the lecture circuit, which had no equivalent on a similar scale in Europe. Their main motive for appearing on this circuit was financial necessity: Herman Melville, for example, touted as the man who had 'lived among the cannibals', began lecturing grudgingly after the commercial failure of his novel, *The Confidence-Man*, while Thomas Starr King stated pragmatically that his incentive for lecturing was 'FAME – Fifty And My Expenses'.[8]

The lecture circuit became crucial to the emergence of literary celebrity after the transformation of the lyceum circuit established in New England in 1826 – on which speakers were poorly paid or unpaid and the principal aim was the education and moral uplift of the audience – into the much more commercial operations which reached their zenith in the 1870s and 1880s. As the circuit developed and expanded greatly after the Civil War, the task of providing lecturers for literary societies and other local organizations was taken up by commercial lecturing agencies run by agents like James Redpath and Major Pond and, under their influence, lecturers' fees rose to as much as a thousand dollars a night.[9] Predictably, the lectures became less obviously educative and took on more and more of the qualities of mass entertainment, a shift which encouraged an emphasis on the idiosyncrasies of the speaker rather than the content of the speech. Aaron Fogel compares the nineteenth-century lecture to the contemporary talk show, because in both forms the purpose is 'not narration ... instruction, drama, or debate, but the suggestion and witness of personality'.[10] The most successful speakers were those like Twain who, rather than simply reading from the lectern on worthy topics, produced a winning 'performance' –

his lectures came complete with stage costume (his famous white three-piece suit) and a highly marketable persona which was virtually a carbon copy of the blunt, coarse, iconoclastic figure presented in his work, a performance which is still imitated in one-man performances by Mark Twain impersonators across America today. The verisimilitude of this persona, itself an attack on affectation and cant and the belletristic veneer of the New England tradition, belied the well-rehearsed, structured nature of the speeches. According to Louis Budd, Twain analysed and perfected his lecture performances as carefully and self-consciously as he did his writing.[11]

A key element in the popularization of the lecture circuit was the promotional power of the press, which effectively transformed the early lyceum movement – which drew on local speakers with reputations fostered by word of mouth – into a much more organized system of national celebrities.[12] The dominance of American magazines and newspapers during this period can also be largely attributed to the book publishing industry's problems with copyright. In lieu of a healthy market for books, authors naturally looked to this thriving print culture for publication and publicity.[13] Apart from the fact that authors wrote for these magazines and newspapers, the latter also reported on the lectures, or sometimes reprinted the speeches in their entirety, accompanying them with illustrations or cartoon caricatures of the speaker, helping to turn the circuit into one frequented by recognized 'names'. One British journalist calculated in 1878 that Twain's speeches were 'probably read by a larger number of men and women in America than any public document, the President's message not excepted'.[14] Twain's lecture tours, as well as being lavishly and expensively advertised in themselves, employed his frequent press interviews as free advance publicity, in the same way that the main purpose of a contemporary celebrity interview is often to 'plug' a book or film. Dickens's tours also received blanket coverage in American newspapers and magazines, anxious for any copy about one of the most famous men in the world – as the author's ship pulled into Boston Harbour on his first visit in 1842, a dozen newspaper editors, according to one contemporary account, 'came leaping on board at the peril of their lives' in search of an exclusive interview.[15]

The Author as Commodity

This developing celebrity culture industry created a number of patterns and tensions which were perhaps best exemplified in the figure of the most famous American author at this time, Mark Twain, and which continued into the twentieth century. The relationship between the press and the lecture circuit represented an early example of the intertextuality of celebrity – the way in which different media can mutually reinforce a person's fame – in the sense that newspapers and periodicals created a textual representation or image of the author which then stimulated a desire to meet the 'real' celebrity in person. As Linda Haverty Rugg has written of the images of Twain which appeared in newspapers:

> Photographs of celebrities arouse longing in viewers. Celebrity images promote the body as product, the self as marketable commodity. These photographs and engravings ... promoted recognition among the public of a face that would then be associated not only with a name, but with the power of making money through the body's appearance onstage. Twain's most successful product was his pseudonymic self, born of an association between his body's image and his literary and lecturing persona; later he would establish its use as a representative for various commercial ventures. Crowds paid money to see this body reunified and identified with its disseminated image and name.[16]

In its intertextual nature, then, Twain's fame anticipated twentieth-century manifestations of celebrity. Hollywood celebrity, for example, did not properly develop until the popularity of cinema was supported by the growth of illustrated entertainment magazines in the 1920s, which reported on and gossiped about the stars. As John Ellis defines it, a star is 'a performer in a particular medium whose figure enters into subsidiary forms of circulation, and then feeds back into future performances'.[17] In other words, stardom is created by a variety of different media which feed off each other and collectively generate interest in the star.

The lecture circuit and the popular press were also clearly creating and consolidating a cultural dominant, manufacturing a very specific notion of what an American author should be. With a few exceptions, like Harriet Beecher Stowe, the author-lecturers on the circuit were male (not the 'damn scribbling women' derided by Nathaniel Hawthorne, whose books sold in their thousands), white and originating from or based in the prosperous northeast of the United States. Although Midwestern newspapers often sought to redress the balance by giving publicity to lecturers from their own region, audiences increasingly preferred the recognizable, branded product of the already well-known eastern lecturers.[18] As Donald M. Scott argues:

> Though it was believed to be the embodiment of an all-embracing national culture, the public lecture system was in fact an institution for

the consolidation of the collective cultural consciousness by which this group [white, eastern, male culture] came to assert a claim that it was the real American public.[19]

The best example of this is Twain, who came from the Midwest but managed to reinvent himself for eastern audiences as a quintessentially American figure – 'a sort of arch-type of the national character',[20] in Van Wyck Brooks's words, an American natural dispensing cracker-barrel philosophy and homespun wisdom. This notion of Twain as the epitome of all-American values continues today as his after-image is disseminated through advertisements, television shows and other forms of popular culture. In the 'American Adventure' attraction at the EPCOT Center in Disney World, for example, an 'audio-animatronic' figure of Twain, complete with white hair, squeaking rocking-chair and cigar, co-presents (with Benjamin Franklin) the story of the nation from the Mayflower onwards. Twain is thus employed, as Bruce Michelson puts it, 'as our national Emcee … presenting "America" to hordes of visitors … at the world's one and only perpetual world's fair'.[21]

Most importantly, though, the emergence of literary celebrity provoked intense discussion about its uneasy negotiation between marketability and cultural authority, a debate which has continued through all the various expressions of literary fame since then. Although they were driven by commercial priorities, the lecture circuit and popular press also sought to popularize 'serious' culture. They thus exploited what Merle Curti calls 'the cult of self-improvement'[22] flourishing amongst much of the American population from the mid-nineteenth century onwards as a consequence of such factors as increasing rates of literacy, improved education and the growth of an aspirant professional middle class. The work of Joan Shelley Rubin and Janice Radway has shown how these various factors led to the emergence of a 'middlebrow' culture industry around this time – 'a vast infrastructure for cultural pedagogy … devoted to the business of commodifying and marketing taste'.[23] Twain's unparalleled popularity, as Justin Kaplan points out, was partly due to the fact that he seemed to transcend so effortlessly the divide between high and low culture, 'both gratifying his audience's hunger for "literature" and reassuring them that he [was] not littérateur, that fancy talk and three-dollar words [were] just as alien to him as to any storekeeper or clerk'.[24]

However, the permeability of these boundaries between high and low culture also raised concerns about the descension of art and literature into the murky sphere of exchange. The fear that America's peculiar economic and cultural situation might create a monopoly of homogenized literary products, manufactured wholly for commercial ends and sold through hype and publicity, was raised in different forms from an early stage. In *Democracy in America*, for example, Alexis de Tocqueville expresses his concern that the extreme egalitarianism of democratic capitalism would 'introduce a trading spirit into literature', which would undermine any notion of the author as culturally authoritative – 'since, in democracies, a writer may hope to gain moderate renown and great wealth cheaply. For this purpose he does not need to be admired; it is enough if people have a taste for his work.'[25] As authors forged a close relationship with popular media from the mid-nineteenth century onwards, these anxieties about the relationship between art and money were heightened. Josiah G. Holland, editor of the highbrow *Scribner's Monthly*, published a series of pieces in 1871 and 1872 which attacked the increasingly commercial nature of the lecture circuit and the decline of the old lyceums, denouncing 'literary jesters and mountebanks' and 'buffoons' who reduced the lecture system to 'a string of entertainments that have no earnest purpose', having 'a ... degrading influence upon the public taste'. Other commentators similarly accused the performers of being 'itinerant retailers of stale platitudes', 'old hacks' and 'humbugs and charlatans', one of them describing the author-lecturer as 'a literary strumpet, subject for a greater than whore's fee to prostitute himself'.[26]

The resilience of these debates can be seen in the way that the central figure of Twain (a reluctant lecturer who spoke of being forced by 'pecuniary compulsions' to 'crucify myself nightly' and 'rob the public from the platform',[27] and who only returned to the circuit after filing for bankruptcy in 1894 when a business venture failed) was frequently invoked by twentieth-century critics as a way of lamenting the colonization of culture by the marketplace. The principal argument of Van Wyck Brooks's classic *The Ordeal of Mark Twain* (1920), for example, is that the author was forced to play the low comic by a vulgarized American culture, against his better judgement and to the huge detriment of his talent, while Dwight Macdonald accuses Twain of hamming it up shamelessly as a 'hillbilly ignoramus'. Theodor Adorno and Max Horkheimer, in an influential essay on mass culture, also refer tellingly to the 'Mark Twain absurdity with which the American culture industry flirts with itself'.[28]

These debates can be linked to broader concerns about the loss of authorial autonomy in the transformation of the author into celebrity-commodity, concerns which were more usually voiced by authors themselves. As William Dean Howells (a friend of Twain's who was worried about the effects of the latter's stratospheric celebrity), expressed it:

The writer's authorial freedom ... is fatally compromised by the success of his own writings; the more his work is read, the more he himself becomes a celebrity, a public figure to be admired or reviled on his own, apart from his books, almost as a public property.[29]

Susan Gillman argues that the writer's new status as exchangeable commodity in the late nineteenth century meant that 'the problems of an emerging technology of mass reproduction were ... intertwined with analogous concerns with artistic identity'. Apart from the fact that Twain struggled for the whole of his career with people trying to reproduce his image and otherwise make a profit out of his celebrity name without his permission – by pirating his books, for example, or by impersonating him as a lecturer – even his own, authorized celebrity image began to circulate in ways that he was not happy with and could not always control.[30]

At the same time, this image was presented as the 'natural', individual self of the author – as Mary Poovey argues, 'the anti-individualizing effect' of the literary marketplace at this time was offset by the strenuous efforts to 'conceptualize [authorship] as an individualistic activity'. According to Poovey, the author-commodity was further naturalized by the attempt to connect it to the author's work, since one of the crucial elements of this individualization of authorship was 'the commercial marketing of books by linking a writer's name to a unique and recognizable image – often an "autobiographical" image derived from the writer's work'.[31] The lecture circuit and popular press, in particular, created a sense that the author's work and life were inextricably interrelated. American newspapers and magazines encouraged authors to work in journalistic, reportorial forms which implicitly connected writing and personality and which appeared in close proximity with more direct attempts to manufacture a persona through news, reviews, interviews and photographs. Twain's journalism, developed during his early career working for newspapers in Iowa, Nevada and California, created a persona which complemented his lecturing self – as in *The Innocents Abroad*, which first stimulated public interest in him as a speaker in 1869. This book grew out of a series of letters written for newspaper serialization and employed a new journalistic mode in which the figure of the 'author-at-large' was interpolated into the text. This mode, incorporated into later works like *Roughing It*, *A Tramp Abroad* and *Life on the Mississippi*, played on and helped to sustain Twain's public image as a rough-and-ready, folksy, no-nonsense character.

The problem for authors, then, is that they were themselves complicit in this manufacture of their public image, and this complicity was underscored by the necessarily entrepreneurial nature of nineteenth-century

American authorship, the fact that financial imperatives encouraged them to sell themselves and their work vigorously. Authors like Mark Twain and Walt Whitman were tirelessly energetic self-publicists – publishing themselves, composing their own 'blurbs' and placing self-penned rave reviews of their work in other media. Whitman, drawing on his earlier experience as a printer, had published *Leaves of Grass* himself, and virtually invented the notion of dustjacket copy, embossing Emerson's paean of praise to the book, 'I greet you at the beginning of a great career', on the spine of the second edition.[32] The book's frontispiece, containing the celebrated Samuel Hollyer etching of Whitman wearing an open-necked shirt, worker's trousers and cowboy hat, also did much to foster the public image of its author as free-spirited folk hero. Twain's commercial nous was even more impressive: he made his own name a legal trade mark to safeguard the value not just of his books but of the many products manufactured in that name, including postcards, cigars, tobacco, whisky, a patented self-pasting scrapbook and a board game, 'Mark Twain's memory builder'. Many of these products profited from and reinforced Twain's public persona – the slogan for the Mark Twain Cigar, for instance, was 'Known to Everyone and Liked by All'.[33]

The symbiotic relationship between promotion and self-promotion in the public construction of authors like Twain makes any attempt to distinguish between the 'public' author and the 'private' self a deeply problematic exercise. Since Twain's death, there has been a whole series of biographies and other accounts which have sought to reveal the 'real' Samuel Clemens behind the celebrity mask, the most notable being Justin Kaplan's appropriately titled *Mr Clemens and Mark Twain* (1966). But as Gillman points out, Twain's public performance was far too internalized and unconscious for us to be able to make such distinctions confidently: she uses the term 'imposture' to describe Twain's presentation of himself because it suggests 'the pose of a pose, the fake of a fake: the word implies no possible return to any point of origin'.[34] Twain himself said as much as early as 1869: 'I am in some sense a *public* man ... but my private character is hacked, & dissected, & mixed up with my public one, & both suffer more in consequence'.[35] In Chapter 4, I point to the ways in which this dangerously interdependent relationship between the 'real' person and the commoditized image remains a central source of concern for contemporary literary celebrities.

The Rise of the Massmarket Magazine

The close connection between literary celebrity and the sphere of commercialized print continued into the twentieth century, partly because the

American book industry still lagged behind magazine and newspaper publishing as a vehicle for promoting and publicizing authors. From the 1880s onwards – about the time the lecture circuit began to decline – there was a second great expansion in the number of newspapers and periodicals as America's transformation into an economy based around mass consumption brought about a huge increase in potential advertising revenue. This created a new kind of magazine – the cheap, massmarket, illustrated weekly. Although this new magazine continued to provide markets for authors' work, its main significance in the development of literary celebrity was to consolidate and extend the popular interest in 'personalities' and to co-opt authors into a new kind of celebrity journalism inspired by the stars of stage and screen.

The most important purveyors of literary celebrity for several decades of the twentieth century were the sister publications, *Time* (1923–) and *Life* magazine (1936–), both owned by the media magnate, Henry Luce. In their prime (between the 1930s and the 1960s), both these publications had circulations of four or five million – which in practice probably meant 20 million readers each – and were thus one of the most significant sources of news and entertainment for Americans at the time.[36] Before television became the dominant mass medium, such magazines were the only truly nationwide media in a country without national newspapers, and an appearance in them, especially if reinforced by a cover portrait, brought immediate celebrity. Perhaps the most significant characteristic of these magazines was the influence of advertising over their editorial content. As W.A. Swanberg argues, their huge reliance on revenue from advertising (which was much greater than any profits gained from newsrack sales) meant that they 'created a news product slanted to draw the advertiser and *his* product', and indeed *Time* was not averse to honouring many of its main advertisers with cover stories in the hope of drumming up more business.[37]

The need for these magazines to sustain the attention of the mass audience their advertisers demanded led to a new kind of personality journalism, based on William Randolph Hearst's principle that 'names make news'. *Time* and *Life* were particularly interested in personalities, as exemplified by *Time*'s 'Man of the Year' awards and their cover stories, which were almost always about an individual. Massmarket magazines during this period practised a type of journalism which Richard Schickel calls 'emblematic', by which personalities were reduced to the convenient shorthand of readily identifiable symbols, and *Time* and *Life* were the first and most influential magazines to treat 'serious' figures like authors in this way. As Schickel says, they 'were the carriers of emblematic journalism from its place of origin, reporting about show people, into new realms – the political, the social, even the literary'.[38]

Time and *Life* achieved this by implicitly connecting life and art, visiting the author at his place of both work and residence – following William Faulkner to Oxford, Mississippi, for instance, or Ernest Hemingway to Key West – and providing an anecdotal treatment of the author's life, detailing his childhood, college career, marriage(s) and current work routine, followed by textual exegesis. *Time*'s celebrated cover portraits also often placed the subject on a fictional backdrop associated with his writing – J.D. Salinger in a field of rye, for example, or Hemingway with a marlin looping around his head. In this simplistically anecdotal approach, truth value was less important than the creation of entertaining stereotypes. Many of the anecdotes circulating about Hemingway in massmarket magazines, for instance – concerning his running away from home as an adolescent to live as a tramp, engaging in heroic military exploits in the First World War as a member of the Arditi (the crack Italian fighting force), or working as both a professional boxer and bullfighter[39] – were wholly fictitious (though initiated by Hemingway himself) and designed to perpetuate the popular image of him as Byronic adventurer and 'man's man'.

The captioned photographs which illustrated the texts of the profiles communicated this emblematic quality even more directly than the prose. Malcolm Cowley complained that the series of photographs and captions which accompanied his 1949 *Life* profile of Hemingway – showing the author in a boxing ring, drinking straight from a bottle of Scotch while in Spain during the Civil War or walking into a bar in Cuba – were 'pretty God-awful' and 'surrounded, submerged, and ... changed in import' his own words.[40] The photographs accompanying the two *Time* cover stories of Hemingway similarly picture him fishing and shooting, posing behind kudu horns, steering his yacht on the open seas, standing barechested at his typewriter and slugging from a bottle at a bullfight.[41] The connection between this emblematic effect and the brand naming of the advertising industry is clear, and for some of the authors covered, the move from magazine profiles to full-page advertisements proved a natural progression. Hemingway, whose public persona was created almost exclusively by magazine profiles and who advertised many products within the same media, was so often invoked in advertisements for clothes, guns and other products after his death that his family made his name a registered trademark.[42] John Cheever's endorsement of Rolex watches in glossy magazines similarly played on his media image as opulent New England patriarch. 'I'm a brand name', he later commented, 'like corn flakes, or shredded wheat'.[43]

Time and *Life*'s singular most important contribution to the creation of the author as public personality, however, was to foster a notion of a characteristically 'American' author in an era when the United States was rising inexorably to the status of economic and political superpower. Luce had famously urged his compatriots, in a *Life* editorial of 17 February 1941 entitled 'The American Century', to 'accept wholeheartedly our duty and our opportunity as the most powerful country in the world and in consequence to exert upon the world the full impact of our influence, for such purposes as we see fit, and by such means as we see fit'.[44] This message was disseminated not merely in the United States but internationally in the form of the several foreign editions of both magazines. As *Der Spiegel*, one of *Time*'s impersonators, wrote in March 1961:

> No man has more incisively shaped the image of America as seen by the rest of the world, and the Americans' image of the world, than Henry R. Luce. Every third U.S. family buys every week a Luce product; 94% of all Americans know *Time*. Luceforic printed products are the intellectual supplement of Coca-Cola, Marilyn Monroe and dollar diplomacy.[45]

No wonder, then, that Robert Coover referred to *Time* caustically as 'the National Poet Laureate'.[46]

Although the authors profiled in *Time* and *Life* were not exclusively American, those that were tended to be defined as quintessentially so in their personality or subject matter. The consistent sponsorship of literary realism by Luce magazines was also a product of their belief that authors should faithfully reflect a specifically national reality. Thornton Wilder, praised for his ability to reproduce 'authentic Americana', and John Dos Passos, who 'has taken as his subject the whole U.S. and attempted to organize its chaotic, high-pressure life into an understandable artistic pattern', were typical *Time* subjects.[47] *Life*'s plea, similarly, was that authors should be 'spokesmen for a virile, confident America', and it concentrated on those authors, like John Steinbeck, Thomas Wolfe, Carl Sandburg and Stephen Vincent Benét, who sought to 're-create the variety of America anew'.[48]

The authors themselves were often presented as highly talented but essentially ordinary, representatively American citizens. The *Time* cover story on John Cheever, for instance, was instrumental in fostering a popular image of the author as a kind of leisurely New England squire whose life revolved around his family, gun dogs and country estate, the Episcopal church and suburban social events. 'Cheever', it says, 'has all the mannerisms of the proud landowner. He fiddles with his rotary mower or chain saw, or flails away with limited competence with an ax ... He worries about his unpruned apple trees, or Dutch disease in the elm where the orioles nest.' The importance of authors like Cheever and his fellow New Englander

John P. Marquand to *Time* and *Life* stemmed from their status as exemplary members of the white, Protestant, newly ex-urban, New England bourgeoisie – an important section of these magazines' readership, and the one most consistently targeted by its advertisers. *Time* and *Life* claimed this readership as typically American: *Time*, for instance, stated that Cheever's tales of 'commuterland' had 'dimensions and echoes far beyond their relatively small compass', and that Marquand mirrored the concerns of 'millions of decent, middle-class U.S. citizens'.[49]

As with the earlier examples of literary celebrity from the nineteenth century, *Time* and *Life* negotiated skilfully between culture and commerce in their selection and championing of certain authors. Both magazines not only tended to pick commercially successful authors as subjects, but also showed an intense interest in the details of this success in the profiles themselves – sales figures, positions on the *New York Times* bestsellers list, the size of print runs, the profitability of subsidiary rights and so on. However, they also wanted authors with serious 'literary' pretensions, even if their notion of seriousness was dependent on market-oriented criteria such as the major literary prizes, the commercial book clubs and favourable reviews in mainstream media like the *New York Times Book Review* and *Saturday Review*.

Hemingway's unparalleled popularity with the Luce magazines (he appeared twice on the cover of *Time* and three times on the cover of *Life*) is a good example of this tension. In many ways, his celebrity was similar to that of a film star – the profiles often foregrounded his friendships with screen idols like Gary Cooper and Ava Gardner and, according to a 1959 *International Celebrity Register*, his face was 'as familiar to millions as the countenance of Clark Gable or Ted Williams'.[50] However, the coverage of Hemingway in these media, particularly at the height of his celebrity in the 1940s and 1950s, was still based on an albeit caricatured notion of a recognizably 'writerly' figure – his stereotyped persona of the authoritative but benevolent old sage, 'Papa'. Hemingway himself bought into this image fully: his *Life*-serialized *The Dangerous Summer*, which describes the author taking a bullfighter under his wing before a *mano à mano*, feeds on an idea of him as 'a man ripe in the wisdom of years and steadfast in his integrity',[51] in John Raeburn's words, and clearly owes much of its style and tone to its need to support the 'Papa' myth circulated through the same magazine.

This need to represent cultural value as well as mere commercial success sometimes created tensions and ambiguities in the magazine's coverage of authors. For example, the Luce magazines were occasionally able to accommodate recusant voices and more technically difficult work if the authors could be presented as authoritatively 'authorial'. 'Confessional' poets like John Berryman and Robert Lowell, for example, were defined as Baudelairian *poètes maudits*, an idealization of artists as suffering, self-destructive, complex, brilliant individuals. Jane Howard's *Life* profile of Berryman refers to 'whiskey and ink' as the fluids he needs 'to survive and describe the thing that sets him apart from other men and even from other poets: his uncommonly, almost maddeningly penetrating awareness of the fact of human mortality'.[52] The *Time* cover story on Robert Lowell, a similarly atypical subject because of the complexity of his work and its modest sales (although he had won the Pulitzer Prize and the National Book Award) claims that 'the bulk of his best poetry is seared with a fiery desperation, fed by rage and self-laceration'. At the same time, the magazine hedged its bets by justifying its choice of Lowell as subject with the unlikely proposition that poetry was 'moving out of the academy – out of college lit courses and esoteric coteries – back to where it was when minstrels sang their verses in the marketplace. It exists once again in an ambience of instant feeling.'[53] The Beat writers were treated similarly – *Life*'s profile of Allen Ginsberg, for example, positions him as a Byronic artist-adventurer, experimenting with drugs and petty theft, and producing work which is wholly personal and heartfelt – after one of the poet's campus readings, *Life* claims, 'the whispers of his secret mind are the possession of everyone present'.[54]

Middlebrow Culture and its Discontents

Time and *Life* thus formed part of what Rubin calls a 'culture of the middle-brow', which flourished particularly in the US in the 1920s, 1930s and 1940s – exemplified by phenomena like the Book-of-the-Month Club, the Literary Guild, *Saturday Review* and the *New York Times Book Review* – and helped to manufacture literary celebrities out of this culture. According to Rubin, this period saw the creation of 'an unprecedented range of activities aimed at making literature and other forms of "high" culture available to a wide reading public', as a consequence of 'the United States' shift from a producer to a consumer society'.[55] (Many of these phenomena were either part of magazine publishing or were sponsored and sustained by it, during a period in which magazines were heavily funded by advertising.) *Time* and *Life* were consciously 'middlebrow' in that they sought to emphasize both seriousness and commercial appeal in their coverage of the arts and literature, and aimed to be both informative and entertaining by providing a weekly digest of essential knowledge, synthesizing a large amount of specialized information for a broadly based, though still predominantly white and middle-class, readership. In Luce's words, his magazines were 'for the lady from Dubuque ... and for the President of the United States'.[56] *Time* and *Life* tended to promote authors who had been well-reviewed and supported by other examples of this middlebrow culture – the favourite indicator of an author's worthiness as a cover story subject was invariably the regular selection of his work by the Book-of-the-Month Club. (Cowley, in a 1946 essay, 'Limousines on Grub Street', also notes the phenomenal effect of the book clubs in bringing fame and success to a limited number of serious authors such as Hemingway, Steinbeck and Marquand – while most authors remain chronically underpaid, he argues, 'those who achieved or blundered into popularity have been living like speculators in a bull market'.[57])

These elements of literary celebrity sponsored by *Time* and *Life* – the brand-naming of 'personalities', the promotion of specifically 'American' cultural values, the 'middlebrow' aesthetic – were made all the more powerful for the fact that they were promoted quite subtly. Luce magazines, in fact, worked in a way similar to many advertisements, by endorsing a particular lifestyle or viewpoint implicitly and suggestively. This suggestiveness was all the more powerful because of the air of unquestioned authority that surrounded the reportage in these magazines. *Time* and *Life*'s profiles of authors tended to be 'in-depth', the result of a team of researchers or 'legmen' conducting multiple interviews with the subject himself and a wide circle of friends, relatives and acquaintances, and the article then being written up by one or more editors at the central bureau. The evidence of teamwork and the use of numerous and occasionally anonymous sources encouraged the impression that the magazine had pinned down the authentic personality of the subject. It is worth noting as well that *Time* had no bylines (unlike *Life* and *Newsweek*), allowing it to claim in its own advertising slogan that it was written 'as if by one man for one man'[58] – an authorless, omniscient and commonsensical voice. (A *Playboy* joke ran: 'We didn't go to Europe this year – *Time* gave it a bad review.'[59]) *Time*'s promotion of its country's literary figures was certainly made more persuasive by its own authorial invisibility.

The great influence of middlebrow culture in deciding which authors were worthy of public attention led many dissenting voices to protest about the role of these cultural intermediaries in creating literary fame. Left-liberal magazines such as the *Nation* and the *New Republic* expressed concern from the 1920s onwards, for example, about the 'standardization' of American cultural life threatened by the basically commercial imperatives of the book clubs. An anonymous editorial in *The Bookman* in April 1927 claimed that these clubs were a self-appointed literary establishment, representing 'a real attempt to standardize and to corral the authority to make literary fame'.[60] This debate was continued with greater force by a group of radical critics usually referred to as the 'New York intellectuals' – a loose-knit cultural establishment which initially formed around limited circulation journals such as *Partisan Review*, *Commentary* and *Dissent*, and which gradually rose to prominence and influence after the Second World War. Many members of this group were former communists, disillusioned with Stalinist Russia after the Nazi-Soviet pact, who were particularly influenced by the critique of mass culture formulated by the Frankfurt School, whose major figures – Theodor Adorno, Max Horkheimer and Herbert Marcuse – had settled in the United States to escape from Nazism. Sharing the hostility of these critics to 'that mass-produced pseudo-art characteristic of industrialized urban society',[61] the New York intellectuals' greatest concern was not so much mass culture in itself as the commodification of ostensibly 'serious' culture represented by the 'middlebrow'. William Phillips, co-editor of *Partisan Review* from 1936, for example, had criticized the trend emerging in America after the First World War for 'serious writing with a popular touch', epitomized by F. Scott Fitzgerald and Hemingway who, 'impatient for recognition, money, love, popularity ... helped bring serious fiction into the middle range of audience appeal'.[62]

This kind of cultural crossover is clearly the main topic of Clement Greenberg's celebrated essay, 'Avant-Garde and Kitsch', which attacked the development in Western capitalist societies of

> an ersatz culture, kitsch, destined for those who, insensible to the values of genuine culture, are hungry nevertheless for the diversion that only culture of some sort can provide. Kitsch, using for raw material the debased and academicized simulacra of genuine culture, welcomes and cultivates this insensibility.[63]

As George Cotkin argues, postwar American intellectuals have been persistently concerned with these sorts of questions, spending 'an inordinate amount of time trying to define boundaries, to make distinctions, to test their authority in opposition to the foes of mass culture and anti-intellectualism'.[64] The New York intellectuals also attacked the kind of partisan Americanism which the Luce magazines exhibited and which they saw as synonymous with the concept of the middlebrow itself. According to Norman Podhoretz, the family, many of whom were New York Jews, 'did not feel that they belonged to America or that America belonged to them', and they therefore attacked '*Kitsch* ... middlebrowism ... commercialism ... mass culture' as 'contaminating influences from the surrounding American world'.[65]

The kind of literary criticism practised by the New York intellectuals was a conscious reaction not simply to literary celebrity, but to the whole confusion of cultural value and promotional hype on which they believed it was based. Their continual complaint was that book reviewers were not critical enough and were letting the commercial power of book clubs, publishers and massmarket magazines win out in the battle for readers. In a 1959 essay, for example, Elizabeth Hardwick deplores the fact that 'sweet, bland commendations fall everywhere upon the scene; a universal, if somewhat lobotomized, accommodation reigns. A book is born into a pudding of treacle; the brine of hostile criticism is only a memory.'[66] In place of what the New York intellectuals saw as this capitulation to bestsellerdom, the reviews of contemporary literature in periodicals like *Partisan Review* and *Commentary* were highly opinionated, polemical and often openly hostile – adopting an attitude, as Podhoretz (editor of *Commentary* from 1960) describes it, 'of great suspiciousness: a book is assumed to be guilty until it proves itself innocent – and not many do'.[67]

A particularly influential two-part article by Dwight Macdonald, 'Masscult and Midcult', published in *Partisan Review* in 1960, is a typical example of the writings of the New York intellectuals in its attack on mass culture ('Masscult') as a prefabricated, standardized product, and in its particular concern with the commodification of 'serious' culture as an effect of the growing influence of Masscult. The article therefore reserves its fiercest disdain for the development of 'Midcult', a hybrid cultural form represented by middlebrow phenomena such as *Time*, *Life* and the book clubs, which 'has the essential qualities of Masscult – the formula, the in-built reaction, the lack of any standard except popularity – but it decently covers them with a cultural figleaf'.[68] Significantly, Macdonald also spends much of the article attacking what he sees as the recent emergence of the author as public personality. He argues that, since both Masscult and Midcult create uniformly mediocre products which encourage people to respond to them as a passive, undifferentiated mass, a sense of connection between product and audience needs to be established by marketing the 'personality' of the author, since 'the more literature [becomes] a branch of industry, the more the craving for the other extreme – individuality. Or rather, a somewhat coarser commodity, Personality.' Macdonald claims that:

in Masscult (and, in its bastard, Midcult) everything becomes a commodity, to be mined for $$$$, used for something it is not ... Once a writer becomes a Name ... the Masscult (or Midcult) mechanism begins to 'build him up,' to package him into something that can be sold in identical units in quantity. He can coast along the rest of his life on momentum; publishers will pay him big advances just to get his Name on their list; his charisma becomes such that people will pay him $250 and up to address them (really just to *see* him); editors will reward him handsomely for articles on subjects he knows nothing about. Artists and writers have always had a tendency to repeat themselves, but Masscult (and Midcult) make it highly profitable to do so and in fact penalize those who don't.[69]

The author's 'personality', then, becomes primarily a means of product differentiation aimed at concealing the repetitiveness of a corporately organized, assembly-line mode of production.

There are problems with this argument, however, which are indicative of Macdonald's unwillingness (along with many of the New York intellectuals) to distinguish between very different kinds of cultural production. Because he sees 'Midcult' as simply the illegitimate child of 'Masscult', literary celebrity becomes primarily an invention of the latter which inveigles its way into the former, when in fact (as I have attempted to show in this chapter) it has emerged out of a much more interlocked relationship between culture and commerce. This reluctance to acknowledge that cultural as well as economic capital plays a part in the production of literary fame means that it is dismissed as being entirely the product of profit-minded overpromotion. In a strategy which supports Bourdieu's theories about the link between social class and the acquisition of cultural capital, Macdonald's solution to the insidious influence of Masscult seems to be to restore class boundaries in order to revive a notion of 'the informed, interested minority'.[70] This odd manoeuvre for a Marxist like Macdonald – which ends with him pining for the class divisions of British society where at least five per cent of the population appreciates 'culture' – is part of his inability to recognize the increasingly provisional character of the boundaries between 'highbrow' and 'lowbrow'.

Just as he sees mass culture as monolithically bad, Macdonald's definition of its heroic opposite, the 'avant-garde', is also neither theorized nor historically specific – he argues that avant-garde culture represents simply 'the expression of feelings, ideas, tastes, visions that are idiosyncratic and the audience similarly responds to them as individuals'.[71] If the Masscult/Midcult literary celebrity is the commodified 'personality' sold to a mass audience, then, the avant-garde still demonstrates the possibility of an authentic self speaking to a cultivated individual reader. This simple dualism belies the contested nature of cultural production and the position of the literary celebrity as a central figure in that contestation. As Bourdieu puts it: 'The most intolerable thing for those who regard themselves as the possessors of legitimate culture is the sacrilegious reuniting of tastes which taste dictates shall be separated.'[72] (In fact, as I suggest in the next chapter, Bourdieu's own comments on 'middlebrow' culture and on French writers and intellectuals who appear regularly in the mass media have been quite scathing, and risk reproducing the same cultural hierarchies his theoretical models seek to deconstruct.)

One example of the fluidity of these categories of 'high' and 'low' is the way that many of the New York intellectuals eventually became celebrities themselves. Jules Feiffer, an insider in the New York cultural establishment, refers to this group as intensely social and 'pretty much in the business of putting themselves on the map. As individuals they were fiercely competitive, energetic, ambitious.'[73] Podhoretz similarly claims that, amongst the New York intellectuals, success had replaced sex as what D.H. Lawrence called 'the dirty little secret',[74] and this concern with status and achievement expressed itself in an alternative cult of celebrity based around Manhattan literary life and fashionable get-togethers. Under the impact of changes in publishing and the media world from the early 1960s onwards, however, the influence of the New York intelligentsia spread into magazines and newspapers with a much wider circulation than *Partisan Review* and *Commentary*. A key development was the founding of the *New York Review of Books* in 1963, early issues of which included contributions from many New York intellectuals including Macdonald, Podhoretz and Irving Howe. Howe himself later accused the *New York Review* of having too cosy a relationship with New York publishing and society circles, and of forging 'a link between campus "leftism" and East Side stylishness', and Tom Wolfe famously dismissed the magazine as 'the chief theoretical organ of radical chic'.[75]

Whether or not these criticisms are fair, it is certainly true that the *New York Review* granted much wider recognition to previously marginalized intellectuals, having from the beginning a larger circulation than *Partisan Review*, *Commentary* and *Dissent* put together. Many of the younger critics who published there, like Richard Poirier and Susan Sontag, were less dismissive of mass culture and popular forms, leading Hilton Kramer to complain about high culture being attacked 'from within',[76] and although it rarely included interviews or profiles it developed a more relaxed attitude to literary 'personalities' – exemplified best, perhaps, by the David Levine caricatures of authors which still accompany many of the reviews. The *New York Review* ushered in a new kind of highbrow magazine which was much more at ease with the increasingly interconnected relationship between culture and the market.

What I have tried to show in this chapter is that literary celebrity is not simply a contemporary phenomenon, but the product of a historically close relationship between certain kinds of authors and a 'middlebrow' print culture, which was ultimately answerable to the marketplace but which also aimed to make literature accessible to the broader populace. Because these forms of publicity for authors were not directly related to book publishing, celebrity authors became not simply marketable commodities but cultural signifiers, mediating and reinforcing ideas about the role and significance of books and authors in American society and culture. The existence of this middlebrow culture qualifies the traditional attempt to link literary celebrity to the decline of public discourse in an 'age of showbusiness' – what Neil Postman has described as the transformation of the US from a 'word-centered' print culture in the nineteenth century to an 'image-centered' one based around visual media in the twentieth.[77] It is clear that the fears currently being expressed about the promotional pressures placed on authors are nothing new in themselves – similar concerns were raised about Twain and others over a century ago. In the next chapter, however, I want to point to more recent developments which continue these long-standing debates about the relationship between literature and the marketplace while also extending them into new and even more problematic areas, produced by the intersection between sophisticated forms of book publicity and the efforts of seemingly non-commercial institutions to sponsor authors and their works.

3
The Reign of Hype: The Contemporary Star System

The last few decades have seen the proliferation of an extraordinary range of activities aimed at publicizing and promoting American authors. This chapter investigates some of these activities by exploring the specifically contemporary aspects of the literary 'star system'. It begins by looking at the implications for literary celebrity of recent changes in the media industries, specifically book publishing's absorption into a global entertainment and information industry under the control of a handful of large conglomerates. It goes on to explore how the commercial imperatives of major publishers are complicated by the continuing importance of cultural capital in the literary marketplace, and considers finally how this negotiation between pure profit making and 'higher' cultural values has produced intense debates and conflicted meanings around literary celebrity in contemporary culture. I want to argue that the contemporary star system, far from being a closed shop populated by mutual log-rollers and backscratchers and number-crunching accountants, is an evolving organism which is not immune to intense self-scrutiny and soul-searching about its more malign aspects.

The Mediagenic Author

There is now an unprecedented series of opportunities for authors to receive public attention in the US, and many of these new opportunities can be linked to shifts in the economics of literary production – what one observer has described as

> the unrestrained reign of hype, with its seemingly irresistible attraction for opportunistic and big-money writers, and its eerie capacity for

luring and ensnaring unwary artists and for turning them, often against their better judgment, into travelling salesmen and TV pitchmen.[1]

The recent transformation of the publishing industry from a large number of family-run houses to a small number of major publishers owned by giant, multimedia parent companies has completely transformed the nature of authorship and publishing in America and, increasingly, throughout the world. Although outside interests have been involved in American publishing since the 1960s, with companies like CBS, ITT and RCA leading the way, the mergers which took place in the 1980s and 1990s brought all the major trade book publishers into the hands of large, transnational communications conglomerates with holdings and interests in many other, usually more profitable, areas of the mass media. As a parallel phenomenon occurring steadily since about 1960, these major publishers have also been purchasing small or medium-sized independent houses, so that there are now few areas of book publishing which do not, either directly or indirectly, come under the control of seven main conglomerates: Bertelsmann, Pearson, Viacom, Rupert Murdoch's News Corporation, Time Warner, Hearst and Holtzbrinck. These large corporations have made more venture capital available to publishers, thus solving the perennial cash-flow problems of the small independently owned houses while also increasing the pressure for commercial success, so that sophisticated forms of book publicity have been developed to market books more effectively.

In order to appreciate the impact of conglomeration in this area, it is worth stressing that, until recently, book promotion was widely viewed as one of the most inefficient areas of the industry. Lewis Coser, Charles Kadushin and Walter Powell, in a definitive 1982 survey of book publishing, pointed to the erratic and unresearched nature of book marketing, particularly within what publishers generally regarded as the unpredictable area of trade books.[2] Jacques Barzun, in a 1984 Library of Congress colloquium, similarly claimed that 'if cornflakes were sold like books, nobody would eat breakfast'.[3] This inefficiency was partly a product of the widespread belief that books were all distinct products and therefore unmarketable anyway, but it was also due to the survival within many houses of the genteel image of the 'gentleman publisher', working for the love of literature rather than mere financial gain. While the publishing industry became progressively more commercially astute throughout this century, it also became more strenuous in its efforts to professionalize itself, producing a hierarchy which sealed off the most prestigious areas of publishing from its commercial aspects. Publishers, as James L.W. West III argues, 'gained dignity and status by removing themselves from the inkstains of the printshop, the blue pencil of the editor, and the cashbox of the book-seller'.[4] In this urbane, old-boy network, a publisher like Alfred Knopf could say that he preferred not to publish any author whom he would not want to invite to dinner.[5] This attitude encouraged a lack of coordination in the marketing of books, particularly since responsibilities for public relations, advertising, sales and distribution were often located in separate depart-ments, and made book publicity, as one of the elements in the chain closest to the consumer, a low status area of responsibility. Publicists, who were predominantly female, were often referred to disparagingly by insiders as the 'airline stewardesses' of the industry.[6]

In the last two decades, however, the status and significance of these departments within publishing houses has steadily risen. Publishers have also realized the cheapness and effectiveness of forms of publicity which concentrate on the author – magazine and newspaper features and tele-vision and radio appearances – over paid advertising. For example, a ten-city author tour costs about the same as, and reaches considerably more pro-spective customers than, a full-page advertisement in the *New York Times Book Review*.[7] Among these forms of cheap publicity, the superiority of television over newspapers and magazines as a book marketing tool has also long been recognized. As long ago as 1981, Thomas Whiteside described an appearance by an author on a major talk show as 'one of the biggest promotional prizes around for any publisher', second only to being selected by the Book-of-the-Month Club.[8] In recognition of this clear relationship between book sales and personal television appearances, the major publishers are even beginning to introduce authors on to direct-mail advertisements – usually 'infomercials' in talk-show format – and home shopping television channels like QVC, on which viewers can phone to order copies by credit card.

The large number of recent novels written by (or, more usually, ghost-written for) celebrities such as Ivana Trump, William Shatner, Martina Navratilova and Joan Collins suggests the increasing importance of the recognizable, media-friendly personality as a kind of brand name with which to sell the literary product.[9] A variation on this theme is the bestselling author producing work from beyond the grave – after the death of Alistair MacLean in 1987, for example, HarperCollins decided to perpetuate his bankable name by turning some of his old story ideas into novels, for which task they chose an unknown, first-time author with the suspiciously simi-lar name of Alastair MacNeill. (After a court ruling in 1991, though, the publishers were forced to make MacLean's name smaller than MacNeill's on the book jacket.) Some publishers can be influenced by the attractive-ness or screen presence of an author in deciding whether or not to accept a book for publication. The *New York Times* has reported cases of authors being sent to speech tutors and image consultants by publishers, and of literary agents providing publishers with dummy videotapes of their clients along with book proposals, acceptance or rejection of the manuscript sometimes hinging on the author's performance.[10]

These still seem to be isolated cases, however, if only because the publishing industry produces too many books to vet all its authors this closely. As Richard Schickel has shown, the modern phenomenon of celebrity developed in early American cinema partly because the popular demand for personalities, unlike the demand for particular plotlines or genres, was relatively stable. As films became more costly and studios needed to take out loans in order to make them, 'star names came to lead the list of collateral that bankers looked upon with favour when their assistance was sought'.[11] The involvement of a particular star can still decide whether a film project goes ahead because of his or her ability to 'open' a movie – to guarantee that audiences will go and see it in the crucial first few weeks of release. The fact that the book publishing industry does not require such a large initial investment as a Hollywood film, however, encourages the speculative overproduction of books. About 80 per cent of the titles produced every year are commercial failures, a ratio which would quickly bankrupt a Hollywood studio or television network. Because the initial cost of publishing a book is quite small, however, a house usually requires only one 'blockbuster' in a season to counterbalance all its other losses, and it is this kind of work which therefore receives the biggest promotional effort. Sales representatives decide in marketing meetings which few books among a publisher's many titles get 'the full treatment – the six-figure print run, the lavish book jacket, the pressure on the news media, the 10-city tour, the television interviews, the advertisements, the four-color posters and bookstore displays'. In these meetings, they may well be influenced by extra-literary factors – especially since, to aid them in their decision making, they are often sent not only proof copies of the books but also videotapes on which editors and authors pitch the book to them.[12] Publishers will therefore only make serious efforts to publicize a small percentage of their list, and the gap between the so-called 'leads' and the 'midlist' (the books with modest advances and modest sales) is becoming wider.

While supporters of the conglomeration of the industry often maintain that the blockbusters help to subsidize the loss-making books, and it is certainly true that the ratio of books produced to those which actually make a profit is extremely high, this argument does not take account of the headstart given to a small number of books by the hugely varying sums spent on book publicity. As Whiteside explains this growing disparity in the publishing industry: 'If you are not in show business, you are really off-Broadway.'[13] The increasingly large advances paid out to star-name authors also help to encourage this inequality, because publishers naturally spend more on promoting these authors in order to recoup their initial outlay. In addition, since the largest of these advances are often reported in the press, they can function by themselves as an important source of publicity. Many publishers admit that even bestselling authors are not always expected to earn back their huge advances, which are used as a way of obtaining free publicity not only for the author but for the publishing house.[14]

The opportunities this creates for the book publishing industry to decide which authors are noticed and read by consumers are given added significance by the influence of the parent companies. All the major conglomerates involved in American book publishing have extensive additional interests in newspapers and magazines, satellite and cable television stations, CD-Roms and on-line services and, in some instances, movie, video and music production and distribution. The real significance of these conglomerates lies in the increased opportunities they afford for cross-subsidization between different strata of the same company. As Joseph Turow suggests, the critical change in the communications industries in the 1980s was that 'conglomeration was now seen as a way to link media holdings actively in the interest of greater profits'. The term commonly used to describe this kind of cooperation is *synergy*, which denotes 'the coordination of parts of a company so that the whole actually turns out to be worth more than the sum of its parts acting alone'.[15]

There is clearly great potential for synergy in the area of book publicity, which involves selling books through other mass media – magazines, newspapers, television and radio – often owned by the same parent company. Possible (although unverified) examples of such cooperation are the cover story on Scott Turow which *Time* magazine published in June 1990, at the same time as its corporate sibling Warner Books distributed *Presumed Innocent* in paperback and Warner Brothers released the film version of the same book, or the extensive profile of the then unknown Donna Tartt in the September 1992 edition of *Vanity Fair* which, like Tartt's publisher, Knopf (an imprint within Random House), was owned by Newhouse. Such profiles and interviews are prearranged long before books are subjected to press reviews or appear in bookstores, the intention being to bypass the normal critical responses which books receive, either in print media or through word of mouth, by pitching the book directly at the individual consumer.

There is also evidence that publishers have used their corporate muscle to influence the process of book reviewing, which can function as a powerful intermediary between reader and author. The complaint that commercial considerations, and in particular the power of the parent companies, can affect the production and placement of book reviews in other media has been made since the late 1960s.[16] As the synergetic interconnections between books and other kinds of media become greater, this accusation – that book reviews are inextricably linked to the process of book promotion – is likely to become even more insistent. Before Newhouse sold Random House to Bertelsmann in March 1998, for example, one independent publisher suggested that Random House had 'cornered the review space' in Newhouse-owned magazines such as the *New Yorker*, *Vanity Fair* and *Vogue*.[17] There is no suggestion that the influence of the parent company is in any way altering the content of the reviews, but since most books are wholly ignored by book reviewers, even bad reviews can be good publicity. Of the 8,000 books sent to the *New York Times Book Review* every year, for instance, only about 2,500 receive even a mention and only a fraction receive a full review.[18] A review on the front page of this magazine, for many years a site of 'unparalleled positional power',[19] can virtually guarantee a book's commercial success, regardless of the review's content.

The conglomerates, in other words, have put pressure on publishers to create the largest possible readership for a small number of books, by pushing commercially successful authors on to mainstream television and other media. There is thus a danger that media interest will only be generated for the kinds of authors who have a chance of making the bestsellers lists, leaving the majority of them to manage with little publicity other than press releases. Frank Rich, in a recent *New York Times* op-ed piece bemoaning the star system in publishing, puts it more forcefully when he writes that 'these days, even *Moby Dick* might not be enough to get Melville booked on *Good Morning America*'.[20] These trends have been reinforced by the growth of large book chains like Barnes and Noble and Borders, which are forming increasingly close ties with publishers, and which aim similarly to foster and promote a small number of bestselling authors by giving them particular attention through book signings and 'dumpbins' (special displays for prioritized books).[21]

The relatively concealed nature of these processes makes them even more effective in controlling the cultural marketplace. Richard Dyer, in a study of Hollywood stardom, distinguishes between two ways in which studios market films – *promotion*, or paid advertising, and *publicity*, or profiles and interviews with the stars of the film in the media – and suggests that the public tends to see the latter as less consciously manipulated by the studio and therefore more authentic.[22] The marketing strategies outlined above come under the definition of publicity rather than promotion: cover stories, book reviews and talk show appearances by authors are presented not simply as public relations exercises but as (to some extent at least) spontaneously generated by popular interest in these authors. Journalists and television interviewers thus serve, with varying degrees of willingness or unwillingness, as conduits for astutely controlled publicity.

The increasing power of publishers in this context has led George Garrett, among many others, to suggest that 'the great corruption ... of the last half of the century has been the attempt on the part of the publishers to *create* (by fiat as much as fact) its own gallery of stars and master artists'.[23] These lavish promotional campaigns, which give an unfair advantage to certain authors in the quest for public recognition, point to a wider pattern in the media industries in general, in which the response of consumers is stabilized and standardized through the 'name recognition' of certain prominent figures. The increasing importance of book publicity in promoting authors as 'personalities' is therefore a symptom of the continuing integration of literary production into the entertainment industry, making authors and books part of the cultural pervasiveness of celebrity as a market mechanism of monopoly capitalism – the celebrity in this case being 'anyone whose name and fame have been built up to the point where reference to them, via mention, mediatized representation or live appearance, can serve as a promotional booster in itself'.[24] In this context, stardom becomes wholly self-fulfilling: the visibility of the author's celebrity name is used to bankroll products, making it harder for unknown or first-time authors and their work to gain recognition.

These developments appear to point to the ascendancy, in Bourdieu's terms, of the large-scale field of cultural production, a market in which 'success goes to success' and 'announcing a print run contributes to making a bestseller'.[25] In fact, Bourdieu's most recent work reveals a change in emphasis from his earlier accounts of literary production by critiquing what he sees as the 'regressions to heteronomy' of the cultural field, resulting from the 'increasingly greater interpenetration between the world of art and the world of money'. According to Bourdieu, this is threatening to undermine the traditional division between avant-garde and commercial production which has been in place since the mid-nineteenth century. He argues that 'the holders of cultural capital may always "regress" ... the claim of autonomy which is inscribed in the very existence of the field of cultural production must reckon with obstacles and powers which are ceaselessly renewed'. The transformation of the American publishing scene in the last few decades would seem to support Bourdieu's concerns about the triumph of the 'doxosophes' – the media-oriented, heteronomous producers who seek to manoeuvre their way into the restricted field and challenge its traditional autonomy and independence.[26]

The Trade in Cultural Capital

While these developments in conglomerate-owned publishing are highly significant, however, they are only one aspect of the highly diversified environment in which books are marketed and consumed in the US. It is worth stressing, perhaps, that people have been criticizing the American publishing industry for many of these same flaws – trend-chasing, bestseller-fixation, excessive hype, rampant commercialism – for at least a century, if not longer. These criticisms have often originated from within the industry itself: as long ago as 1905, the publisher Henry Holt commented in an essay in the *Atlantic Monthly* that his profession was 'as crazy about advertising as the Dutch ever were about tulips'.[27] As Ken Worpole writes, 'the complaint – that publishers ignore new writing, preferring to play safe with a stock-list of general titles – dates back almost to Caxton'.[28] In fact, book publishing has proved remarkably adaptable to these commercial pressures, remaining one of the few areas of the mass media where market values have not triumphed wholesale – there are still many editors committed to 'literary' fiction even within commercially minded publishing houses, as is shown by the survival and growth of prestigious imprints such as Scribner's and Flamingo within corporate-owned publishers like Simon and Schuster and HarperCollins. The familiar argument that media conglomeration produces the triumph of short-term profit over artistic merit is thus qualified by the peculiar status of book publishing within the culture industries.

More important, perhaps, literary celebrity is not simply an effect of the increasingly promotional nature of the publishing industry – the cultural field is characterized by a perpetual conflict between internal demands and external pressures, and celebrity authors continue to ply their trade in the middle ground between cultural kudos and commercial success. Indeed, this middle ground has flourished in recent years as cultural and economic capital have become increasingly interchangeable in progressively diverse and stratified capitalist societies like the US. This has been most evident in the 1980s and 1990s in the growth of 'serious' literature as a marketable commodity, the product of a whole series of economic and cultural factors. Jason Epstein's founding of Anchor Books in 1953 initiated a 'quality paperback' revolution in the US, in which publishers exploited the low risk, more prolonged shelf life and higher returns of quality paperbacks as compared with their massmarket counterparts. (A similar development had already taken place in Britain, after the creation of Penguin Books in 1935.)

The pace of this revolution was stepped up in the 1980s, a key event being the establishment of Random House's innovative *Vintage Contemporaries* series by Gary Fisketjon in 1984, which attempted to combine commercial clout with literary prestige by marketing a stable of new and semi-established authors such as Raymond Carver, Jay McInerney and Thomas McGuane. The highly successful positioning of this series 'at the center of the crossroads of culture and commerce',[29] in Stephanie Girard's words, has since been duplicated by many other publishing houses. These new conditions have put pressure on 'literary' authors, even publicity-shy ones like Don DeLillo, Cormac McCarthy and William Gaddis, to do some promotional work by at least submitting to print interviews. 'These days', as the *New York Times* puts it, 'the most ardent apostles for art roll up their sleeves, hold their noses against the meretriciousness of the marketplace and practice a little economic determinism'.[30]

The current situation in American publishing is particularly difficult to unravel because its macro-tendencies have been accompanied by micro-tendencies. In other words, while collectivization within the industry promotes the vigorous marketing of books to as wide a readership as possible, American media have also militated against this trend by diversifying and demassifying as a product of technological and sociological change, as evidenced by the growth of interactive multimedia, so-called 'narrowcasting' on cable and satellite channels and 'niche' market magazines. In particular, more specialized magazines have proliferated and thrived in recent years because of their attraction to potential advertisers (due to the clearly defined nature and relative affluence of their readerships), and their increasingly cheap production costs. The long-term decline in circulation of popular, general interest 'consensus' magazines like *Time* and *Life* has been accompanied, therefore, by the emergence of a huge range of publications interested in writing about 'serious' authors. These range from the highbrow *Paris Review* (which has run a prestigious series of 'Writers at Work' interviews since 1953), to tabloidy outlets like *People*, to glossies like *Esquire* and *Vanity Fair*. With its annual 'Hall of Fame' ('the thirty-five people who made the year') and combination of elaborate photo spreads and higher gossip, this latter magazine has been extremely influential in bringing some of the elements of entertainment celebrity into the sphere of high culture – as David Wyatt says, it 'gives off heat precisely by confounding the distinction between copy and ad [and] trades openly on the irresistible habit of validating taste by confirming it through the visibility – the celebrity – of authors'.[31] *Vanity Fair*'s approach has been contagious – the previously staid *New Yorker* broke its long-held rule against combining text with photographs in the mid-1980s, and introduced a much more gossipy, celebrity-friendly element to its pages after Tina Brown (previously at *Vanity Fair*) became editor in 1992. Newspapers such as the *New York Times* and *Washington Post*, meanwhile, have also expanded their arts, books and culture pages in recent years to incorporate author interviews, profiles and other similar features.

The willingness of both the book industry and other print media to exploit the potential of literary prizes is another factor which points to the interconnectedness of cultural and economic capital in the creation of contemporary literary fame. (Indeed, book publishers have directly sponsored and even been involved in the judging of prizes like the National Book Awards and the ABBY, the American Booksellers' Book of the Year.) These prizes help to create a kind of 'major league' of literary heavyweights by stimulating sales and inspiring media coverage, while also appealing to the existence of higher values which surpass mere commercial considerations. This direct negotiation between commercial and cultural worth is often at the root of the controversies surrounding the awards, particularly the suspicion that they provide only a veneer of intellectual and aesthetic authority, rubber-stamping bestselling success and ignoring innovative, challenging authors – a suspicion reinforced in 1974 when the Pulitzer committee rejected the judges' recommendation for the fiction prize, Thomas Pynchon's *Gravity's Rainbow*, and gave no award. But the way that publishers invest heavily in the prestige attaching to such prizes makes it clear that they are far from only being concerned uncomplicatedly with the 'bottom line'.

Their penchant for list-making is further evidence of this: Random House's recent roll-call of the hundred 'best' novels of the twentieth century, compiled with the help of authors such as Gore Vidal, A.S. Byatt and William Styron, was clearly both a successful publicity-grabbing exercise (it received wide newspaper coverage) and an attempt to claim the cultural high ground. The continued growth of literary festivals where readers can meet famous authors – such as the Arizona and Los Angeles Times Book Festivals, and the Miami Book Fair, begun in 1983 and still the largest, attracting hundreds of authors and over 400,000 people – also attests to this interlocked relationship between literature and the market. As one festival organizer puts it, these events are 'mongrels – part commerce, part art, part street fair', including book 'plugs' and signings as well as weightier lectures and panels. Clearly their main function from the publisher's viewpoint is to promote books, but the people who attend them have a variety of more elevated motives – as one author-participant, Allan Gurganus, says, they are indicative of 'a kind of righteous remnant, of people looking for some kind of spiritual existence apart from the sandpaper of the culture'.[32]

The major impetus behind the interdependent relationship between cultural and economic capital in contemporary American culture has, however, been the increased clout of the academy – one of the prime symbols and disseminators of cultural capital in capitalist societies – and its institutional sponsorship of authors. The huge growth of college bookstores after the Second World War, stimulated by a rise in enrolment on the back of the GI Bill and then the Baby Boom, has made universities a large and significant factor within the broader literary marketplace. Indeed, as Philip Fisher says, the success of the quality paperback revolution in the United States has largely been a product of the commercial success of college course texts.[33] In an era of mass education, there is a constant demand for new authors as raw material for undergraduate courses, doctoral theses, critical monographs and articles in journals like *Modern Fiction Studies*, *Contemporary Literature* and *Critique*. More generally, the postwar rise in college enrolment has greatly enlarged the educated reading public who are interested in buying work by new authors.

Just as important, universities have also been involved in more direct forms of sponsorship of authors through the setting up of creative writing courses and workshops, which are largely a postwar phenomenon and have mushroomed particularly over the last 20 years. The first and most celebrated writer's programme, at the University of Iowa, now stands, according to the *New York Times*, 'unshakably in the mainstream of our literary life'.[34] Although the work produced out of some of these courses is destined never to reach beyond the readerships for university quarterlies, little magazines and small-press publications, the more prestigious of them are far from being an ivory tower, a haven from the corrupted world of commerce – they are designed to feed organically into the marketplace, producing professional authors who will be of interest to mainstream magazines, agents and major publishers. It is striking, in fact, how many of the most successful literary celebrities of the last 25 years are products of writers' workshops – Raymond Carver, Jay McInerney and John Irving, to name only a few.

Perhaps the most telling indication of the influence of the universities in American cultural life is the fact that tenured academics have often become mainstream celebrities themselves: critics such as Edward Said, Harold Bloom and Camille Paglia are recognized media figures and even occasionally make the bestsellers lists in the US. Paglia is perhaps the best example of this crossover success – she has transformed herself into a media celebrity by appearing on MTV, television talk shows and both writing for and being profiled in popular magazines like *Wired*, *Harper's* and *Penthouse*. Her own account of the cultural resonance of female film and pop stars –

most famously her claiming of Madonna as a feminist icon – has clearly contributed to her own celebrity, as has her talent for producing punchy soundbites which make their way regularly into newspapers' 'quotes of the week'. She has also developed a particularly distinctive, aggressively self-promoting public image, posing in extravagant attire on the covers of magazines and including cartoon caricatures of herself in her books.[35] Celebrities like Paglia are often controversial figures within the academy, criticized for pandering to base commercial tastes and reproducing the conservative politics of the mass media. bell hooks, for example, has suggested that Paglia's books are 'bought not for their ideas but because the hype surrounding the author entices', and accuses her and other media feminists like Katie Roiphe and Naomi Wolf of being white, privileged women presuming to speak for women in general in an 'opportunistic bid for stardom', and producing 'revamped patriarchal logic passing for "new feminism" that the mass media hypes, and that sexist men and women cheer'.[36] Paglia, meanwhile, has attacked academic critical theory, particularly the work of Jacques Lacan and Michael Foucault, and what she calls the 'PC feminism' formulated within university humanities departments.[37] Allan Bloom is another example of an academic who has achieved bestseller status (with *The Closing of the American Mind* in 1987) and a considerable degree of media attention – but not generally professional approval – by vehemently criticizing current paradigms in the humanities.

'The New Mediocracy'

The phenomenon of intellectual celebrity is not, of course, unique to the United States. The peculiar status of intellectuals in French society, for example, has helped to produce a whole group of celebrity thinkers (the most famous being Bernard-Henri Lévy), who appear as frequent guests on late-night television chat shows. The most influential of these shows was Bernard Pivot's book review programme, *Apostrophes*, which ran between 1975 and 1990 and had a huge effect on the public prominence and book sales of leading intellectuals.[38] The power of television to make or break intellectual reputations in France has led Godfrey Hodgson, among others, to suggest that it is a country in which '40 mediacrats have the power of life and death over 40,000 authors'.[39] The debate in France about the role of these intellectuals offers a useful way into a discussion not only about the celebritization of academics in the US but also, more generally, the complicated mediation between cultural and economic capital I have been discussing above.

Régis Debray first criticized these developments in France in the late 1970s, deploring the way in which his country's intellectuals had forged an alliance with 'the new mediocracy'.[40] (In fact, though, the French tradition of denouncing intellectuals as 'sellouts' and traitors to their calling dates at least as far back as Julien Benda's 1927 *La Trahison des Clercs*.[41]) According to Debray, the wholesale appropriation of intellectual production by the media has produced 'an Americanized intelligentsia in European-ized France [which] puts the emphasis on smiles, good teeth, nice hair and the adolescent stupidity known as petulance'. Debray suggests that intellectuals have been corrupted by the broadening of their constituency beyond the narrow confines of their own peer group. He argues that

> by extending the reception area, the mass media have reduced the sources of intellectual legitimacy, surrounding the professional intelligentsia, the classic source of legitimacy, with wider concentric circles that are less demanding and therefore more easily won over ... The mass media have broken down the closure of the traditional intelligentsia, together with its evaluative norms and its scale of values.[42]

One of Bourdieu's most polemical works to date, *On Television and Journalism*, is also an attack on French media intellectuals (although, like Debray's book, it mentions none of them by name). Bourdieu notes witheringly that

> television rewards a certain number of *fast-thinkers* who offer cultural 'fast food' – predigested and prethought culture ... Like the Trojan horse, [such intellectuals] introduce heteronomous agents into autonomous worlds. Supported by external forces, these agents are accorded an authority they cannot get from their peers.[43]

In fact, these comments on the usurpation of intellectual life by the journalistic field form part of Bourdieu's overall criticisms of any kind of culture which attempts to bridge the distinction between high and mass culture – what he calls the 'partial revolutions in the hierarchies' created by 'the new cultural intermediaries' who 'have invented a whole series of genres half-way between legitimate culture and mass production'. He defines 'la culture moyenne', or middlebrow culture (typified by such cultural phenomena as literary prizes, 'light' classical music and intellectual talk shows), as an 'imposture' which relies on the 'complicity of the consumers'. This kind of culture, according to Bourdieu, simply exploits the inferiority complex of an aspirant petit bourgeoisie which 'bows, just in case, to everything which looks as if it might be culture', a knee-jerk reaction which he defines as a 'cultural allodoxia, that is, all the mistaken identifications and false recognitions which betray the gap between acknowledgement and knowledge'.[44] As David Swartz points out, there is a tension in Bourdieu's work between the unmasking of the provisional nature of cultural hierarchies in his 'field' theory, and a much more prescriptive view of how intellectuals and authors should critically engage with society and culture,[45] and these comments seem to belong to this latter aspect of his work.

American cultural critics have tended to follow Bourdieu's approach in arguing that the new cultural conditions in the US represent the appropriation of high culture by mass consumption – a 'dumbing down' rather than a 'wising up'. As early as the mid-1970s, Richard Ohmann argued that a diverse network of academic and journalistic book critics, literary prize committees, editors, book publicists, metropolitan book buyers and authors now constituted 'a cultural establishment, inseparable from the market, both influencing and influenced by it', creating a literature produced and received within what he called 'a nearly closed circle of marketing and consumption, the simultaneous exploitation and creation of taste, familiar to anyone who has examined marketplace culture under monopoly capitalism'.[46] In particular, the close link between university writing courses and the broader marketplace has been condemned for promoting only certain kinds of books and authors, creating a kind of invisible screening process for contemporary fiction and poetry. Donald Morton and Mas'ud Zavarzadeh, in an article which seeks to expose the cultural politics of the fiction workshop, argue that writer's courses are 'colonized by the mass media. Cultural representations that sell in the marketplace, such as realist fiction, dominate university humanities programs.'[47] Charles Newman also points to this cosily interdependent relationship when he states that

insofar as literature ever provided a social frame of reference, it has been obliterated by the two growth industries of the Post-Modern era – the democratized academy and the mass entertainment industry. The academy absorbs literature as a subsidiary, a paper acquisition in which assets are not redeployed but only displayed more attractively on a newly consolidated balance sheet.[48]

One of the most sustained critiques of this new situation is made by John Aldridge in his book, *Talents and Technicians*, an attack on 'assembly-line fiction', exemplified for him by such celebrity authors as Raymond Carver, Ann Beattie, Bobbie Ann Mason, Louise Erdrich, Lorrie Moore, Jay McInerney and Bret Easton Ellis. Aldridge argues that 'such reputations as [these writers] have acquired are mainly the products of book reviews, literary gossip, and publishers' advertising and have scarcely come under examination or been ratified by serious criticism'. He sees them as a by-product of the commodification of the book business, which is now run by 'merchants operating a vast corporate enterprise engaged in the mass manufacture and promotion of books', and, echoing Boorstin's well-used phrase, claims that they 'have become familiar names mostly for being familiar names'. However, Aldridge then goes on to examine the connection between book publishing and other areas of the mass media and a new cultural establishment originating out of the universities, suggesting that this new breed of authors 'belong[s] to the first generation in American history ... ever to be created almost exclusively through formal academic instruction in creative writing'. The writers' workshops, he argues, produce not authentic literary talents but 'clonal fabrications' of authors, whose appeal is precisely that they are standardized and safe – there is thus an almost perfect fit between the authors churned out by a process of academic accreditation and the broader demands of the marketplace.[49] To summarize: the argument in all these accounts is that various overlapping spheres or institutions – journalism, book publishing, academia – have been able to function as a kind of self-contained literary establishment helping to determine which authors receive the most public attention in contemporary American culture.

The problem with these accounts is that they suppose the existence of a 'pure' form of literary and intellectual production without the corrupting influences of money or the craving for prestige. Aldridge, for example, posits a highly romanticized vision of the 'real writer' who has been displaced by the processes he describes, someone who 'becomes a witness and an incurable isolate, doing his work alone and in secret, and being in the end not only fully aware of his otherness but coming to coddle and cultivate it'.[50] In this sense, his critique is broadly similar to the jeremiads against celebrity by Boorstin and others discussed in the introduction to this book, in its assumption of a prelapsarian state in which major figures rise to prominence 'naturally'. Debray's unexamined notion of 'intellectual legitimacy' similarly seems to assume that literary and intellectual expression can be mediated transparently, and that when intellectuals themselves control the means of mediation, this transparency is achieved. Even Bourdieu – despite the overall emphasis in his work on the relational nature of different fields, and on the 'interestedness' of all forms of cultural production, whether obviously commercial or not – ultimately nails his cultural elitism to the mast. As R.M. Shusterman puts it: 'Bourdieu rigorously exposes the hidden economy and veiled interests of the so-called disinterested aesthetic of high culture but nonetheless remains too enchanted by the myth he demystifies to acknowledge the existence of any legitimate popular aesthetic.'[51] All these critics, then, implicitly support a dubious notion of authors or intellectuals as ethereal, detached individuals, which overlooks the kinds of capital, either economic or cultural, at stake in all forms of cultural production – the fact that writers who disseminate their ideas to a public, however narrowly defined, have always been at least partly concerned with presenting themselves competitively.

A Promotional Culture

It is true that there have been significant changes in the American cultural landscape in recent years, partly as a consequence of the trends to which Aldridge and others refer. The range and diversity of authors who achieve fame in contemporary culture, however, shows that American literary culture is too complex and contradictory to allow for the formation of a sealed-off cultural establishment, conspiratorially determining the rise and fall of literary reputations. In fact, the highly specific celebrity constructions of 40 or 50 years ago – notably the white, male, representatively 'American' author championed by *Time* and *Life* and epitomized in figures like Hemingway and Faulkner – have been increasingly challenged, allowing many different kinds of authors, including the less obviously 'mainstream', to be marketed as public personalities. To give one example, the celebritization of African-American women authors like Toni Morrison shows how questions of simple market appeal can merge with broader social, cultural and racially inflected issues in the construction of celebrity authorship. Morrison's transformation over the last 20 years into what the *New York Times* calls 'the nearest thing America has to a national novelist'[52] has been supported by a wide range of phenomena. Her name was clearly established by critical discussion of her work within the academy: the increasing marketability of black women authors as a whole, in fact, has been greatly stimulated by the movements towards canon revision in American universities since the 1960s. Morrison and other authors have thus benefited greatly from the growth in black studies, multicultural studies and women's studies courses (the latter being particularly receptive to black writers), as well as their integration into more general literature courses.[53]

In more recent years, however, Morrison's celebrity has been significantly reinforced by two events outside the academy – the huge media interest surrounding her Nobel Prize success in 1993 (after she had already received a series of smaller, national prizes like the Pulitzer and the National

Book Award), and her promotion on Oprah's Book Club, a monthly part of Oprah Winfrey's talk show. The effects of *Oprah* on book sales were first recognized in 1993, when 250,000 extra copies of Robert James Waller's *The Bridges of Madison County* were sold after it was featured on the show. Oprah's Book Club, established soon afterwards, was one of the most important innovations in book promotion in the 1990s. Winfrey focuses on one book a month – with a bias towards black and/or women authors, who make up a large part of her audience – and every volume featured so far has gone on to make the bestsellers lists. Morrison's *Song of Solomon* became a bestseller 19 years after its first publication, as did her more recent novel, *Paradise* – a much more complex, technically innovative text which would not normally be expected to appeal to so wide a readership.

Unlike many of the other celebrities discussed in this book, Morrison has largely welcomed her own fame and bestsellerdom, and that of other black women authors such as Terry McMillan and Alice Walker, as a way of opening up literature to wider readerships and challenging established canons. She took part in the hour-long *Oprah* special on *Paradise*, leading a study group of 20 viewers in a discussion of the novel, and says approvingly: 'Oprah uses her show to promote books to the kind of people who might be intimidated by bookshops, the people I want to reach and am keen to address.'[54] Morrison has also used her celebrity to speak out on race and gender issues provoked by such events as the Clarence Thomas – Anita Hill hearings of 1991 and the O.J. Simpson trial of 1995. In particular, she has sought to challenge the dominant representations of mainstream media on these issues, dedicating herself to the task of 'representing one's own race to, or in spite of, a race of readers that understands itself to be "universal" or race-free'.[55]

Morrison's fame – both in the way it has been constructed and the way she has sought to use it as a model of public, socially engaged authorship – shows that recent changes in the cultural marketplace have, at least in some cases, allowed different literary traditions to reach new audiences and previously marginalized authors to achieve fame and success. Morrison's celebrity has been accompanied by the new prominence of black public intellectuals like Cornel West, Henry Louis Gates, Jr and Michael Eric Dyson, who have written for general interest magazines and newspapers in debates over such issues as the Rodney King riots, 'political correctness' and canon revision. This has spilled over into bestselling books (West's *Race Matters* made the *New York Times* bestsellers list in 1993 and he received lengthy profiles in both *Time* and *Newsweek* as a consequence) and television appearances (Dyson has guested on talk shows such as *Today*, *Good Morning America* and *Oprah*).

Aside from these shifts in contemporary canon formation, there is another problem with the conspiratorial model put forward by Aldridge and others – the sheer complexity of the way that literary celebrity circulates in contemporary culture, the fact that it amounts to much more than the cumulative effect of the promotional strategies of publishing companies and other institutions. In this context, Andrew Wernick employs the useful term 'promotional culture' to describe the increasing consolidation of a system of competitive exchange in ostensibly non-commercial institutions – by which he means the permeation of the *logic* of the marketplace into all areas of cultural life rather than the straightforward co-opting of culture into commodity production. Wernick, for example, outlines a number of key stages in 'the promotional constitution of the authorial name': first, the name of an individual author is assigned to a work (a relatively recent innovation, as Michel Foucault also points out in his essay, 'What is an Author?'); second, the author's name enters the business of authorship and publishing, where it can be used to sell a recognized product in a competitive marketplace; finally, this promotional name becomes detached from the book or other product it sells, and starts to circulate separately, becoming part of 'the vast discourse constituted by promotion as a whole'.[56]

Wernick is suggesting that, although there are direct ways in which authors can be promoted as part of the marketing strategies of publishers and other media, the general dissemination of different forms of publicity in contemporary culture makes it increasingly difficult to distinguish these from other means by which the author's name can circulate. This is a general pattern in celebrity culture as a whole: the 'imaged name' of the celebrity represents 'a banked and transferable store of promotional capital', useful in many different contexts. According to Wernick, this is what distinguishes contemporary celebrity from older types of fame – not so much its 'mediatized artificiality' (as Boorstin might argue) but the fact that it is 'freefloating'. The celebrity is not just the product of promotional strategies, then, but is part of 'the vortex of promotional signs ... a great, swirling stream of signifiers whose only meaning, in the end, is the circulatory process which it anticipates, represents and impels'.[57]

I want to argue that the intertextuality of celebrity – the fact that it is, as Richard deCordova points out, a discursive as well as a narrowly economic phenomenon[58] – makes the star a site of considerable ambivalence and contestation. A number of critics have examined this intertextuality through recent controversies surrounding copyright law, created by the simultaneous growth of trademark rights to protect celebrities and a more nebulous and less controllable sphere of publicity.[59] These controversies emerge from the fact that more and more institutions are seeking to market the celebrity for profit (either for economic or cultural capital), and using trademark law to protect the unauthorized appropriation of his or her 'image', at the same time as they are also losing control over that image as it disseminates inexorably through many different media. These tensions – between the exchange value of celebrity and its status as a site for disputed cultural meanings – mean that it functions as 'an ambiguous sign in contemporary culture that inscribes within and between its various forms a tension of signification'.[60] In other words, celebrity works through its own contradictions, critiquing and commenting on the tenuousness of its claims to single people out for special attention.

This allows the celebrity to function at the centre of debates about what constitutes an individual, and specifically an exceptional individual, in contemporary society, clustering around polarities such as depth and surface, authenticity and superficiality, cultural capital and commercial value. One example of this is the entertainment media's schizophrenic attitude to the stars – the same publications which publish *Hello*-style, uncritical profiles of celebrities will also frequently complain that celebrity as a whole is a shallow and trivial phenomenon, accompanying this with a debunking of stars for their inflated salaries, huge entourages, on-set tantrums and extravagant lifestyles. Similarly, although publishers and other institutions may attempt to sponsor particular authors over others, this process is not uncontested: there are countless articles in newspapers and magazines deploring the barrage of hype, the way that overrated star authors can deprive the humble foot-soldiers of attention and sales. In one sense, then, the critical comments of Aldridge and others about literary celebrity feed back into the phenomenon, reinforcing the familiar notion of celebrities as contentious figures.

In addition to this, literary celebrities are particularly controversial figures within celebrity culture as a whole because of their position at the centre of an ongoing battle about the relationship between art and money in contemporary culture. Bourdieu may argue in the comments quoted above that the balance has shifted towards the large-scale field in recent years, but one of the defining characteristics of the cultural field is still this 'chiastic structure' in the distribution of cultural and economic capital, based on the perpetual contest between two competing principles of legitimacy: autonomy and heteronomy.[61] Bourdieu's seminal work on the 'field' – as opposed to his later protests about the triumph of heteronomy – is valuable here because it recognizes the contested nature of literary production, showing the importance of border positions between different fields as a source of struggle and change. As a structuralist, Bourdieu concedes that the field of cultural production does function as a star system, in which 'what "makes reputations" is not ... this or that influential person, this or that institution, review, magazine, academy, coterie, dealer or publisher ... it is the field of production, understood as a system of objective relations between agents or institutions.'[62] However, he suggests that this system (as with the structure of other fields) is constantly open to negotiation and debate by individual and collective agents within the field. These debates are particularly fiercely fought in the cultural field because one of its chief characteristics is its 'weak degree of institutionalization', which means that the various positions it offers are diverse, constantly changing and always up for grabs.[63] The cultural field is also unstable because (like celebrity itself) it is constituted symbolically as well as materially, and is therefore always liable to be altered by the discourses and debates produced by the agents within it.

The role of author-recluses in celebrity culture – where the authors' apparent distance from celebrity seems to contribute to their fame – is perhaps the most obvious example of this symbolic struggle between the restricted and large-scale fields. As Philip Stevick has written:

> A substantial number of figures from the age of electronic media ... have been famous in ways that owe nothing to television ... it is the supreme paradox of literary fame in our century that, insofar as writers have elected to act out such marginality, they have become more central; as they have acted out such alienation, they have become integrated and embraced; and as they have acted out a kind of cultural nihilism, their culture has made them famous.[64]

The most celebrated of these recluses, of course, are J.D. Salinger and Thomas Pynchon. Salinger has given no interviews since the mid-1950s, has not published any new work since 1965, and has banned all blurbs and dustjacket photographs on the covers of his four published books, fiercely resisting any other kind of reprinting or commercial exploitation of his work. (In 1986, he took Ian Hamilton and Random House to the Supreme Court to prevent the publication of a biography which used quotations from some of his private letters.) Pynchon, while continuing to publish at longish intervals, has proved similarly elusive: there are only two widely available photographs of him and he never appears in public (he sent a stand-up comic to receive his National Book Award for *Gravity's Rainbow* in 1974). The rarity of these authors' appearances in print seems to be particularly valued in contemporary culture. The news that Salinger was to publish a short novella with a tiny Virginian publisher, Orchises Press – even though it was only a reprint of his last published story, which appeared in the *New Yorker* in 1965 – merited front-page coverage in many newspapers in January 1997.

This kind of mystique surrounds not simply authors who are never seen, but even authors who, for a variety of reasons, do not publish for long periods. Harold Brodkey's novel, *The Runaway Soul*, had a celebrated 27-year gestation period (sustained by lucrative contracts with several publishing houses) which provoked a considerable amount of media interest – the *New York Times* and the *Washington Post* both ran front-page headlines at various times reporting (mistakenly, as it turned out) that the novel was nearly finished.[65] The book, when eventually published in 1991, was an inevitable anti-climax and garnered mostly poor reviews – one critic wrote that 'death would have been a smarter career move'.[66] Truman Capote's *Answered Prayers*, which was never finished and appeared only in shortened form three years after his death, also had a very long and well-publicized incubation period. This kind of figure has become a familiar element in mainstream celebrity culture – a recent episode of *Frasier*, for example, has the eponymous radio shrink and his brother, Niles, pursuing a reclusive and rarely published author, T.H. Houghton, around the bars of Seattle, pouncing on a beermat doodle which they wrongly believe has been drawn by him, and then stealing the manuscript of his long-awaited book.

Of course, it is possible to argue that these cultural phenomena provide an indication of the all-consuming nature of the culture of celebrity, its ability to incorporate diverse and apparently unassimilable elements to its own ends. There were certainly those who argued that authors like Brodkey and Capote were inverting the terms of celebrity for their own self-promoting purposes; some saw Brodkey, in particular, as 'an amusing fraud, whose celebrity in Manhattan literary circles was a classic case of the emperor's clothes'.[67] Brodkey did prove adept at publicizing himself in various ways, telling interviewers that *The Runaway Soul* was 'too brilliant', and that he had been the inspiration for both the character of Satan in John Updike's *The Witches of Eastwick* and the Sean Connery role in the film *Indiana Jones and the Last Crusade*.[68] However, this does not explain the *peculiar* fascination with such authors in celebrity culture, which would seem to run counter to the perpetual impulse towards commodity production in monopoly capitalism. Although Brodkey's publishers, for example, were clearly able to use the publicity surrounding the book's non-appearance as a marketing strategy, the celebrity industry would not normally be able to sanction such underproduction – no Hollywood star, for example, could afford not to make films for so long without dropping off the A-list.

The appeal of such authors, then, rests primarily in the ability of celebrity to critique itself from within. As Ron Rosenbaum puts it:

Their varieties of reticence and concealment and self-effacement cumu-
latively constitute a provocative dissent from the culture of self-promotion
that has swept contemporary publishing, a reproof to the roaring 'white
noise' ... of the publicity-industrial complex that dominates contemporary celebrity culture.[69]

Of course, the fact that Rosenbaum's comments come in a long *Esquire*
profile of Salinger – one of many to follow the author to his home in
Cornish, New Hampshire and make a vain attempt to contact him by leaving
a message in his mailbox – shows the extent to which this particular brand
of dissent has become implicated in what it condemns. Author-recluses
are thus particularly indicative of a tension (evident to a lesser degree in
other kinds of literary celebrity) between what Walter Benjamin refers to
as 'cult value' and 'exhibition value' – in other words, between the uniqueness and particularity of art and culture, and its reproducibility to as wide
an audience as possible.[70] They represent a kind of routinization, for the
purposes of the celebrity industry, of the high-culture ideal of the artist as
authentic, individual genius, and of what Bourdieu calls 'the autonomous
principle ... which leads its most radical defenders to make of temporal
failure a sign of election and of success a sign of compromise with the
times'.[71]

These examples show that conflicts about the meaning and purpose of
literary celebrity – whether they are discussions about the commercialization of literature and the ubiquity of the publicity machine, or the
attempts by authors like Salinger and Pynchon to extricate themselves
from that machine – are part of the whole fabric of literary fame itself. The
contemporary literary star system is still a system, then, but one with considerable internal dissonance and fluidity, which makes it difficult to view
celebrity authors as simply the product of publishers' and media hype. As
Jennifer Wicke puts it in a different context, 'celebrity visibility per se
should not be automatically associated with corruption or selling out –
our mass-cultural tag sale took place long ago. The logic of celebrity construction is complex, rich and historically specific.'[72] This is not to say that
the unequal wielding of power and influence is not significant in literary
reputation making: it is clear that there are vast disparities in the prominence (or lack of prominence) achieved by contemporary authors which
have little to do with differences in talent, ambition or cultural relevance.
Some of the processes analysed above raise important questions about the
relationship between culture and the marketplace in advanced capitalist
societies and the way in which certain authors can, almost imperceptibly,
achieve a disproportionate share of commercial and critical attention. What

I am suggesting, though, is that the market will not triumph in a straight-forward, mechanical way, because cultural capital plays such a pivotal role in the construction of literary celebrity, with often surprising consequences not caught by simple oppositions between markets and cultures. Above all, the contemporary literary star system attests to the persistence of the notion, in spite of the changes to the cultural marketplace outlined above, of the world of art and culture as what Bourdieu describes as 'a sacred island systematically and ostentatiously opposed to the profane world of production, a sanctuary for gratuitous, disinterested activity in a universe given over to money and self-interest'.[73]

4
Disembodied Images: Authors, Authorship and Celebrity

The notions of authorship formulated within the academy and outside it have radically diverged in recent years – while academic criticism has formulated theories about the death, disappearance or absence of the author, this figure still seems to be very much alive in non-academic culture. This chapter discusses literary celebrity in relation to some of these apparently conflicting notions of authorship, examining theoretical perspectives in relation to the actual effects of the literary marketplace and the way that authors themselves have responded to the phenomenon of celebrity. It begins by examining how the transformation of authors into media images connects with the efforts within academic literary criticism to question the figure of the author as the authoritative originator of texts and to view individualistic notions of authorship instead as culturally and historically determined. It then goes on to examine a number of texts in which authors have dealt with these issues, which tend to pivot similarly around questions of authorial intention and agency. If the main contention of anti-intentionalist textual criticism is that a text 'is not the author's (it is detached from the author at birth and goes about the world beyond his power to intend about it or control it)',[1] a similar case might be made for the way in which celebrity has impacted on the work and public personality of authors. The academy's scepticism about the figure of the author thus has more similarities than might at first be apparent with celebrity's appropriation of the authorial personality.

The Death of the Author?

Several critics have already pointed to the irony that the kinds of publicity about authors discussed in the previous chapter seemed to emerge at roughly the same time as academic criticism was becoming increasingly suspicious of essentialist notions of the individual author. Malcolm Bradbury, for example, suggests that we now live 'in two ages at once: the age of the author hyped and promoted, studied and celebrated; the age of the author denied and eliminated, desubjected and airbrushed from writing'.[2] Others have drawn attention to the transformation of literary critics and philosophers who have proclaimed the death of the author-subject into media celebrities, even suggesting that this represents a kind of bad faith on their part. Peter Washington, for example, argues that the most enthusiastic sponsor of the 'death of the author', Roland Barthes, 'brought to theory a journalist's sense of publicity and a decorator's eye for effect ... how appropriate that the author of the Author's Death should be a narcissist whose only subject is himself!'[3]

In fact, though, the irony would not have been lost on Barthes himself: the kind of 'anti-authorial' criticism with which he is associated is actually useful to this discussion in pointing to the ways in which the figure of the author can function as a vehicle for ideologies which promote the autonomy and singularity of the individual subject, and which attribute value and authority to certain texts (and authors) but not others. Barthes urges the death of the author as a project for literary criticism precisely because, he says, 'the image of literature to be found in ordinary culture is tyrannically centred on the author, his person, his life, his tastes, his passions'. He aims to show that the privileged figure of the author is a modern invention, the product of bourgeois society's discovery of 'the prestige of the individual'.[4] Barthes's demystification of *Le Figaro*'s lionization of André Gide in *Mythologies*, for example, points to 'the glamorous status which bourgeois society liberally grants its spiritual representatives (so long as they remain harmless)'.[5]

Similarly, Michel Foucault's essay, 'What is an Author?' traces the conditions by which contemporary literary discourse has come to be dominated by 'the sovereignty of the author' back to the seventeenth and eighteenth centuries, when literary texts began to be attached to the name of a single author as part of their transformation into legally reinforced, marketable cultural properties. According to Foucault, 'in our culture, the name of an author is a variable that accompanies only certain texts to the exclusion of others ... the function of an author is to characterize the existence, circulation, and operation of certain discourses within a society'.[6] Both Barthes and Foucault, then, are criticizing not so much the common-sense notion that individual authors write texts, but the kinds of mystical associations which cluster around them in capitalist societies, naturalizing them as the only authoritative source of textual meaning and as a locus of power and authority within a culture.

As I have attempted to show in previous chapters, this is precisely how literary celebrity functions, reformulating authorship within the literary marketplace and using it as the repository of all kinds of conflicting cultural meanings and values. The same might be said, in fact, for celebrity culture in general, which reifies individuals and allows them to be used by capitalist society in a variety of ways – as market stimuli, as representations of ideal social types, as focal points for the desires and longings of audiences, and so on. This emphasis in Barthes's and Foucault's work on the social construction of the individual thus has similarities with the theories of the Frankfurt School of cultural criticism, which deal more generally with the way in which capitalism has valorized a particular form of individualism, making 'the peculiarity of the self ... a monopoly commodity determined by society'. In particular, Adorno and Horkheimer attack the American culture industries for producing a star system of 'pseudo individuality ... a shallow cult of leading personalities'.[7] In his essay, 'The Work of Art in the Age of Mechanical Reproduction', Walter Benjamin similarly comments that the Hollywood film industry

> responds to the shrivelling of the aura with an artificial build-up of the 'personality' outside the studio. The cult of the movie star, fostered by the money of the film industry, preserves not the unique aura of the person but the 'spell of the personality', the phony spell of a commodity.[8]

It is not difficult to see how early studies of stardom by Boorstin and others were influenced by the Frankfurt School critics in their definition of the celebrity as devoid of depth or individuality, a 'human pseudo-event'.

Both Jane Gaines and Celia Lury have looked more specifically at these developments in the culture industries in relation to contemporary authorship. Gaines explores the shift in emphasis in American law from questions of copyright (ownership of a product by its author) to trademark (ownership of an image by a corporation) as protection for cultural products, pointing out that the 'legal displacement of the author', a product of the growing power of corporations to control the production of literature and culture, is 'roughly contemporaneous with what postmodern theory has diagnosed as the eclipse of the author by his or her own text'.[9] Lury also examines the repositioning of intellectual property rights from copyright to trademark law and argues that this is a response to the increasing importance, in Benjamin's terms, of 'exhibition value' over 'cult value'. As Lury explains it, the cultural producer's protected position as originator has been under-mined by the commercial exploitation of the possibilities of replication offered by the technologies of culture ... The development of market relations can thus be seen to have been a factor in both the emergence and the decline of the author-function as a form of asymmetry in cultural reproduction.[10]

Lury suggests that entrepreneurial capitalism created the individual author with the consolidation of copyright law in the eighteenth century, reinforcing this ideologically with the invention of a romantic notion of an 'author-god', but that monopoly capitalism is now threatening to destroy this figure with its promiscuous exploitation of new markets. This is true, up to a point: in the areas of popular culture that Lury and Gaines examine – films, broadcast media, commercials, comics – the 'author-function' is indeed becoming less important as large corporations increasingly control the output of the entertainment industry. In the literary sphere, however, the figure of the author (as we have seen, a complex synergy of 'cult value' and 'exhibition value') is still very much alive. Within this sphere, a more pressing problem is that the name of the author herself can become merely an image, either used to market a literary product directly or as a kind of freefloating signifier within contemporary culture. Although the most extreme example of this is provided by the celebrities who opportunistically adorn the dustjackets of novels ghost-written by other people, this is only one of the many ways in which an author's name can be used for promotional effect.

There is a danger, then, that the anti-individualizing effects of the literary marketplace – the creation of the author as a 'personality' by a vast network of cultural and economic practices – will actually threaten the whole notion of authorship as an individualistic activity, taking away agency from the author at the same time as it apparently celebrates that author's autonomy as a 'star author'. The author becomes gradually less in control not only of her work but also of her image and how it circulates, at the same time as the machinery of celebrity asserts what literary critics call 'the intentional fallacy', which assumes that she is wholly in control of it. This cuts to the heart of the paradoxical nature of celebrity culture as a whole, which promotes individualism at the same time as it undermines it, being founded on what Leo Braudy calls 'a public rhetoric of individualism that offsets an increasingly pervasive web of institutional and corporate relations', with celebrity being seen as 'the only way out of increasingly complex political and economic dependence on others ... in a more crowded, corporate and collective world'.[11] As Stuart Ewen has written:

It is this objectification of the person that, most probably, explains much of the turmoil and grief, the identity crisis that often accompanies stardom. Perhaps celebrities, too, become uncomfortable in their own skins as they, in the eyes of others, become frozen images; as their faces and bodies and mannerisms become icons; always the personage, never the person. It is difficult to be a disembodied image.[12]

Public and Private

A further complication is presented by the fact that celebrity attempts to authenticate its image of the author by a fascination with the 'private' self, which means that there is sometimes little escape for authors from the imaging effects of celebrity. It is often suggested that, in contrast with historical forms of fame which have emphasized public achievements, 'the machinery of celebrity recognizes no boundaries between the public and private realm'.[13] This pattern can be traced back to early Hollywood publicity texts of the 1920s and 1930s, which broke with earlier accounts of the stars of stage and screen by celebrating the 'natural' charisma of the celebrity rather than any exceptional acting talent or technical ability, and which therefore sought to show that the star's on-screen persona and off-screen behaviour were broadly similar.[14] As Richard Dyer shows, however, celebrity texts also began to tease the fault line between the public and private lives of the stars, as if recognizing that the two were not always identical and that much journalistic mileage could be gained from this discrepancy. (*Time* and *Life*'s in-depth profiles of authors, with their assumption of a privileged, behind-the-scenes look at the star, are an example of this.)

Dyer argues that stardom has developed as an intertextual phenomenon, produced by the interchange between 'official' celebrity texts such as movies and TV shows and a subsidiary sphere of journalism, publicity and gossip. He suggests that the audience's relation with the star is a compulsive search for the 'real' – an attempt to distinguish between the 'authentic' and the 'superficial' in the star's personality by playing off these different sorts of texts against each other. In doing so, he argues, people use celebrity as a way of speculating about the nature of the individual in contemporary society – specifically, stars 'enact ways of making sense of the experience of being a person in a particular kind of social production (capitalism), with its particular organisation of life into public and private spheres'.[15] Joshua Gamson, similarly, has pointed out that the attractions of 'celebrity tourism' (turning up at film premieres or going on coach tours of Beverly Hills residential areas in the hope of spotting stars taking out their garbage, for example) are partly generated by a search for the 'excitement of proof' – the desire 'to confirm and reconfirm that surfaces have something, in this case someone, beneath them'.[16] The appropriation of the 'private' by celebrity culture, then, is partly a result of the continuing commodification of the self in monopoly capitalism as described by Adorno and Horkheimer and others, but is also a product of celebrity culture's own recognition that the image it presents of the star is somehow 'false'.

This latter characteristic is most notable, perhaps, in the public fascination with scandals involving stars – a feature of celebrity culture since Fatty Arbuckle's fall from grace in the 1920s. The biography specializing in salacious disclosures about much-loved celebrities, by writers like Kitty Kelley and Albert Goldman, in which nothing is sacred and every kind of private misdemeanour is grist to the celebrity mill, is one of the more securely lucrative areas of the publishing industry. While not nearly as intrusive or prurient, literary biographies also often sell themselves through the promise of 'revelations' about their subject. Recent biographies of Hemingway, for example, have sought to expose the author's macho public image as a sham, concealing a much more complex, tormented figure with a lifelong interest in lesbianism and androgyny.[17] Similarly, John Cheever's posthumously published journals and letters, and memoirs by members of his family, revealed his alcoholism, drugtaking, unstable marriage and affairs with both men and women, casting doubts on the notion of Cheever as patrician family man or, in the words of one reviewer, as 'part of the Hudson Valley squirearchy – a kind of laminated placemat figure complete with hunting dogs, country estate, staff and saddle horses'.[18] This new idea of Cheever as closet bisexual quickly became the received image of him, even finding its way into an episode of the sitcom, *Seinfeld*, entitled 'The Cheever Letters', which involves the discovery of love letters between Cheever and a male friend.

Even as these biographical accounts (and, more significantly, the media interest they inspire) unmask the celebrity personae these authors assumed when they were alive, they also reproduce a central premise of celebrity by satisfying our desire to know the 'reality behind the legend'. Celebrity's fascination with the 'private' self connects with attempts by theorists of postmodernity to explain the loss of a 'depth model' of the human personality as the product of a culture dominated by self-referential signs. A chief interpreter of the primacy of simulacra, Jean Baudrillard, has described the postmodern moment in terms which seem to encapsulate this characteristic of celebrity culture:

This loss of public space occurs contemporaneously with the loss of private space. The one is no longer a spectacle, the other no longer a secret. Their distinctive opposition, the clear difference of an exterior and an interior ... is effaced in a sort of *obscenity* where the most intimate processes of our life become the virtual feeding ground of the media.[19]

This confusion between public and private spheres is again evident in the perpetual interest in author-recluses in contemporary culture. Although much of Boorstin's book, *The Image*, concerns the extraordinary power of the media in dictating the cultural habits, thoughts and everyday lives of most Americans, he also recognizes that people are often aware of the artificiality of celebrity and 'will not so supinely allow themselves to be deprived of the last vestiges of spontaneous reality'. He suggests that

> in a world where the public acts of politicians and celebrities become more and more contrived, we look ever more eagerly for happenings not brought into being especially for our benefit. We search for those areas of life which may have remained immune to the cancer of pseudo-eventfulness.[20]

Author-recluses clearly tap into this longing because their 'private' selves seem to be more authentic than that of other celebrities, untouched by the contaminating effects of the publicity machine. Baudrillard makes a similar point in his analysis of postmodern culture:

> When the real is no longer what it used to be, nostalgia assumes its full meaning. There is a proliferation of myths of origin and signs of reality: of second-hand truth, objectivity and authenticity. There is an escalation of the true, of the lived experience; a resurrection of the figurative where the object and substance have disappeared.[21]

The preoccupation with figures like Salinger and Pynchon amounts similarly to a fascination with the absence of these authors, the rarity of their image in a culture saturated with images. This is evident even in the early profiles of Salinger in *Life* and *Time*, which represented their inability to penetrate the author's fortified retreat in New Hampshire by taking pictures of his mailbox, the family Jeep parked in a clearing or his dog taking an 'un-Salingerlike peek at passersby'.[22] A huge amount of media interest followed the publication of a photograph of Salinger which appeared on the front page of the *New York Post* in 1988 under the headline 'Catcher Caught', picturing the author as he was caught unawares by two journalists while coming out of his local supermarket.[23] The Salinger photograph was clearly interesting in part because it seemed to point to the existence of a 'real' Salinger existing outside of the media's representation of him, particularly since it contrasted so sharply with the only other widely circulated photograph of the author – the young, brylcreemed figure on the cover of early editions of *The Catcher in the Rye*. A roughly similar amount of attention was attracted by the appearance of a photograph of Thomas Pynchon in *New York* magazine in 1997. (The magazine's reporter used an open-access Internet service which cross-references credit card and telephone numbers and located Pynchon in about ten minutes, an apt demonstration of the way in which the information overload in postmodern culture is making it increasingly difficult for author-recluses to escape from celebrity.)

The media also seem to fasten on any detail of the private lives of these authors, however banal, in recognition of its rarity. In 1998, for example, Joyce Maynard published an intimate biography of her nine-month affair with Salinger, *At Home in the World*, which related the story of their life together in New Hampshire. This book was heavily excerpted in *Vanity Fair* and inspired lengthy speculation and punditry even before its publication, most of it hostile to Maynard for betraying the author's privacy but nevertheless happily reproducing many of the choicest anecdotes from the book. In fact, the book's interest seemed to rest not only in the gossipy details of their sexual relationship but also in the mundane, everyday account of Salinger's life, relating his passion for homeopathic medicine, organic foods and junk TV.[24] (This approach can permeate into relatively highbrow spheres: in 1981 *Paris Review* printed a piece by Betty Eppes, a reporter from the 'Fun' section of the *Baton Rouge Advocate*, in which she tracks Salinger down to a general store in his hometown of Cornish, takes some long-range photographs and manages to have a brief conversation with him, with a tape recorder hidden under her blouse, about his hatred of publication and his fondness for cold-pressed peanut oil.[25]) As well as creating an appetite for these apparently inconsequential revelations, the absence of any substantive information about such authors has also produced a proliferation of rumour and counter-rumour, as in the frequently touted canard that Salinger and Pynchon are the same person, or that Salinger is still publishing under the name William Wharton (another reclusive author). *Weekly World News*, the tabloid that broke the story, 'Elvis is Alive', and which announces sightings of the King regularly, has also reported sightings of Pynchon, and the Internet, that popular source of urban myth, even initiated a rumour that he was the Unabomber.[26]

The urge to interpret and explain the silence of author-recluses is also a perennial feature of journalistic and other kinds of writing on this theme. The way in which cultural commentators rushed to decipher the *New York*

Post photograph of Salinger in various ways, describing it as 'sad and fright-
ening', or revealing the author as 'a scared little old man, arm thrown up
as if to ward off a blow',[27] shows how the apparent paucity of information
in a cultural text can sometimes inspire a plethora of different interpretations. There is a tendency among critics to use Salinger's invisibility as a
kind of master key which opens up and unravels his life and work, and
this seems to go hand in hand with a readiness to pass judgement on his
silence by portraying it as either a heroic gesture or a publicity stunt. In
Ian Hamilton's *In Search of J.D. Salinger* (1988), for example, the biographer justifies his invasion of the author's privacy with the argument that
Salinger's anonymity has been 'consciously constructed', and that his life-
time love of performance has extended to a 'heavily theatrical "man of
mystery" stance'. One of Hamilton's friends even speculates that the letter
he receives from Salinger declining to be involved in any way in his biography and warning him off approaching members of his family, may be 'a
kind of come-on'.[28]

   This propensity to overinterpret Salinger's silence also extends to his
admirers. Ron Rosenbaum, for example, is typical in suggesting that the
author's seclusion is 'an eloquent work of art ... [which] betokens some
special knowledge, some wisdom, the penetration of some unutterable
mystery beyond words, beyond speech, expressible only in silence'.[29]
Steffen Hantke has explained the celebritization of the reclusive author
in terms of this refusal in postmodern culture to let silence speak for itself:

> Since the power of [the publicity] machinery is geared toward textual
> and commodity production, just as the author himself, isolation and
> silence alone are not sufficient means of throwing sand into its gears.
> Rather, silence and absence open up a space that remains a potentiality,
> a site that remains, as of yet, uncolonized until it is noticed and taken
> advantage of. In the absence of prior claims, postmodern culture will
> attempt to invade that space by staging the author as celebrity.[30]

Authors and Their Images

What is the future of authorship as an individualistic activity, then, in an
age in which authors are themselves (whether they like it or not) the
intertextual creations of promotion and publicity? Given that these
intertextual creations often assume an almost inseparable connection
between the author's life and work – what Albert Camus describes as 'the
modern mania of identifying the author with his subject-matter'[31] – it
would seem that the possibility for both authorial and readerly confusion

is limitless. Although the work of theorists like Barthes and Foucault is useful in showing how the figure of the author is culturally constructed, then, my specific concern here is to examine the relationship between the 'real' author and this mythicized image. Most importantly, I want to explore how questions of authorial intention can be understood within a cultural context in which the author and her image have become completely interconnected. The problem, as Andrew Wernick suggests, is that the 'concrete-historical individual' who 'wrote' the text interacts with

> a name, an identification tag, which circulates independently of the phantom individual, and which functions at once as the signatured assertion of a property right, and as a vehicle for whatever significance, reputation, or myth (including, generically, the myth of the author-creator itself) that name has come to acquire.

According to Wernick, a promotional culture constructs authors 'ab initio', making them inescapably caught up in a process by which the 'sign-exchange value' of their name circulates competitively as part of marketing and publicity.[32] The promotional culture affects authors in every aspect of their subjectivities, creating

> a self which continually produces itself for competitive circulation ... an inextricable mixture of what its author/object actually has to offer, the signs by which this might be recognized, and the symbolic appeal this is given in order to enhance the advantages which can be obtained from its trade.[33]

Wernick's position is therefore somewhat similar to poststructuralist arguments that texts produce authors as much as authors produce texts, although his approach is more historical-contextual than textual, suggesting that the significance of promotion in contemporary culture means that 'the author authors the "author", even as he or she writes'.[34] If literary celebrity is as all-pervasive as Wernick suggests, any attempt by authors to write or talk about their fame critically is condemned to circularity: they will never be outside the promotional loop.

Bourdieu's 'field' theory, by attempting a negotiation between structure and agency which he defines as 'genetic structuralism',[35] suggests that authors have slightly more room for manoeuvre than Wernick allows for. While arguing that they are always constrained by specific conditions within the field of cultural production – and are thus unavoidably situated within the struggle for cultural and/or economic capital – he also maintains that authors can alter the nature of the field by their actions, statements and works. Bourdieu's notion of the 'habitus', another important concept in his work, explains the process by which agents within each field have a 'feel for the game', a socially constituted disposition to behave in a certain way depending on their position within a particular field. The habitus exists because fields are inherently competitive and positions between agents arise 'quasi-mechanically' according to the power struggles within them.[36] According to Bourdieu's model, then, authors are not only caught up in promotional practices but also very much want to be famous and successful, whatever their protestations to the contrary – or as John Cheever put it more succinctly, 'the rivalry among novelists is quite as intense as that among sopranos'.[37] Moreover, according to Bourdieu, an author's work will reflect these power struggles and position-takings:

> The relationship between a creative artist and his work, and therefore his work itself, is affected by the system of social relations within which creation as an act of communication takes place, or to be more precise, by the position of the creative artist in the structure of the intellectual field.[38]

However, because Bourdieu's model of the field also argues that it is dynamic, improvisatory and provisional, he shows that agents within particular fields are not simply slaves to strategic moves but can also transform their social conditions. Since the field is a site of symbolic contestation, authorial interventions can become as much a part of the make-up of the cultural field as the broader structural factors which constrain authors. My argument, similarly, is that authors are often deeply concerned about their own complicity with celebrity and address these concerns usefully in their writings. Celebrity authors are also likely to be particularly ambivalent about their own fame because, as I have suggested, they are situated in a contentiously in-between position in relation to different subfields of the field of cultural production. Their unease about celebrity thus often has less to do with an objection to being noticed *per se* than to a vulgarized fame which seems to borrow its methods and assumptions from the sphere of commercial entertainment.

Despite Camus's advice that 'an artist should cheerfully resign himself to allowing what he knows is an unworthy image of himself to lie about in dentists' waiting and hairdressers' waiting-rooms',[39] then, American authors have repeatedly nagged away at the subject of their celebrity, as though compulsively tonguing a sore tooth. It is notable, when reading comments in interviews by authors about their fame, how often loss of control and agency asserts itself as a common theme – even apparently publicity-friendly celebrity authors seem to voice the concern that their authorial identity is undermined by its status as public property. Truman Capote's comment is typical:

> All [celebrity] means is that you can cash a small check in a small town. Famous people sometimes become like turtles turned over on their backs. Everybody is picking at the turtle – the media, would-be loves, everybody – and he can't defend himself. It takes an enormous amount of effort for him to turn over.[40]

Authors have also continually explored these themes in their work. Many critics have seen the current vogue for autobiography and autobiographical fiction by authors, often dealing with their own fame, as a pernicious effect of celebrity culture. Christopher Lasch has criticized the confessional mode in much contemporary fiction as part of what he calls a 'culture of narcissism':

> The increasing interpenetration of fiction, journalism, and autobiography undeniably indicates that many writers find it more and more difficult to achieve the detachment indispensable to art ... Instead of working through their memories, many writers now rely on mere self-disclosure to keep the reader interested, appealing not to his understanding but to his salacious curiosity about the private lives of famous people.

Lasch argues that, in works by celebrity authors such as Norman Mailer and Erica Jong, the authors are 'trading on [their] own celebrity and filling page after page with material having no other claim to attention than its association with a famous name. Once having brought himself to public attention, the writer enjoys a ready-made market for true confessions.'[41] James Atlas agrees that

> in an era when *Oprah* reigns supreme and 12-step programs have been adopted as the new mantra, it's perhaps only natural for literary confession to join the parade. We live in a time when the very notion of privacy, of a zone beyond the reach of public proving, has become an alien concept.[42]

According to critics like Lasch and Atlas, authors who write about their celebrity merely reproduce it uncritically by pandering to the popular pastime of star-watching. Although clearly there is a danger that authors may use their work as a form of self-publicity, and it is true that such authors often 'walk a fine line between self-analysis and self-indulgence',[43] I would suggest that many of these works are a necessary working through of the problems of being a public author – perhaps not merely necessary but unavoidable, since authors are inextricably caught up in promotional practices anyway. These texts often provide a productive way of dealing with anxieties about the survival of authorship as a meaningful activity in an age when ideas and images are often corporately owned, and the dangers of being trapped in a persona which assumes simplistic connections between writer and work. Although it is true that the activity of writing may be bound up in varying degrees with the machinery of celebrity, it is still a more powerful tool than many other cultural workers possess with which to examine and interrogate that celebrity.

The Power of Celebrity

To use one example that Lasch cites, the tension between propagandistic self-invention and critical engagement with celebrity is particularly evident in Norman Mailer's life and work. Mailer protests in an early prose collection, *Advertisements for Myself* (1959), that success and celebrity have performed a 'lobotomy on [his] past', making him 'prominent and empty', someone to whom people react not as a person but as 'a node in a new electronic landscape of celebrity, personality and status'.[44] This is part of his larger complaint that literature has become a business in which

> there was no room for the old literary idea of oneself as a major writer, a figure in the landscape. One had become a set of relations and equations, most flourishing when most incorporated, for then one's literary stock was ready for merger.

As Mailer himself admits, though, this way of presenting himself solely as a victim of celebrity culture has 'a protective elegance' which avoids the question of how far the author himself has created 'Norman Mailer'.[45] Up until at least the mid-1950s, he had been, in his own words, 'a nice young literary man [with] manners ... the equal of anyone's', and had told the *New Yorker* after his first novel was published that 'getting your mug in the papers is one of the shameful ways of earning a living'.[46] Mailer's persona of a literary *enfant terrible*, which flourishes today well into his 70s, was created first not by the mass media but in his work – the literary 'bad boy' first mooted in *Advertisements for Myself* was 'my search to discover in public how much of me is sheer egotism', an attempt to overcome his early version of literary niceness, and cast off the yoke of 'the one personality he found absolutely insupportable – the nice Jewish boy from Brooklyn'.[47]

In a later work, *The Armies of the Night* (1968), Mailer deals in greater depth with the way in which this persona has become an inseparable combination of self-creation and media invention. This book, written in the third person, is all about Mailer as a celebrity – he spends the whole of the narrative in public settings during the anti-Vietnam War march on the Pentagon in 1967, accompanied all the time by a film crew. Mailer writes at the beginning of the book that by now he has

> learned to live in the sarcophagus of his image – at night, in his sleep, he might dart out, and paint improvements on the sarcophagus. During the day, while he was helpless, newspapermen and other assorted bravos of the media and the literary world would carve ugly pictures on the tomb of his legend.[48]

There are examples of this throughout *Armies* – of Mailer's words being diced up by reporters so that their sense is lost, and of newspapers distorting his actions to play up to his persona. In fact, the book begins with an excerpt from *Time* magazine describing Mailer's appearance at the Ambassador Theater on the eve of the anti-Vietnam march, which portrays the author as a drunken, opportunistic oaf, and the rest of the narrative presents itself as a response to this conventional characterization of Mailer: 'Now we may leave *Time* in order to find out what happened'.[49] Mailer recognizes, though, that he is both controlled by this image and complicit with it, since his

> remaining funds of sensitivity went right into the war of supporting his image and working for it. Sometimes he thought his relation to this image was not unlike some poor fellow who strains his very testicles to bring in emoluments for his wife yet is never favored with carnal knowledge of her.[50]

Although Mailer is often derided as a shameless self-publicist – Braudy has described his career as 'a series of disjunctures held together thinly by his raucous public personality'[51] – it would be more accurate to say that he has thought deeply and written at length about the ways in which his celebrity is the product of a tension between (freely admitted) authorial ambition and the demands of the literary marketplace. This was particularly the case in the 1970s, when Mailer's financial difficulties led to his work being constantly affected by the need to meet contractual deadlines and then publicize his books vigorously. (The way Mailer's books have been packaged and sold has always contributed significantly to his public persona: the dustjacket cover of the first edition of *An American Dream* shows Mailer shadow-boxing, for example, while the cover of *Why Are We in Vietnam?* carries a picture of its author sporting a black eye.) His admission of his own collusion with celebrity culture in his promotional appearances on the late-night talk show circuit at this time – his 'wretched collaboration with the multimillion-celled nausea-machine, that Christ-killer of the ages – television'[52] – make it clear that his celebrity has always been partly self-inflicted and partly imposed by external forces.

Mailer's work is a good example of the way in which celebrity authors are often concerned about their uneasily intermediate position between the restricted and large-scale fields, which in his case manifests itself as a desire to be successful while still being taken seriously. He wants to be famous but not at any price – empty 'celebrity' means little to him, since 'fame, unless one [has] a mission, [is] equal to the taste of aspirin in one's death'.[53] In fact, part of the overreaching ambition for which he is often disparaged stems from Mailer's decision to stop being 'an amateur literary politician' and write a 'big novel' which will be more than just that publishing season's blockbuster.[54] In the 1950s, Mailer was associated with some of the New York intellectuals and had written for their house journals like *Dissent* and *Partisan Review*, but was also often dismissed by this group for being a sellout. As Midge Decter, a member of the group, summarizes it, Mailer was 'not only a best seller, he was a celebrity too. He was in gossip columns. *Ipso facto*, he was middlebrow.'[55] Mailer has always reserved his fiercest scorn for literary 'politicians' like William Styron, who he claims 'has spent years oiling every literary lever and power which could help him on his way, and there are medals waiting for him in the mass-media'.[56] Throughout his career, he has been concerned that he might be perceived in this way, as a mere hack – this partly explains his awkwardness with his fellow anti-Vietnam demonstrator, Robert Lowell, in *The Armies of the Night*, because Lowell enjoys the kind of highbrow prestige, particularly amongst the New York intelligentsia, that he lacks. Contemplating the poet's winning performance with the audience of protesters, Mailer feels

hot anger at how Lowell was loved and he was not, a pure and surprising recognition of ... how much simple and childlike bitter sorrowing emotion had been concealed from himself for years under the manhole cover of his contempt for bad reviews.[57]

Mailer's principal fear about his celebrity, therefore, is that his serious literary ambitions will be compromised. He begins many of his non-fiction
works of the 1970s – *The Prisoner of Sex* (1971), *Marilyn* (1973) – with an
explanation of the financial constraints or contractual obligations which
have required him to write them and the admission that he would rather
be at work on the 'big novel' than producing the work we are reading.

A less common strategy used by celebrity authors seems to be to revel
in the superficiality of fame – a tactic employed throughout Nicholson
Baker's *U and I* (1991), a very funny account of his fan-worship of John
Updike and his own literary ambitions. This book is about how celebrity
culture envelops authors, turning more than averagely intelligent and
sensitive human beings into ambitious, insecure obsessives. Although
the book's title suggests that it will be an account of a literary friendship,
Baker in fact has only had two brief meetings with Updike, at two quin-
tessential celebrity bashes – a literary party and a book signing – during
which he pushily imposed himself on the author, telling him exactly who
he was and where he had published. Despite this, he constantly compares himself with Updike at the same stage of his career, supposes all
kinds of connections with him – psoriasis, insomnia, their strong relationship with their mothers – and even at one point imagines himself as
Updike's golfing partner. Baker's admiration for Updike is based not so
much on a reading of his work – he admits that he has read less than half
of his books – as on the fact that he is 'top of the heap', not only at the
apex of the literary establishment but more broadly famous as well, 'a
complete tweeter-woofer crossover success'.[58] What he wants most of all
from his hero, he decides, is not so much his literary achievements but
the 'responses to pert queries from *Mademoiselle* and the *New York Times
Book Review* ... I wanted more of these monocellular living appearances.
More awards-acceptance speeches!'[59] In other words, Baker wants Updike
as celebrity man-of-letters to compare his own career against: in fact, the
book is as much to do with Baker's attempts to establish himself as a famous
author as it is with Updike.

From the book's jokey epigraph onwards (a quote from Cyril Connolly
on the subject of literary fandom: 'It may be *us* they wish to meet but it's
themselves they want to talk about') Baker self-consciously portrays himself as shallow and self-serving. Even before he establishes himself as a
published author, he is in promotional mode – he imagines interviews with
Paris Review about his literary influences, wonders how precisely he will
word the acknowledgements page on his first published novel and, after
reading some of Updike's awards acceptance speeches, lies awake at night
rehearsing the acceptance speech for *his* National Book Award.[60] Baker's

refreshing strategy seems to be to tackle the subject of fame head-on and to recognize its influence over the creative process – to make the author's involvement with celebrity part of the book's conceit. His work is similar to Mailer's, then, in its combination of careerist manoeuvres and high-minded literary aspirations – for there is no denying his love of literature and his ambition to be a fine writer as well as a famous one – but there is a greater acceptance of the reality of celebrity and less willingness to inter-rogate structurally the causes of the phenomenon.

Authors and Reclusiveness

An uneasiness with the constraints of celebrity often produces a fascina-tion with withdrawal and silence in authors who are not themselves recluses. Jay McInerney's *Brightness Falls* (1992), for example, is an extended reflec-tion on these themes by an author who achieved full-scale media celebrity in the mid-1980s. McInerney formed part of a so-called 'Brat Pack' of very young, fashionable novelists (also including Bret Easton Ellis and Tama Janowitz) which took its name from a similar grouping of young Holly-wood actors. With their glamorous, nightclubbing lifestyles and frequent appearances in the gossip columns, the literary Brat Pack were often dis-missed as superficial and self-publicizing – a pure product of the 1980s, a decade of merger frenzy and media hype. Gerald Howard, for example, criticized this group for representing

> the writer as photo opportunity, the self-huckster as literary waif ... The so-called promotability of an author – one with an interesting personal story, a mediagenic profile, a set of powerful friends, a snappy line of patter – is routinely taken into consideration by publishers these days and may well obscure certain literary failings in the work even as it enhances its dollar value. Shall we call these young writers Capote's children?[61]

Writers like McInerney and Bret Easton Ellis were also often accused, in works like *Bright Lights, Big City* (1984) and *Less Than Zero* (1985), of recycling their fashionable lifestyles in their fiction, using their work itself as a form of self-promotion, a seamless by-product of their celebrity. Elizabeth Young and Graham Caveney, while acknowledging the connection between these authors' celebrity and their work, offer a more sympathetic reading which recognizes that authors can no longer be seen as separate from their public images in a mediatized world:

What needs to be thought through about these writers is the critical implications of their relationship to the media, the ways in which their positions as literary socialites has worked as a *para-text* to their fiction ... Rather than dismissing their work because of their public profiles, it is necessary to look at how the conflation of these two elements works as a new and often productive model of literary relations ... The profiles of McInerney, Ellis and Janowitz exist at the junction where the autobiographical concerns of 'intention' and 'personality' meet the postmodern world of fiction and representation: where the faceless power of narrative is counterbalanced by the performance of the literary ego ... What has been read as the indulgence of youth is in fact an engagement with the realities of literature *as an event* ... In short, these writers have made it their project to strip away disguise, enabling us to read the rhetoric of their fiction over the shoulder of their self-advertisement.[62]

It is interesting, though, that *Brightness Falls*, widely read (as Young and Caveney point out) as the work of an author who has 'come of age' and 'settled down' after his wild, party-going years,[63] apparently expunges these 'autobiographical', self-advertising elements in a mature reflection on authorship. One of the characters in *Brightness Falls* is a literary celebrity, Victor Propp (loosely based, one presumes, on Harold Brodkey), whose fame has been achieved by a massive work-in-progress which, thanks to Propp's efforts at self-publicity, 'gained stature and renown with each passing year in which it failed to appear, while the fame of his contemporaries waxed and waned according to the conventional market principles'.[64] Propp's failure to deliver the manuscript has turned him into a celebrated figure – 'the Boo Radley of American letters',[65] in his own words. In fact, he is anything but a recluse, the source of his creative stagnation being his own relentless and time-consuming craving for publicity and the willingness of the book industry and the mass media to indulge it. Propp, sensing that his publisher is losing patience with him, persuades the novel's central character, Russell Calloway, an underpaid editor at the same firm, to set up his own publishing house with Propp as its star author. The company that Russell subsequently founds goes bankrupt during the Wall Street Crash of October 1987, largely because of Propp's failure to deliver the promised manuscript which, as Russell discovers after Propp's death, only ever existed in note form.

Propp's charlatanism is countered in the novel by a shadowy, non-speaking appearance by the 'real' J.D. Salinger. Russell's wife, Corrine, recalls having lunch with a man when she was a student, 'a nice old guy named Jerome' whom she met in the Dartmouth library while trying to escape from an obnoxious boyfriend; he invites her to lunch and they talk about organic food and Zen. Salinger does not announce himself as the famous author, and Corrine only realizes who he is when he shows her the bunker where he writes.[66] While Propp is a mere self-publicist, this opposition seems to imply Salinger's reclusiveness has an unshowy integrity. McInerney seeks to demystify the idealization of authorial reclusiveness by pointing to its links with the promotional machinery of books, while also nostalgically reasserting the existence of a 'purer' form of silence. Although McInerney's early work may, as Young and Caveney suggest, be a much more direct engagement with his own celebrity, his purpose here seems to be to distance himself from the beau monde out of which he emerged in the 1980s, and which formed the subject matter for his books, and construct a space outside celebrity.

Salinger also makes an appearance in W.P. Kinsella's unashamedly sentimental novel, *Shoeless Joe* (1982). This book is narrated by an Iowa farmer, Ray Kinsella, who, when out in the fields one day, hears from nowhere the voice of a baseball announcer telling him to 'ease his pain'.[67] Assuming that 'he' must be his favourite author, J.D. Salinger, Kinsella sets off for New Hampshire, kidnaps Salinger outside a grocery store and takes him to a baseball game at Boston's Fenway Park. Kinsella tells Salinger that he feels a special kinship with him, that he has 'touched [his] soul', but Salinger replies with a classic exposition of literary fame's autobiographical fallacy:

> I didn't ask you to feel the way you do ... the words on the page have no connection with the person who wrote them. Writers live other peoples' lives for them. I don't write autobiography. I'm a quiet man who wrote stories that people believe. Because they believe, they want to touch me, but I can't stand to be touched. They would have been chipping little pieces off me before I knew it, as if I were a statue, and pretty soon there wouldn't have been anything left of me. That's why I chose to drop out.[68]

Improbably, though, Salinger puts up little resistance to being kidnapped and eventually befriends Ray, being initiated into a bizarre scheme to build a magical baseball park in Iowa out of his cornfield in order to summon back to life the great stars of the past, Moonlight Graham and Shoeless Joe Jackson. While purporting to be a critique of literary celebrity, the novel arguably fuels the fire of all the Salinger fanatics who have followed him to New Hampshire, presuming that they alone can understand him. The book is founded, then, on the 'illusion of intimacy' which Richard Schickel has defined as the principal characteristic of the relationship between celebrities and fans.[69] Like McInerney's book, it seeks to negotiate a way out of the fame machine, but ultimately reiterates one of its central assumptions.

Paul Auster has also written about reclusiveness in the three linked stories of his *New York Trilogy* (1987). In the final novella, *The Locked Room*, an unpublished and reclusive author, Fanshawe, goes missing for several months, presumed dead. The story is narrated by Fanshawe's closest childhood friend, who is contacted by Fanshawe's wife after his disappearance so that she can pass on his unpublished manuscripts to him. The narrator, also a published author, realizes quickly that they are works of genius, goes on to publish them with the help of his editorial contacts, and Fanshawe becomes posthumously famous. The narrator then receives a letter from Fanshawe, thanking him for his help, promising that he will never be in touch again, and threatening to kill the narrator if he does succeed in tracking him down. Despite this, the narrator becomes determined to find his old friend and to kill *him*: after some years of fruitless searching, he receives a final letter from Fanshawe requesting a meeting. He locates Fanshawe in a dilapidated house in an unfashionable area of Boston, but Fanshawe (who now even refuses to let the narrator call him by this name) will only talk through locked double doors, promising to shoot the narrator if he tries to open them. Fanshawe claims that he took poison some hours ago and is near to death, and has only invited the narrator here to give him an explanation of why he disappeared. This explanation is contained in a red notebook which the narrator finds under the stairs: the story ends as he reads the notebook on his way home, failing to make any sense of it.

At the heart of the book is the contrast between the narrator and Fanshawe as models of public and private authorship. The narrator is a successful critic, publishing review articles to order for magazines, and wanting constantly to 'impress people with the empty signs of my ambition: good grades, varsity letters, awards for whatever it was they were judging us on that week'. He regards what he produces as 'little short of hack work ... so much dust ... the slightest wind would blow it away', when he really wants 'to write something that would touch people and make a difference in their lives'.[70] While he plods away carefully, Fanshawe is effortlessly brilliant at everything he touches, but does not feel the need for public approval. He is attempting to control the public image of himself totally, by separating his life from his work – when his texts enter the public arena and take on a life of their own, it is the narrator who picks up the pieces, as the Fanshawe bandwagon gets out of hand:

One thing kept leading to another, and before I knew it a small industry had been set in motion ... I was the mad scientist who had invented the great hocus-pocus machine, and the more smoke that poured from it, the more noise it produced, the happier I was.[71]

Spurred on by the promotional machinery of the publishing house with which he has placed Fanshawe's work, the narrator produces articles on his friend, and is then contracted to write a biography of him. Knowing that this will be a sham because it will have to pretend that Fanshawe is dead, he feels 'like a man who had signed away his soul'. The rumour mill even speculates that he has invented Fanshawe as a front for his own writing. He is thus made to think hard about 'what it means when a writer puts his name on a book, why some writers choose to hide behind a pseudonym, whether or not a writer has a real life anyway'.[72] The Fanshawe industry he has inadvertently established eventually makes him deeply resentful of his absent friend – hence his wish to kill him.

The New York Trilogy represents a much more complex engagement with the question of authorial identity than Kinsella's or McInerney's books. Auster's text has none of the redemptive quality of *Brightness Falls* or *Shoeless Joe* – the unsettling nature of the stories lies in the fact that no essential 'private' self can be salvaged by retreating from the public sphere: both Fanshawe and the narrator seem equally trapped. All Auster's characters in the trilogy, in fact, are attempting to escape from their 'public' selves – like the author, Quinn, who writes under a pseudonym, assumes various identities and disappears at the end of *City of Glass*, or the writer in *Ghosts* who hires a private detective to spy on him, perhaps to assure himself that he really exists – but the escape provides them with no release or sense of certainty, because the self itself is seen as provisional and textual. As the narrator in *The Locked Room* says:

Every life is inexplicable ... No matter how many facts are told, no matter how many details are given, the essential thing resists telling ... as our lives go on, we become more and more opaque to ourselves, more and more aware of our own incoherence. No one can cross the boundary into another – for the simple reason that no one can gain access to himself.[73]

All the same, there is a certain romanticization of Fanshawe in his very impenetrability, and the narrator gives the impression that Fanshawe's identity is unfathomable simply because it is out of the reach of ordinary mortals:

You felt there was a secret core in him that could never be penetrated, a mysterious centre of hiddenness. To imitate him was somehow to participate in that mystery, but it was also to understand that you could never really know him.[74]

Clearly there is much more going on in *The New York Trilogy* than a speculation on literary celebrity, but part of its postmodern self-reflexiveness around the notion of authorship – 'Auster' even appears as both a friend of the narrator of all three stories and an assumed name for one of the characters – is a recognition of the way that postmodern culture assumes control over authorial identity and dissolves distinctions between 'public' and 'private'.

In varying ways, then, these writers use surrogate author figures to explore the inescapably public nature of contemporary authorship and the issues surrounding authorial intention and agency which this raises. Many of them seek to locate a 'private' self for the author beyond celebrity while recognizing, at the same time, that they are still implicated in the systems and practices through which their fame is produced. In the second part of this book, I want to look at four contemporary authors – Updike, Roth, DeLillo and Acker – who raise similar questions in being unavoidably involved in the construction of their own celebrity, yet continually aware of the problems caused by this involvement. Running the gamut from the comfortably mainstream to the politicized avant-garde, this group of authors has adopted a variety of strategies to make sense of their often highly problematic relationship with mediatized fame. There is, however, a consistent element in their writings and comments on this theme: as with some of the authors examined above, the professed struggle for authorial autonomy, often accompanied by a moralistic, disdainful attitude to celebrity itself, is used as a way of asserting their own non-involvement in the discourses they examine. In fact, this strategy only reaffirms what they are often already uncomfortably aware of: that they are not separate from but wholly implicated in their own fame. The second part of this book thus aims to show that contemporary literary celebrity can only be understood as the effect of a whole range of discourses, from publicity material to literary texts, which authors themselves are not merely produced by but also help to produce.

Part Two
Star Authors

5
The Scribe of Suburbia: John Updike

John Updike has been a literary celebrity for almost all his adult life – a professional author since leaving college, nationally famous soon after, and now perhaps the most consistently successful and well-known 'serious' author in the United States. His works regularly make the bestsellers lists, he is profiled, interviewed and reviewed in a huge range of publications (being the only living American writer to appear twice on the cover of *Time*) and has won all the major American literary prizes. As Frederick Crews puts it: 'With the possible exception of ... Norman Mailer, no living American writer has been more closely watched.'[1] Updike's popularity is partly due to the ways in which his work reaffirms a realist literary aesthetic which Janice Radway has associated with the Book-of-the-Month Club and other mainstays of 'middlebrow' culture.[2] Those works that have earned Updike wealth and celebrity tend to be based, at least in the minds of their readers, around 'lived experience' and the reflection of a concrete and tangible external reality – notably in the Rabbit tetralogy for which he is most famous – an aesthetic which Updike himself sponsors in his own literary criticism, undertaken as chief book reviewer for the *New Yorker*. 'What we want from fiction', he writes, 'and what fiction is increasingly loath to give us, is vicarious experience'.[3] Updike's novels are particularly noted for their microcosmic recreation of everyday American life – what Hermione Lee calls the 'dazzling thinginess' of his work.[4] One *Saturday Review* critic, for instance, praises the fact that, in Updike's work, 'there is no hysteria, no sense of apocalyptic posturing, just the quiet recording of American middle-class life as it was actually lived between the headlines'.[5]

However, Updike's fame – precisely because it is seen as being the product of these elements in his work – has been accompanied by a great deal of adverse criticism. In particular, he has been attacked throughout his career by many New York critics (in magazines like *Commentary*, *Partisan Review* and, to a lesser extent, the *New York Review of Books*) for prospering within a celebrity culture which confuses popular success with literary merit – a sphere of commercial book clubs, literary prizes and magazines like *Time*, *Life* and *Saturday Review*. He has also been accused of presenting, in both his work and public persona, a particular version of Americanness (white, male, middle-class and suburban) which specifically appeals to this culture and does not attempt to extend beyond its narrow concerns – a critique summarized in this comment by one reviewer: 'Great issues aren't at issue in Updike's fiction. When ignorant armies clash by night, his people are somewhere else on the beach, skinny dipping, perhaps ... Updike is our genteel Gentile: the sweet, lonesome singer of Protestant mediocrity.'[6] Updike's star has also descended within academia recently: as literary and cultural critics have sought to open up the canon to previously marginalized literary traditions, his work has been seen to focus too insistently on middle-aged, middle-class, white male angst. This chapter discusses the ways in which Updike has dealt with his celebrity and shaped his career as public figure – in both his work and public persona – in order to make sense of both his own fame and this critique of it.

'Rancid Advice from my Critical Betters'

The public Updike gives the impression of coping easily with celebrity, producing a book a year throughout his career, working without the assistance of literary agents or large advances, and generally wearing his critical sores lightly. One critic has complimented him for remaining

> one of Augustine's 'fair and fit' – and never more so than when viewed alongside his male literary colleagues who often tend to show the lump and bump of gene, bad habits, the spread and paste of a lifetime spent taking one's own dictation ... he is the true and sweetly acceptable celebrity of art, that world of the always self-made where attitude and pose have a license as plain as that of a mosquito.[7]

At the same time, though, Updike has often discussed the debilitating effects of both good and bad publicity in his work. I want to suggest that the conflicted nature of Updike's fame – his success in one celebrity sphere seemingly being inversely proportional to success in another – accounts in part for his considerable ambivalence about his status as a public figure. In particular, Updike's opposition to what one of his narrators calls 'the narrow precincts of the Manhattan intelligentsia, a site saturated in poisonous envy and reflexive intolerance and basic impotence',[8] has fundamentally influenced his career and also affected his attitude to more vernacular forms of celebrity.

On the one hand, Updike has frequently written about the pernicious influence of mainstream celebrity, lamenting 'the drain on the brain, the assumption that a writer is a mass of opinions to be trucked in and carted off for his annual six minutes on the pan-American talk show'.[9] Updike was apparently so 'mortified' by the massive fame he received after the publication of his 1968 novel, *Couples* – his only number one bestseller and still the highpoint of his celebrity – that he refused even to look at the royalty statements from his publisher.[10] This experience inspired sections of the long autobiographical poem, 'Midpoint', written immediately after *Couples* was published, which describes him 'cring[ing] in the face of glory':

> For conscientious climbing, God gave me these rewards:
> fame with its bucket of unanswerable letters,
> wealth with its worrisome market report,
> rancid advice from my critical betters ...
> From *Time*'s grim cover my fretful face peers out.[11]

After writing 'Midpoint' Updike began work on an eight-hour long historical play, *Buchanan Dying*, which has not been professionally produced and is widely regarded as unperformable, and which he describes in an afterword to the published script as 'an act of penance for a commercially successful novel set in New England'.[12] Updike has also spoken in interviews of his hatred for publicity – that 'funny kind of marriage between writing and television, promotion and production' in which 'someone who's trying to unpack his heart through the device of fiction' finds that 'what counts is really the aggrandizement of himself as a figure, a celebrity, a name brand'.[13]

Generally, though, Updike's professional demeanour is well-mannered and obliging – apparently ever-willing to give interviews, make speeches, appear on talk shows, pose for photographs and accept awards in person – and his prolific output of book reviews and other occasional pieces for magazines as diverse as the *New Yorker*, *Popular Mechanics* and *TV Guide* keeps him constantly in the public domain. Updike also involves himself at every stage in the production and marketing of his books, from dustjacket design and copy to publicity tours. Despite some misgivings, he seems comfortable with the more straightforwardly commercial aspects of book production and reception, as demonstrated recently by his sanguine response to the possibility of appearing on home shopping channels ('The whole business of authorship is becoming ... aggressively entrepreneurial ... It doesn't seem to be worse than some other things we're asked to do'), and his expression of pleasure at winning the Pulitzer for the first time because it was 'the one prize your Aunt Edna has heard of'.[14]

At the same time, Updike is opposed to the kinds of celebrity produced by the restricted field of cultural production, with its claims of autonomy from the market – the kinds of writing favoured by what he sees as a New York intellectual clique and 'the immense captive audience of academia', the artificial marketplaces created by the postwar institutionalization of American authorship, which 'can only deflect artists from their responsibility to find an authentic market for their products'.[15] In an interesting reversal of the romantic *artiste maudit* persona, Updike equates the marketplace itself with artistic disinterestedness, contrasting it with the 'modernist' pose of literature as suggestive of 'saintly suffering' and of writers as aloof from their potential readerships.[16] In fact, one of Updike's first *New Yorker* pieces links what it sees as the wretched state of contemporary American literature with a cult of the author's personality and a tendency for self-mythologizing inspired by this kind of elitism. He complains of the 'fever of self-importance' afflicting American writing, an atmosphere in which 'failure is the only possible success, and pained incapacity the only acceptable proof of sincerity'.[17]

Updike's notion of writing as a job of work, demanding a fixed number of hours and an end-product like any other trade, has led him to accept and naturalize certain forms of literary celebrity while rejecting others as elitist and self-promoting. In fact, Updike's edgy relationship with more rarefied literary circles could be viewed as a perfect paradigm of Bourdieu's account of the struggle between the heteronomous and autonomous ends of the cultural field, each subfield attacking the other's supposed 'disinterest'. Where Updike sees the self-interested shoring up of cultural capital in the 'rancid advice from my critical betters', his left-oriented critics have seen him colluding with American capitalism and a conservative politics which rewards its spokespersons with mainstream critical and commercial success. Their different attitudes to literary criticism, which Updike also writes as chief book reviewer for the *New Yorker*, are indicative: his more relaxed and generous approach can be contrasted with the New York intellectuals' perception of themselves as a critical bulwark against the commercialized art which Updike's own work is seen as exemplifying. Updike refers to this kind of criticism disparagingly as 'holier-than-Thou second-guessing in the *New York Review of Books*',[18] although there is a deliberate element of confrontationalism here, since he now writes regularly for the *New York Review*.

The Nostalgia for Failure

Some of this ambivalence about New York fame is evident even in Updike's earliest work. The short stories and novels set in Olinger (based on Updike's hometown of Shillington, Pennsylvania) construct a kind of speculative self around the idea of the bright young smalltown hope leaving for the metropolis. (Of these stories, Updike once said that 'not an autobiography, they have made one impossible'.[19]) They veer between nostalgic recollection and the dream of escape, typically employing a young male central character who anticipates leaving the town in late adolescence, or who returns to the town in young adulthood. In 'Flight', for instance, Allen Dow's domineering mother pushes her son to succeed. 'There we all are, and there we'll all be forever', she tells him as they view Olinger from a hilltop. 'Except you, Allan. You're going to fly.' Although his mother's influence and guidance make Allan conscious of his own 'special destiny', he also rebels against her ambitious plans for him by going out with an Olinger girl, thus symbolically attaching himself to the town.[20] Similarly, in 'A Sense of Shelter', the central character confesses his love to his beautiful classmate, the high school 'queen', Mary Landis, as an expression of loyalty to the town he is leaving behind. As one reviewer puts it, the main character in the Olinger stories typically adopts a 'priestly, in-between role', never risking isolation by acknowledging the fact of his intellectual superiority: 'He won't let himself fly ... like a man who, ashamed of his inherited riches, develops a limp.'[21]

These early 'portraits of the artist' point to a conscious attempt to situate himself in the middle ground between fame and obscurity which Updike has exhibited throughout his career. His 'Rabbit' books similarly express this ambivalence about success. In the first book of the series, *Rabbit, Run* (1960), Updike (by then already a celebrity) creates a central character who would ordinarily be viewed as a 'failure' – an ex-basketball star talking through his former sporting glories with his alcoholic high-school coach, demonstrating 'the Magipeel kitchen peeler' in a local store and attempting to escape from a dead-end marriage by moving in with a local prostitute. Updike has frequently expressed his sympathy for this mid-American everyman, often dismissed by his critics as bigoted, misogynistic and jingoistic. Sanford Pinsker is one of many to suggest that Rabbit is 'a profile of what Updike might have become had he stayed in Shillington, Pa., married a local girl and lived out his life as dozens of his high school classmates did'.[22] This may account for what Philip Stevick has identified as the unevenness of the books' narrative register, in which Updike, using first and third person alternately, injects his own highly lyrical, syntactically complex style into Rabbit's thought patterns.[23]

Updike tackles the subject of celebrity more directly, however, in his series of books concerning the famous American author, Henry Bech. Beginning in 1970, this series was one of the first to explore the ways in which the extra-curricular activities of celebrity authors could function as a lucrative substitute for their work. Bech is a famously blocked author whose 'reputation [has] grown while his powers [have] declined',[24] and who now spends his time doing anything other than writing – appearing on television talk shows, filling out questionnaires from doctoral students, teaching creative writing, speaking at colleges and functioning as a kind of unofficial American cultural ambassador on trips across the globe. In a familiar pattern of literary fame, Bech's lack of productivity is turned into a cultural commodity. As he writes less and less, he finds that he is

> more and more thickly hounded by homage, by flat-footed exegetes, by arrogantly worshipful undergraduates who hitchhiked a thousand miles to touch his hand, by querulous translators, by election to honorary societies, by invitations to lecture, to 'speak', to 'read', to participate in symposia trumped up by ambitious girlie magazines in shameless conjunction with venerable universities.[25]

This situation had already been anticipated by John Aldridge in his 1966 book, *Time to Murder and Create*:

> A point can indeed be reached where it is practically inadvisable for a young writer to continue writing and far more strategic for him just to lean back and enjoy the advantages that come simply from being well known and going through the motions, putting in the appearances necessary to keep himself in the public eye. Celebrity, after a certain amount of it has been achieved, tends to become self-perpetuating. As it grows in size, it comes to depend less and less on the specific act or gift that may initially have called it into being, and more and more on skillful public relations ... It is therefore not so very surprising that there should be young one- or two-book writers today who seem to feel no particular obligation to settle down to their proper business of writing more books, since they already enjoy most of the advantages of having written them without having had to.[26]

Although Updike makes use of his own experiences as a celebrity in these books, he clearly means Bech to be a kind of joke anti-self, who draws mainly on the reserves of cultural capital available in New York literary circles. Bech is a *Commentary* essayist, a favourite of its reviewers, a disciple of 'the gaunt Titans of modernism ... Joyce and Eliot and Valéry and Rilke'[27] and a native New Yorker at ease in the metropolis. Updike thus inverts his own celebrity as the scribe of suburbia – when Henry moves to the small town of Ossining in upstate New York (home of John Cheever), he becomes restless and homesick. Updike also inverts his own famous prolificity by writing about an author who seems to acquiesce in his own transformation into inert cultural symbol, even at one point accepting 'the Melville medal' from a literary society for 'the most meaningful silence'.[28] Indeed, Bech's submission to this process seems to be partly responsible for his writer's block, a connection which is shown symbolically when, hired by 'Superbooks' to autograph thousands of tip-in sheets for a special edition of one of his books during an all-expenses paid holiday to the Caribbean, he clams up and cannot even write his own name.[29]

These books are fundamentally about Bech's inability to situate himself outside the promotional machine – the ways in which celebrity culture has exploited his vanity and ambition and overtaken his personality, leaving him feeling alienated and helpless, unsure of where his celebrity self ends and his 'real' self begins:

> It was his fault; he had wanted to be noticed, to be praised. He had wanted to be a man in the world, a 'writer'. For his punishment they had made from the sticks and mud of his words, a coarse large doll to question and torment, which would not have mattered except that he was trapped inside the doll, shared a name and bank account with it. And the life that touched and brushed other people, that played across them like a saving breeze, could not break through the crust to him.

Bech has thus himself become 'a character by Henry Bech',[30] a confusing mixture of self-invention and media stereotyping. Updike compounds the misery by turning Bech into an author who, unlike himself, thinks that writers should not readily assimilate themselves into society and who feels intense shame at his conversion from a dedicated disciple of High Modernism into 'a slick crowd-pleaser at whistle-stop colleges'.[31] As Robert Detweiler argues, Bech 'is in constant danger of losing his status as an independent artist and of submitting instead to cultural objectification, to the process whereby a contemporary artist becomes a static showpiece of the society he has sought to unsettle'.[32]

In the second book in the series, *Bech is Back* (1982), Updike changes tack slightly in order to satirize developments in book publishing, as Bech finally breaks his silence by producing a sleazy book filled with titillating sex scenes which is a conscious tilt at the bestsellers lists. Bech is now

consumed by the 'voracious idiot' of publicity which 'dismiss[es] all quali-
tative distinctions and feast[s] off good and bad alike'.[33] His corporate-owned
publishing firm promotes the novel, *Think Big*, through an elaborate promotional campaign centring on the size of the advance and the subsidiary
rights sales, and on the author rather than the book ('Bech is Back!'), turning it into a huge seller despite its decidedly mixed reviews. 'Bech' has now
become a branded, mass-produced product, as his wife suggests when she
tells him: 'Whatever you produce, it'll be Bech, and that's all anybody wants
out of you.'[34]

In the last book in the series, *Bech at Bay* (1998), Bech is even more dismissive about the future of literature in a corporatized age as he prepares
his Nobel Prize acceptance speech. Wanting to speak about 'the timeless
bliss when pencil point touches paper and makes a mark', he is overtaken
by pessimism:

> The printed word? The book trade, that old carcass tossed here and there
> by its ravenous jackals? Greedy authors, greedy agents, brainless book
> chains with their Vivaldi-riddled espresso bars, publishers owned by
> metallurgy conglomerates, operated by glacially cold bean-counters in
> Geneva.[35]

In all these books, Updike offers a deeply cynical view of the literary life
in which journalists, editors, publishers and other hangers-on feed para-
sitically on authors. He also satirizes Bech, who veers between two extremes
of literary celebrity culture – overproduction and underproduction – which
Updike's own career has famously managed to steer between. There is a
sense in which Updike himself remains aloof from the fray: Bech is an
oddly insubstantial character, a curious compound of very different kinds
of fame, and is clearly a cautionary tale rather than a serious attempt by
Updike to work through issues around his own celebrity.

'A Mask that Eats into the Face'

Updike's own equivocal feelings about fame are brought together in a much
more developed way in his autobiography, *Self-Consciousness* (1989), which
claims finally to dispense with the fictionalized selves or anti-selves of his
fiction and present the 'real' Updike. Updike's attitude to celebrity in this
book mirrors a classic surface and depth model formulated by the psycholo-
gist Otto Rank, a member of Freud's circle concerned with the psychology
of creativity. Rank argues that, although they may complain continually
of lack of success, creative artists actually have a fundamental 'disinclination

to fame', which means that those who achieve it will often 'return, artistically or at least spiritually, to an earlier period of their struggle for success ... in which they seem to be set back in their modest beginnings'. Such a tendency has 'a rejuvenation-wish', based on the need to escape from fame which has 'a flavour of death'.[36] This author-centred, psychologistic approach is reiterated in *Self-Consciousness*, with its narrative of a treasured, thoughtful only child leaving a claustrophobic smalltown and upbringing to become a famous author, but then feeling a strong urge to escape from the impedimenta of fame back into the innocence of childhood.

Updike's memoirs are presented not as a conventional chronological narrative but as six themed essays – on his Pennsylvania hometown, his psoriasis, his stammer, his support for the Vietnam War, his family ancestry, and his reflections on death and the possibility of an afterlife. The essayistic nature of the text means that suggestive connections are made between apparently disparate areas of Updike's life, bringing them together into what he regards as the essential components of his 'self'. This creates a sense of the self as innate and immutable – he repeatedly writes of his life in terms of 'fates', 'instincts', 'inheritances' and 'dispositions', as though it is following a prefigurative script written in childhood. Despite Updike's statement in the book's foreword that 'perspectives are altered by the fact of being drawn' (xii), the knowable nature of the book's subject is never finally in doubt.

Self-Consciousness, in fact, follows many of the techniques of traditional autobiography in its apparently transparent recording of a completed life story by what John Haegart calls 'a sovereign or essential presence situated at the still center of his recollected world'.[37] This notion of what Paul John Eakin (in his discussion of the book) identifies as 'a primary *Ur*-self'[38] is reinforced by the contrast Updike makes throughout the book between the celebrated author with whom his readers will be familiar, and the 'ordinary', extra-literary Updike. He writes that he was inspired to write *Self-Consciousness* by the rumour that someone was writing his biography, and might thus 'take my life, my lode of ore and heap of memories, from me' (xi). Updike here implies that, although there are certain aspects of his life which are unavoidably public, there is a private self which remains off-limits.

Updike's notion of this private self, as already explored in much of his other work, is influenced by his readings of Søren Kierkegaard, Miguel de Unamuno and existential theologians like Karl Barth and Paul Tillich, and essentially amounts to a fear and trembling at the individual's unbearable situatedness: 'Billions of consciousnesses silt history full, and every one of them the center of the universe. What can we do in the face of this unthinkable truth but scream or take refuge in God?' (40) This leads on to a notion that this elemental self should be valued above all else, further pointing to another central concern of existentialism: the quest for individual authenticity and genuine 'selfhood' as against socially imposed identities. In a key passage at the end of the book, for example, Updike refers to the ways in which literary fame threatens the ability of authors to write by encouraging them to assume the role of self-conscious public performer, thus separating them from the more authentically personal experience on which they rely for subject matter:

> Celebrity is a mask that eats into the face. As soon as one is aware of being 'somebody', to be watched and listened to with extra interest, input ceases, and the performer goes blind and deaf in his overanimation ... Self-importance is a thickened, occluding form of self-consciousness (252–3).

Updike thus distinguishes clearly between a 'pure' self and the publicly famous author. Significantly, this discrepancy also emerges at book signings, an increasingly common activity for celebrity authors, at which, when writing his autograph, he hesitates instinctively on the 'd': 'This unprompted hesitation, in what should be a fluent practiced signature, I think of as my self – a flaw that reveals my true, deep self, like a rift in Antarctic ice showing a scary, skyey blue at the far bottom' (213).

Updike also explores the nature of his 'essential' self through another connecting theme in the book: his collection of chronic ailments, anxieties and neuroses. The most serious of these, discussed in discrete chapters, are psoriasis and stuttering, but there are others: emphysema, bronchial asthma, hay fever, a tendency to choke, dental problems and arachnophobia. In fact, these various afflictions inspire two conflicting takes on the self. In one sense, they are seen as defining him fundamentally as a person, by giving him a keen awareness of his own self as somehow flawed and inadequate – stuttering, for example, is 'an expression of alarm and shame at sounding like yourself, at *being* yourself, at taking up space and air' (87). Many of them are also aggravated by stress, and are thus somatic effects of his inner moods and desires: when he leaves his first wife and family in 1974, for example, he starts to stammer with his children, has trouble breathing and develops severe psoriasis. More usually, however, these problems point to the uncomfortable gap between the self and its outward performance, suggesting that there is a 'real' Updike which a disfiguring skin complaint or an inability to speak prevents him from revealing.

It is interesting that Updike, in the passage quoted above, describes celebrity as a kind of unwanted extra skin – the phrase, 'a mask that eats into the face' could easily suggest psoriasis, which manifests itself as a series of itchy, scaly patches on the layers of the skin. As with celebrity, psoriasis produces an unhealthy degree of self-contemplation, since the sufferer is 'forced to the mirror again and again; [it] compels narcissism, if we can suppose a Narcissus who did not like what he saw' (45). Like a public self, however, psoriasis is only skin-deep: the pain in his forehead from actinic damage, for instance, reminds Updike that 'my public, marketable self ... the book-autographing, anxious-to-please me ... feels like another skin and hurts also' (238). His stammer is also an external symptom of this awkward division between public and private selves. It tends to surface when he feels that he is being mistaken for someone or something he is not – as when he indignantly protests at a childhood friend who calls him an 'ostrich'. This includes celebrity appearances which seem to be based around 'bad faith', such as reading out a cloying awards citation which he has not written, or appearing on a talk show:

> Viewing myself on taped television, I see the repulsive symptoms of an approaching stammer take possession of my face ... And through it all a detestable coyness and craven willingness to please, to assure my talk-show host and his millions of viewers that I am not, appearances to the contrary, an ostrich (80–1).

Updike's 'true', authentic self is represented most insistently in the book, however, by his constant recollection of the prelapsarian period before he assumed the mask of a public individual – his childhood and adolescence in Shillington. The opening chapter of the book begins with Updike ending up serendipitously on Shillington's Pennsylvania Avenue and then wandering aimlessly around its streets on a spring evening, reminiscing to the reader about incidents from his boyhood. Aside from this opening chapter, though, Updike's memories of Shillington are central to the whole narrative and are interspersed throughout each of the other five chapters. Updike describes the grudge he held against Shillington while growing up – his ambitions to leave and become a famous author, partly as an act of revenge on the town for its snobbishness towards his father, a kindly but ineffectual schoolteacher, and spurred on by his mother, who discouraged his relationship with his first girlfriend because 'my avenging mission beckoned' (37). From the perspective of the famous author returning to his point of origin, however, Shillington now seems to be part of 'my own deepest sense of self' (220).

Shillington also brings the narrative full circle, as Updike returns alone to his old family farmhouse to visit his elderly and ailing mother at the end of the book. In a long passage written in the present tense, Updike sits late at night in the spare room, listening to his mother's breathing as she sleeps next door, and reflecting on his public life. He has stopped over in Shillington on the way home from a public reading at a Midwestern university where he charmed the faculty, students and local dignitaries but left 'feeling dirty and disturbed, as though I have wasted this time away from my desk, posing as an author instead of being one ... it is hard to get back from the academic unreality and ponderous flattery into my own skin' (237). (It is notable that Updike here again compares celebrity to an inauthentic extra skin.) He is also reading a book for review, leading him to reflect further that reviewing is another 'superfluous chore' which he undertakes 'for the money and ... the easy exposure of it, the showing-off, the quick certification from a world that I fear is not hearing me, is not *understanding* me' (238).

At the end of this passage, Updike looks over at a portrait on the wall which pictures him at the age of five, a sepia-tinted studio-style photograph with the edges artificially blurred away. Although Updike reflects that the 'little Johnny' shown here has 'got me into this' (meaning, I suppose, his current position of wealth and worldly success), the main effect is of discontinuity – this boy's 'tentatively smiling mouth, his dark and ardent, hopeful eyes' (238) are contrasted with the world-weary baggage of late middle-age. The whole passage, in which Updike reproaches himself for his other-directedness and eagerness to please, reinforces the sense that Updike's Shillington self stands for what lies 'behind the facade, the human courtesies, my performance, my "act"'(232). For added emphasis, the portrait of 'little Johnny' is reproduced on the front cover of *Self-Consciousness*, with (in the hardback edition) a recent photograph of Updike at a book signing on the back.

Jobbing Author of the Suburbs

As I have already suggested, however, Updike is not uncomplicatedly anti-fame, and the inconsistency of his response to celebrity is also apparent in *Self-Consciousness*, although it is partly concealed behind a nostalgic evocation of his Shillington self. One example of this is the way in which Updike's enthusiasm for the more obviously commercial areas of cultural production is naturalized through its association with a world of childhood innocence and wonderment. Updike links his idea of literature as 'a space one gratefully escaped into rather than ... a burden of wisdom to be gained', to a Shillington childhood steeped in 'the papery self-magnification and immortality of printed reproduction' (108). His love of mainstream popular culture takes various stages which are seen as natural progressions in a child's development: his ABC blocks featuring Walt Disney characters like Mickey Mouse and Horace Horsecollar, his love of cartoons compiled in Big Little Books bought at five-and-ten-cent stores, and his ambitions to be a cartoonist for Walt Disney or the syndicates, and then finally a writer for the *New Yorker*.

Updike argues that this background accounts for the fact that he has no preciousness about the 'pureness' of art, just a delight in 'the general marvel of reproduced imagery, of comic strips and comic books and books and magazines and motion pictures' (105), and an overall reluctance to view the writing of a book as separate from the process of printing, publishing and marketing it. If Updike describes himself in these years as insecure and ambitious, searching in New York magazines for 'the secret passageway out' (33), he now looks back nostalgically on this younger self, who is seeking a kind of salvation through the magic world of print. Significantly, the *New Yorker*, with which his boyhood ambition to reach New York was largely associated, now becomes associated retrospectively not with the metropolis but with Shillington – Updike describes himself gazing at it longingly on magazine racks, and being given it by his Aunt Mary for Christmas – and is seen as a haven from the stormy waters of New York literary life:

> a club of sorts, from within which the large rest of literary America – the many other less distinguished and fastidious magazines, the coarsely striving book trade, the tawdry bestseller lists, the sharp-tongued quarterlies and partisan reviews – could be politely disdained (222).

This antipathy towards New York – in particular, the 'sharp-tongued quarterlies and partisan reviews' – extends into Updike's comments about the purpose and meaning of his fiction. His reply to the accusation by critics like Norman Podhoretz and John Aldridge that he has 'nothing to say' is that he has 'the whole mass of muddling, hidden, troubled America to say', and that all his books are instalments in 'the hymning of this great roughly rectangular country severed from Christ by the breadth of the sea' (103). This reply is an attempt to address the complaint by some critics and reviewers that Updike's middlebrow success is due to his overemphasis on (and uncritical stance towards) the manners and mores of the suburban professional middle class. Since Updike associates this criticism with too-clever-by-half New York critics, it is significant that he should also link this aspect of his work with his move to Massachusetts suburbia in 1957, after a brief and unhappy residence in New York which left him with an abiding distaste for what he saw as its biliously competitive literary world. Updike dives eagerly into the social swim of parties, amateur dramatics, committees and societies in his adopted hometown of Ipswich, and delights in being 'an inconspicuous part of this herd' (59). For Updike, this town is sufficiently distant from the distractions and temptations of literary life to allow him to be 'a literary spy within average, public-school, supermarket America' (53), and Ipswich is indeed the setting (most notably in *Couples*, fictionalized as Tarbox) for the tales of suburban marriage, child-rearing, adultery and divorce for which Updike is still primarily famous. Updike describes Ipswich as being, like Shillington, 'out of harm's way', although now 'harm' is represented by 'Cambridge professors', 'Manhattan word-merchants', 'agents' and 'literary groupies' (52, 61, 253).

Updike's unfashionably hawkish views on the Vietnam War, to which he devotes the longest chapter of *Self-Consciousness*, can also partly be viewed in the context of his hostility towards New York literary life and his identification with what he sees as average, middletown America. In this chapter, the suggestive nature of the book's arguments is most apparent, as his pro-Vietnam views are rendered unchangeable and unchallengeable by their association with a cherished Shillington childhood. Updike intermingles a polemic against the anti-Vietnam protesters with memories of childhood and adolescence, so that his views on Vietnam are linked with a political position 'wormed into on Artie Hoyer's barber's chair' (125) and reinforced by family maxims and Shillington folk wisdom, and a trust in benign authority represented by his father and the other high-school teachers. As Updike puts it:

> My undovishness ... constituted a refusal to give up ... my deepest and most fruitful self, my Shillington self – dimes for war stamps, nickels for the Sunday school collection, and grown-ups maintaining order so that I might be free to play with my cartoons and Big Little Books (141).

Updike goes further, however, in explicitly connecting the peace movement with the eastern cultural establishment and New York literary and cultural figures like Jules Feiffer, Susan Sontag and Norman Mailer, describing it as a 'war ... being waged by a privileged few upon the administration and the American majority that had elected it' (132). Much of the protest, he argues, was based on simple snobbery towards Lyndon Johnson, particularly amongst 'Cambridge professors and Manhattan lawyers and their guitar-strumming children', who 'thought they could run the country and the world better than this lugubrious bohunk from Texas' (120). The debate about the Vietnam War seems to be partly refracted here through the antagonism Updike feels towards his New York critics. (Updike's poem, 'Minority Report' – written in 1968 at the height of the anti-war protests, when Updike also received particularly scathing criticism from New York intellectuals with the publication and popular success of *Couples* – also makes a suggestive connection between the Vietnam protesters and critics of his own work: 'Don't read your reviews, / A*M*E*R*I*C*A: / you are the only land.'[39]) However, in seeking to expose the hidden economy and in-crowdishness of a New York cultural elite – what Bourdieu calls 'the ostentatious impostures of *radical chic*'[40] – Updike neglects to inter-rogate his own position within the cultural field, which leads him to present a highly contentious political viewpoint as straightforwardly commonsensical.

This is not to say that Updike is unquestioning of his motives and inter-ests in *Self-Consciousness*. In fact, the last chapter of the book, 'On Being a Self Forever', is an extended reflection on what he calls 'the frangibility and provisionality of the self' (219), in which he concedes that we have any number of different selves, and that some of his own are not innocent and passive but self-serving and ambitious. In this chapter, fame seems to become something willed by the author himself (or, at least, by one aspect of his self) rather than simply an unhappy side effect of the ambition to write for a living. In fact, Updike links this individualistic, competitive streak in his personality to the very notion of the self as conditional and mortal – his horrified realization that life is 'a futile misadventure, a leap out of the dark and back', inspires the belief that 'there is something intrin-sically and individually vital which must be defended against the claims even of virtue' (97, 211). Updike's account of his Ipswich self in this chap-ter somewhat undercuts his earlier comments about the collegiality and clubbiness of commuter-belt life – as when he describes his position within the 'gang' as

> enhanced by a touch of wealth and celebrity, a mini-Mailer in our small salt-water pond, a stag of sorts in our herd of housewife-does ... he seems another obnoxious show-off, rapacious and sneaky and, in the service of his own ego, remorseless (222).

Updike seems keen here to dispel the public image of him as unassuming and self-deprecating – *Life* magazine's idea of him as the novelist 'who looks so nice and modest on his book jacket photographs'.[41]

Updike clearly reserves a sneaking admiration for, and grudging grate-fulness towards, these ambitious selves, 'the bravest boys' (223) who are largely responsible for writing the works on which he still picks up royalties and on whom his present fame, wealth and comfort depend. Ultimately, though, these ambitious selves are not 'really' Updike, but part of the public self he is stripping away in the narrative we are reading: 'The burden of activity, of participation, must plainly be shouldered, and has its pleasures. But they are cruel pleasures ... The essential self is innocent, and when it tastes its own innocence knows that it lives forever' (35). We may present a multitude of selves to others, he implies, but there is only one 'true' self, as revealed here – 'my most intimate self – the bedrock, as it were, beneath my more or less acceptable social, sexual, professional performance' (214). Updike clearly seeks, then, to use his autobiography in a conventional sense as a way of presenting the self authentically, dispensing with the 'false' self which has been serviceable only for career purposes. Indeed, this dismissal of the ephemera of fame gives *Self-Consciousness* a valedictory, even posthumous quality, particularly towards the end of the book as Updike discusses the end of his life and the inevitability of death.

Can any autobiography, though, seal itself so hermetically from its author's own celebrity? *Self-Consciousness* received a great deal of commercial and critical attention when it appeared in 1989, and has inevitably added to Updike's fame and the associations clustering around him. Updike follows a common technique of autobiography in seeking to individualize a subjectivity which is in fact culturally and historically produced, and this can be linked more generally with an assumption of transparency in his public persona which obscures his own inevitable involvement in the promotional aspects of contemporary authorship. *Self-Consciousness* can thus be read in conjunction with the supposed naturalness of Updike's public self, a performed version of his professed wish 'to cultivate serenely my garden of private life and printed artifact' (129). Interviews and profiles of Updike in newspapers and magazines, and the photographs which accompany them, celebrate the smalltown ordinariness of someone who, 'to ward off the perils of celebrity ... followed Flaubert's advice that in order to be a great writer, one must live like a bourgeois'.[42] They typically show the author gardening, playing volleyball with friends, reading the newspaper outside his local store, snoozing in an inflatable dinghy or 'tossing a hip into his golf swing'.[43] (Updike's celebrated love of golf, with its bourgeois, polyester knitwear image, encapsulates this notion of him as comfortably suburban. As Robert Winder says, for Updike 'capitalism's favourite game represents ... a pleasant minor rebellion against the conventions of bohemia, a way of pooh-poohing the sometimes fastidious manners of the literary scene'.[44])

Since Updike has considerable control over the design and marketing of his books, the photographs of him on their dustjackets show that this image is not merely accidental. The front cover of *Picked-Up Pieces* (1975), for instance, carries a black-and-white photograph of a smiling Updike dressed in jeans and sweater, standing in a nondescript suburban street and holding some leaves up to the camera. As Sanford Schwartz says, this image seeks to convey that the author is 'not doing anything serious ... he's just a fellow out for a walk, picking up stuff, cleaning the neighbourhood'.[45] The cover photographs for *Hugging the Shore* (1983) and *Odd Jobs* (1991) similarly show Updike in summer clothes, sitting in a boat by the banks of a river, and in winter overcoat and woollen hat, raking leaves and twigs on to a garden fire. Accompanied by the hefty page counts and self-effacing titles of these prose collections, such images add considerably to Updike's reputation as the jobbing author of suburbia, an 'anti-persona' which has itself become a prime source of his celebrity. One *Time* cover story on Updike, for example, congratulates him for refusing to be distracted by a public role – suggesting that, while contemporary authors are given financial and other inducements to engage in almost any activity other than writing, Updike has 'lived through and withstood such pressure on his private labours'.[46]

This is not to suggest that the popular image of Updike is merely a public facade, of course, designed simply to increase his own capital in the celebrity marketplace. Among other things, though, it does serve usefully to distinguish between particular kinds of fame and position the author in relation to them. Updike's attitude towards New York literary celebrity, in particular, has focused his unease about celebrity on to specific aspects of the experience of being a famous American author, and allowed him to view other kinds of literary fame in favourable opposition to them. This has meant that, in spite of the anxiety he expresses in *Self-Consciousness* about the unhealthy effects of celebrity, he seems ultimately unwilling to distinguish between writing as solitary activity and as published performance – an attitude which has helped to sustain him as a public figure over several decades. Asked by an interviewer if he ever felt inclined to 'do a J.D. Salinger', Updike replied: 'I love publication ... I am very much in love with printer's ink and could never do what Salinger has done.'[47]

6
Reality Shift: Philip Roth

Philip Roth rose to celebrity in the late 1960s with the publication of *Portnoy's Complaint*, the novel with which (even after 18 further books) his name is still virtually synonymous. Dubbed 'a wild blue shocker' by *Life* magazine on its first appearance,[1] it became notorious primarily because of its comic treatment of a formerly taboo subject: adolescent masturbation. This *succès de scandale* made Roth a huge fortune (the book earned a million dollars even prior to publication through the exploitation of movie, book club and serialization rights) and turned him, albeit briefly, into one of the most famous people in America. This chapter looks at Roth's subsequent career, which has been greatly influenced by the huge gap between the kind of attention he received after the publication of this novel and his own preconceptions about the high-minded seriousness with which books and authors should be publicly discussed.

Celebrity and Scandal

Roth says that his first encounter with literature was by means of a 'priestly literary education', in which the vocation of writing itself was viewed as 'a form of ethical conduct', making him someone for whom 'the postwar onslaught of a mass electronically amplified philistine culture ... look[ed] ... to be the work of the Devil's legions, and High Art in turn the only refuge of the godly'. He assumed that fame would come to him 'as it had to Mann's Aschenbach, as Honor',[2] and up to *Portnoy's Complaint* he achieved this with healthy but modest book sales and generally respectful reviews. On the publication of this novel, however, Roth was catapulted into the much more polymorphous and less manageable sphere of mediatized celebrity. Initially created by publicity overkill for the book itself, this celebrity took on a life of its own as his name began to circulate freely in all kinds of contexts: gossip columnists reported that he was dating Barbra Streisand or Jackie Onassis, or that he had been committed to a mental hospital; he was accosted in the street by fans and detractors alike; his name was used, without his permission, in television advertisements; he became an endless source of innuendo on television talk shows (one guest joked on a late-night talk show that she would like to meet Philip Roth, but wouldn't want to shake his hand).[3] In effect, Roth became fetishized for celebrity purposes as a sex maniac – he complained that

> to become a celebrity is to become a brand name. There is Ivory soap, Rice Krispies, and Philip Roth. Ivory is the soap that floats; Rice Krispies the breakfast cereal that goes snap-crackle-pop; Philip Roth the Jew who masturbates with a piece of liver. And makes a million out of it.[4]

Roth's *Portnoy* fame thus had all the ingredients of a media scandal, as outlined by James Lull and Stephen Hinerman in their book on the subject. Such scandals, they argue, are both an example of the shifting status of public and private domains in celebrity culture (the publicity surrounding *Portnoy's Complaint* centring on the most 'private' act of all), and a way of regulating transgressive behaviour and reinforcing social norms.[5] At the same time, stars are granted more moral latitude than 'ordinary' people since, as Herman Gray puts it, 'ours is a media environment where fame and celebrity, no matter how momentary, are the currency which stimulates desire and fantasy'.[6] In this sense, the *Portnoy* scandal aptly illustrated celebrity culture's simultaneous fascination with and squeamishness about sex. Unlike many celebrity scandals, however, this one was wholly fictional, a pure 'pseudo-event': Roth had almost no public profile at the time, and had retired for several months to the writer's colony at Yaddo immediately after the book's publication, so these 'revelations' were not even based on half-truths about the author. Instead, they were a combustible combination of a traditional characteristic of literary celebrity – the identification of the author with his subject matter, encouraged here by the colloquial first person and confessional tone of *Portnoy's Complaint* – and a celebrity machinery of salacious gossip and rumour more usually associated with the sphere of commercial entertainment than with 'serious' literature. As Lull and Hinerman point out, though, 'a star's moral violations ... are always recontextualized in terms of his or her "image system" ... any particular transgression is constructed and read against an image in circulation'.[7] Insofar as Roth had a public personality at this time, it was as a bookish, intellectual figure who took himself and his work seriously, and the *Portnoy* affair's appeal may have lain partly in the discovery that such a figure also had base desires and shameful secrets. This was celebrity as cheap notoriety, then, involving the almost complete collapse of Roth's cultural authority as an 'author'.

Roth's response to this was to consolidate his persona as a serious figure. Educated to believe that 'the independent reality of the fiction is all there is of importance and that writers should remain in the shadows', Roth has situated himself in 'a midway position' on 'the pendulum of self-exposure that oscillates between aggressively exhibitionistic Mailerism and seques-tered Salingerism'.[8] He rarely appears in public, dividing his time between a Connecticut farmhouse and London and never appearing on American television to promote his work. It is true that he has given many inter-views in every kind of publication from *Paris Review* to *House and Garden*, incorporating some of them (including ones conducted with himself) into a collection entitled *Reading Myself and Others*. However, these appearances are limited and highly controlled – he insists that print interviews con-fine themselves to serious, impersonal queries, maintaining that his life and work should be kept separate. Interviewers often contrast his quiet, professional manner with his fictional personae – as one writer puts it, 'Roth resembles an accountant on his day off more than the globe-trotting neurotic you'd expect from the books'.[9]

At the same time, however, Roth recognizes that his celebrity has partly been a product of his ability to shake off this high seriousness and embrace some of the profane elements of American culture in his work. He character-izes his own writing as 'redface' – combining the traits of 'redskin' and 'paleface', terms coined by Philip Rahv to denote two diametrically oppo-sed, 'highbrow' and 'lowbrow' traditions in American writing. In particular, he suggests that *Portnoy's Complaint* and the novels which followed it grew out of his growing impatience with 'elevated notions' of fiction as 'something like a religious calling', which opposed 'high' art to mass-market 'philistinism'.[10] Alongside his European literary influences (Chekhov, Tolstoy, Flaubert, Mann and Kafka), Roth now embraced a freer verbal facility suggestive of oral performance, influenced by the comedy routines of Abbott and Costello and the Marx Brothers and sev-eral years of psychoanalysis. His work became more 'ego-ridden ... All sorts of impulses that I might once have put down as excessive, frivo-lous, or exhibitionistic I allowed to surface'.[11] This mixture of low comedy and therapeutic excess was a major factor in *Portnoy's Complaint*'s suc-cess, and undoubtedly contributed to the confusion surrounding its 'autobiographical' status, the almost universally held assumption that the author was 'spilling his guts out'.[12] As *New York* magazine saw it, Roth had 'kicked the nice Jewish boy bit, the stance of the Jamesian moral intelligence, and unleashed his comic, foul-mouthed, sex-obsessed demon. His true self'.[13]

This ability to combine elements of 'high' and 'low' culture in his work has meant that Roth has had an uneasy relationship with certain New York intellectuals. These critics have accused him of borrowing a kind of stand-up patter from the world of showbusiness and nightclub comedy and dressing it up as 'serious' literature – Irving Howe, in a famous critical assault which was later fictionalized by Roth in *The Anatomy Lesson* (1983), attacked him for having a 'thin personal culture', and (in Flaubert's terms) choosing an audience over readers.[14] As a fellow Jew from a slightly older generation, Howe also took issue with Roth for trivializing serious issues about the position of Jews in postwar American society – particularly given the very recent memory of the Holocaust – in the pursuit of bestsellerdom and notoriety. Roth's arguments with his Jewish readers are usually partly to do with his mainstream fame – the Rabbis who denounced him from synagogue pulpits and community centre lecterns after the publication of his first book, *Goodbye, Columbus*, for example, did so not so much on the grounds that Roth himself was anti-Semitic but that he would, in his own words, 'fuel the fires of the anti-Semites' by presenting an unflattering view of Jews to a wider audience.[15] These arguments have been important to Roth as a counterweight to the more absurd manifestations of his celebrity. His comment that he has 'a general audience and a Jewish audience', the former of which he has 'no sense of my impact upon' but the latter of which he 'feel[s] intensely their expectations, disdain, delight, criticism, their wounded self-love, their healthy curiosity',[16] implicitly contrasts celebrity's huge constituency with this smaller Jewish readership. I want to argue that Roth brings together some of these tensions produced by his fame in his work after *Portnoy's Complaint*.

Hypothetical Selves

Roth has described the celebrity he received after the publication of *Portnoy's Complaint* as 'one of the oddest misreadings ... that any contemporary writer has run into',[17] and says that much of his fiction since then has been an attempt to deal with this pivotal point in his career. In his subsequent books, Roth has written directly about the experience of fame but has also explored issues raised by the particular kind of celebrity he received for a novel which many readers assumed to be straightforwardly confessional. This has produced a series of progressively labyrinthine explorations of the relationship between autobiography and fiction – much of his writing after *Portnoy's Complaint* has included a recognizable surrogate of its author, in

Roth's words 'a being whose experience [is] comparable to my own and yet register[s] a more powerful valence'.[18] Roth's experiments with 'auto-biographical' fiction have created a kind of 'hall of mirrors' effect which has only added to the public confusion about the relationship between the author and his characters. These issues are dealt with most fully in Roth's novel series, *Zuckerman Bound* (1985), a trilogy and epilogue which follows the career of the author, Nathan Zuckerman, over a 20 year period, taking him through the youthful promise of his 20s, the celebrity of his 30s and the early burnout and creative stagnation of his 40s. There are two competing notions of literary celebrity which are played out in these books: on the one hand, fame is presented as a media invention, which vulgarizes everything it touches and entraps the author in a false and con-fining persona; on the other hand, it is seen as being intimately related to the author's own writing, personality and ambitions, which leads on to broader questions about the relationship between writers and their work, their readerships and their cultural identities.

The first book of the series, *The Ghost Writer* (1979), begins in December 1956, when Zuckerman spends the night at the Vermont retreat of E.I. Lonoff, a reclusive author who has rejected all the trappings of literary fame – prizes, honorary degrees, requests for interviews – and whom Nathan admires for his 'relentless winnowing out of the babyish, preening, insa-tiable self'.[19] As the novel progresses, however, tensions and discrepancies emerge between Nathan's motives and his behaviour, and between his idealization of Lonoff and the reality. While claiming to submit himself 'for candidacy as nothing less than E.I. Lonoff's spiritual son' (9), Zuckerman is really a young author on the make, shamelessly buttering Lonoff up in his letter of introduction and reading his own profile in the 'A Dozen to Keep Your Eye On' feature in the *Saturday Review* 50 times over. He also only mails his stories to Lonoff after being snubbed by another author, Felix Abravanel – who, with his beautiful wives and girlfriends, glitzy lec-ture tours and magazine profiles, is Lonoff's rival and complete antithesis.

Zuckerman's idealism about the renunciation of worldly fame has thus been bought cheaply and has a heavily self-romanticizing quality, even influencing his fantasy about one of Lonoff's students, Amy Bellette, in which he reimagines her as the Anne Frank who survives Belsen, emigrates to the United States and reads about the publication of her diary while flick-ing through the pages of *Time* in a dentist's waiting room. Although her greatest ambition, as announced in her diary, is to become a famous writer, she refuses to ring up *Time* to announce her survival because the diary will be less meaningful to its readers without her death and her symbolic importance as 'the incarnation of the millions of unlived years robbed from the murdered Jews' (150). In the classic adolescent daydream, though, she imagines her childhood friends and acquaintances saying to themselves: 'Who realized she was so gifted? Who realized we had such a writer in our midst?' (135) Although Roth was criticized by many reviewers for using the story of the Holocaust in this way, Zuckerman's unconscious reconfiguring of it as a cheesy and quintessentially American narrative of undiscovered star quality does show clearly the flimsiness of his claims to disinterest. Lonoff realizes this and attempts to steer Nathan away from his own life of 'reading and writing and looking at the snow', lamenting that all he has done for 30 years is 'turn sentences around' (30, 17). In turn, Zuckerman's disillusionment with Lonoff sets in when he speculates that Amy may be Lonoff's mistress. The truth is more subtle – in refusing to sleep with Amy, Lonoff has made his wife feel as though he has only done so out of a per- verted sense of duty, while she has become frustrated by his endless fastidiousness and asceticism. Roth, then, refuses to idealize the life of the author-recluse, portraying it (in both Lonoff's and Zuckerman's case) as an ambiguous mixture of high ideals and *hauteur*.

In the second novel in the series, *Zuckerman Unbound* (1981), set in 1969, Nathan has left the notion of literature as a *sanctum sanctorum* firmly behind him, becoming nationally notorious with the publication of a sexu- ally explicit novel, *Carnovsky*. Zuckerman is now the celebrity equivalent of a sideshow freak – he is stopped in the street by people who either want to insult him or touch his coat adoringly, is discussed in gossip columns and on talk shows, and receives bizarre letters and phone calls, death threats aimed at his family, and photographs of scantily-clad women offering sexual favours. Such a success is 'as baffling as a misfortune' (184), inverting all his expectations about literary success, and is made more traumatic because, for everyone else, it is wholly unimaginable – as Nathan puts it, 'being a poor misunderstood millionaire is not really a topic that intelligent people can discuss for very long' (306). Zuckerman circulates in a media maelstrom in which traditional cultural hierarchies are not respected and the distinc- tion between 'reality' and 'fiction' is routinely ignored. His experience seems to support Rainer Maria Rilke's comment, which Roth is fond of quoting, that 'fame is no more than the quintessence of all the misunder- standings collecting around a new name'.[20]

There are similarities here with another Roth character, David Kepesh, who mutates into a six-foot high mammary gland in an earlier novella, *The Breast* (1972). Roth says that this book

wasn't just about entrapment in the flesh and the horrors of desire, it was also inspired by some thinking I'd had to do about fame, notoriety and scandal. When the idea for the book first came to me, I had myself only recently become an object of curiosity, believed by some to be very much the sexual freak and grotesque.[21]

Interestingly, the novella does end with Kepesh contemplating an escape from the hospital where he is being treated in order to use his affliction in the pursuit of fame and fortune, claiming that 'if the Beatles can fill Shea Stadium, so can I'.[22] Kepesh's metamorphosis is a wholly absurd, meaningless event outside his control, which has no relation to his own life as the archetypal 'nice Jewish boy' with good college grades and brilliant career; similarly, at the beginning of *Zuckerman Unbound*, Nathan remains essentially bewildered, submissive and apparently blameless as events unfold inexorably around him.

Roth suggests that this debased, disposable kind of celebrity has in turn produced a dysfunctional culture of fandom, encapsulated in the figure of Alvin Pepler, a personification of 'how Johnny Carson America sees me', according to Nathan (339). Pepler introduces himself to Zuckerman in a restaurant and then, when their friendship fails to develop, proceeds to harass him with obscene phone calls and handkerchiefs soiled with semen. Pepler is himself a victim of celebrity culture, a former champion on the hugely popular 1950s TV game show, *Smart Money*, who has been forced to 'take a dive' to make way for a wealthy New England WASP contestant, Hewlett Lincoln, while his promised sweetener of a big break in television has not materialized. Roth here uses a fairly accurate rendering of the quiz-show scandals – dealt with more recently by Robert Redford in a 1994 film – as a kind of parable of the corruptions and betrayals of celebrity. Successful contestants appearing on quiz shows in the golden age of network television, the 1950s, were transformed into national celebrities (Charles Van Doren, the most famous participant, was featured on the cover of *Time* and later became a talk show star) in order to create a meritocratic narrative in which fame was conferred on 'ordinary' people through their own hard work and talent. This concealed a bureaucratized and standardized fame machine in which stars were entirely manufactured by the studios: questions and answers were provided in advance, every response and gesture scripted and the contestants instructed to play closely defined roles designed to create dramatic tension, increase ratings and perpetuate popular stereotypes. Herbert Stempel, on whom Pepler is based, for example, played the part of the poor Jewish boy from Queens, before being forced off the show to make way for the WASP golden boy, Van Doren. The quiz shows thus bought into a highly controlled myth of accessibility which surrounds many examples of mainstream celebrity: the mass-produced star represents the potential of all individuals in society to achieve success. As Stuart Ewen puts it:

> In a society where everyday life [is] increasingly defined by feelings of insignificance and institutions of standardization, the 'star' provide[s] an accessible icon to the significance of the personal and the individual ... Celebrity forms a symbolic pathway, connecting each aspiring individual to a universal image of fulfillment: to be someone, when 'being no one' is the norm.[23]

Pepler's celebrity is thus similar to Zuckerman's in being wholly artificial, and designed to perpetuate society's stereotypes about Jews. There the similarity ends: Pepler, a talentless man with a head for useless quiz-show-type facts, stalks Nathan because he has been left embittered by his brief experience of fame. He has constructed an elaborate fantasy life in which he is a brilliant writer and critic, fictional Broadway producers vie for the rights to his life story and Zuckerman steals material from him for *Carnovsky*. Nathan even begins to fear for his life at one point, speculating that Pepler may belong to a long line of assassins of celebrities: 'Bang bang, you're dead. There was all the meaning the act was ever meant to have. You're you, I'm me, and for that and that alone you die' (338). In this connection, Richard Schickel has suggested that the relationship between celebrities and their fans is based around an 'illusion of intimacy'. Celebrities are such omnipresent, apparently accessible figures in contemporary culture, he suggests, that this fosters a dangerous mixture of devotion and envy amongst their fans, epitomized by borderline personalities like John Hinckley, Jr and Mark Chapman who stalk and attempt to kill the objects of their worship.[24] This obsessional model of fandom has itself fed back into celebrity culture, being reproduced in Hollywood films like *The Fan* (1981), *King of Comedy* (1982) and *Misery* (1990). Other critics, though, have attacked this 'othering' of fans, conducted from what Joli Jenson calls a 'savannah of smug superiority'. Jenson argues that

> defining fandom as a deviant activity allows ... a reassuring, self-aggrandizing stance to be adopted. It also supports the celebration of particular values – the rational over the emotional, the educated over the uneducated, the subdued over the passionate, the elite over the popular, the mainstream over the margin, the status quo over the alternative.[25]

In *Zuckerman Unbound*, the 'Zuckermaniacs' (378) who harass Nathan are certainly an ominous sign that the distinctions between these different dualisms have disintegrated. The strength of Roth's novel, however, lies in the fact that it does not merely demonize the people who read *Carnovsky* in this way, but also begins to interrogate Zuckerman's own responsibility for his fame.

The single unifying characteristic of all Zuckerman's fans is that they assume that the author and his character are identical: he is often addressed as 'Carnovsky', and constantly complains that people have 'mistaken impersonation for confession and [a]re calling out to a character in a book' (190). During the second half of *Zuckerman Unbound*, however, when Nathan flies to Miami to be at the bedside of his dying father, the novel considers the extent to which Zuckerman has appropriated his own and other people's life stories in his fiction in such a way as to invite these comparisons. Pepler's accusation that Zuckerman is a 'heartless bastard' who has hurt his family 'in the name of Great Art' (288), now begins to be voiced by the interested parties themselves. Zuckerman's own mother fails to disguise her hurt at the portrayal of a stereotypical 'Jewish mother' in *Carnovsky*, Nathan's father, with his dying breath, apparently calls his son a 'bastard', and his brother, Henry, berates him: 'To you everything is disposable ... everything is grist for your fun-machine' (397).

Zuckerman's exasperation at his new-found notoriety is also shot through with moments of self-insight:

Coldhearted betrayer of the most intimate confessions, cutthroat caricaturist of your own loving parents, graphic reporter of encounters with women to whom you have been deeply bound by trust, by sex, by love – no, the virtue racket ill becomes you (234).

Nathan's agent also realizes that there is a fundamental relationship between his celebrity and the book he has written, and he accuses his client of trying to 'humiliate all your dignified, high-minded gravity', and then protesting 'because nobody aside from you seems to see it as a profoundly moral and high-minded act' (305). He and his wife thus urge Zuckerman to start enjoying his success and to 'come out from behind all that disgusting highbrow disapproval of the fallen people having fun' (257).

In the third novel in the series, *The Anatomy Lesson*, these issues are increasingly played out inside Zuckerman's own head, as he simultaneously complains that the fact 'that writing is an act of imagination seems to perplex and infuriate everyone' and laments the self-centredness of his own writing, which uses his 'life as cud ... Swallow as experience, then up from the gut for a second go as art' (450, 602). His writing has always drawn on personal experience, but now he can only write about the problems of being a famous writer – so his recognition that 'the personal ingredient is what gets you going' is countered by a realization that 'if you hang on to the personal ingredient any longer you'll disappear right up your asshole' (550). Zuckerman now experiences a life crisis, as he becomes paralysed with undiagnosable and untreatable back pain and suffers from severe writer's block. Since no medical cause can be found for his back pain, there is a suggestion that his physical and creative atrophy may be interrelated, and linked ultimately to the experience of fame. Nathan's friends, as well as his analyst, argue that his pain 'is a self-inflicted wound: penance for the popularity of *Carnovsky* ... the enviable, comfortable success story wrecked by the wrathful cells' (440). Nathan, however, strongly resists this interpretation that his illness is 'expiation through suffering' (430). These two views reflect two opposing takes on Nathan's fame in the books – it is either a bizarre, anomalous event which teaches him nothing, or something for which he is, to varying degrees, answerable through his writing.

In *The Prague Orgy* (1985), the final book in the series, Zuckerman's visit to Eastern Europe allows him to contrast the misreadings of his own work with the ruthless censorship endured by his Czech counterparts. Roth himself has made this comparison between writers in totalitarian countries and in 'free' societies in the West, suggesting that 'in my situation, everything goes and nothing matters; in their situation, nothing goes and everything matters'.[26] When Zdenek Sisovsky, a young Czech writer, suggests to Zuckerman that *Carnovsky* is an unacknowledged masterpiece and that 'the weight of stupidity you must carry is heavier than the weight of banning', Zuckerman strongly disagrees: 'It's you ... who's been denied the right to practice his profession. Whatever the scandal, I have been profusely – bizarrely – rewarded. Everything from an Upper East Side address to helping worthy murderers get out on parole' (703, 704). Nathan's involvement with the Prague literary underground also becomes an escape from the enforced narcissism of celebrity – at the height of his life crisis in *The Anatomy Lesson*, for instance, he longs for 'war, destruction, anti-Semitism, totalitarianism ... a martyrdom more to the point ... than bearing the cocktail party chitchat as a guest on Dick Cavett' (550–1). Zuckerman finds such a cause and reverts to being the good Jewish son in *The Prague Orgy* when, attempting to recover the manuscript of an unknown Yiddish writer for publication in the West, he has the stories confiscated by the Czech Minister of Culture and is accused of being a Zionist agent (784). Zuckerman is now the famous author deigning to rescue the forgotten one, who wrote for a higher purpose than worldly renown. Recovering these manuscripts, however, also represents Zuckerman's realization that, although authors are powerless in the face of misreadings of their work, it is better to have any kind of reception than none at all: 'Think of all that his stories will be spared if instead of wrenching his fiction out of oblivion, you just turn around and go ... Yet I stay' (766).

It is clear, then, that this series of books, as an extended speculation on 'the unforeseen consequences of art' (759), is an attempt to deal with some of the issues raised by the spectacular success of *Portnoy's Complaint*. One should be careful, of course, not to reproduce the kinds of assumptions satirized by Roth in these books by claiming them as transparently auto-biographical. In Roth's words, his writing is the 'transformation, through an elaborate impersonation, of a personal emergency into a public act',[27] and his fictional alter egos are 'useful fictions',[28] allowing these issues to be worked through hypothetically in his work – a form of release which is not, of course, available to Zuckerman (hence his writer's block). It may be that the novels comprising *Zuckerman Bound* thus seem more 'autobio-graphical' than they are because they explore the predicament of celebrity and therefore use the public facts of Roth's life most familiar to us – most obviously the fame achieved by a sexually explicit novel presumed by many of its readers to be autobiographical, and the critical controversies surrounding it. Even these elements are deliberately heightened and dramatized – while Zuckerman stays in New York to face the music after the publication of *Carnovsky*, for example, Roth retreated to Yaddo. The distance Roth achieves from his subject matter in *Zuckerman Bound*, then, allows him to interrogate his celebrity in an open and self-questioning way, presenting it as both a wholly alien presence which dislocates the author from his past, and as a more nuanced process which involves the ambition and self-promotion of the author.

'Peekaboo Narratives'

It should come as no surprise to Roth, given the nature of the celebrity culture he is part of and is examining, that his 'autobiographical' reading of reductively autobiographical readings of his work has only exacerbated the tendency of journalists and critics to make these kinds of assumptions. Although Roth has been forthcoming about this issue in his work, his response in interviews has been to resist fiercely any attempt to reference his own life through his fiction. These two approaches – openness and intransigence – are both present in Roth's autobiography, *The Facts* (1988), caught as it is between the imaginative status of fiction and the creative self-presentation of the interview and other aspects of Roth's public per-sona. In this book, Roth describes his disillusionment with novel-writing after suffering a breakdown in 1987, and claims that *The Facts* represents 'the bare bones, the structure of a life without a fiction', conveying 'my exhaustion with masks, disguises, distortions, and lies'.[29] Roth's decision to end the narrative just before the publication of *Portnoy's Complaint*, thus covering only just over half of his life, suggests that he is attempting to write about a former self untouched by celebrity. Much of the book works as a very conventional linear narrative, with separate chapters on Roth's childhood, college days, failed marriage and developing career. However, the book ends with a letter from 'Zuckerman' to 'Roth' which comments on the preceding chapters and problematizes this apparent transparency. Zuckerman complains that the book is too 'steeped in [Roth's] nice-guy side', suggesting that he is not the first novelist who, 'by fleeing the wearying demands of fictional invention for a little vacation in straightforward recollection, has shackled the less sociable impulses that led him or her to become a novelist in the first place'. As Nathan points out, 'with autobiography there's always another text, a countertext, if you will, to the one presented'.[30] While much of the book therefore presumes to be a candid account of the events of Roth's life, then, the coda critiques this assumption of representational innocence.

Roth's more recent fictional works point much more insistently to a notion of the self as unstable and intertextual, and to the genres of fiction and autobiography as infinitely permeable. Although this means that Roth's work is often grouped critically with that of metafictionists like John Barth and Donald Barthelme, one senses that Roth has his own agenda, working through issues which are of fundamental concern to him and which can be traced back to his first experience of celebrity. As Hillel Halkin puts it, 'the impression given by [Roth's] later books is that, had post-modernism not existed, he would have been quite capable of inventing aspects of it by himself'.[31] Roth's next novel after *Zuckerman Bound*, *The Counterlife* (1986), reiterates many of the same themes as the trilogy and epilogue, specifically the supposedly parasitic dependence of authors on their own and other people's life experiences. While Nathan's editor praises his 'gift for theatrical self-transformation', Henry continues to accuse his brother of irresponsibly reclaiming and vulgarizing his family history, and asserts that 'calling [*Carnovsky*] fiction was the biggest fiction of all'.[32] Zuckerman's trip to Israel in the novel is partly inspired by the kind of solipsistic impasse to which his celebrity has brought him, his exhaustion at living 'in the nutshell of self-scrutiny' and desire to escape from 'the writer's tedious burden of being his own cause'.[33] This dialogue takes place, however, at Zuckerman's funeral, and the entire book is made up of different sections in which Nathan and other characters die and are then brought back to life in a series of hypothetical scenarios. Each section undermines the 'truth' of its predecessor, thus reinforcing the notion of Zuckerman as only a fictionalized alter ego – indeed, Roth says that killing off Nathan was partly a way of second-guessing autobiographical readings of his work.[34]

In Roth's next novel, *Deception* (1990), a Jewish-American author named 'Philip' engages in discussions with his English mistress about his previous fictional creations, including Zuckerman, Lonoff and Portnoy, at the end of which she asks him to change his own name in the fiction we are reading to 'Nathan'. But their incessant role-playing, in which he impersonates a whole series of Roth's characters and she acts the part of Zuckerman's and Lonoff's biographer, suggests that the whole book may be an extended game of 'reality shift'. As Philip says bullishly: 'I write fiction and I'm told it's autobiography and I write autobiography and I'm told it's fiction, so since I'm so dim and they're so smart, let *them* decide what is or what isn't'.[35]

This trick of playing selves and counterselves off against each other reaches its apotheosis in Roth's 1993 novel, *Operation Shylock*. In this book, 'Philip Roth', the narrator and central character who shares many biographical details with Roth himself, discovers that a Chicago private detective who looks and sounds uncannily like him is impersonating him publicly in order to preach the gospel of 'diasporism' throughout the Middle East. The impersonator sends the 'real' Philip Roth a clumsily written critique of his reclusiveness: 'I am only spending the renown you hoard. You hide yourself/in lonely rooms/country recluse/anonymous expatriate/garreted monk. Never spent it as you should/might/wouldn't/couldn't: IN BEHALF OF THE JEWISH PEOPLE'.[36] In other words, the imposter is trying not so much to appropriate the private identity of 'Philip Roth' as to use his celebrity for his own purposes – as Jonathan Raban says, the imposter 'is a criminal, not because he steals Roth's "identity" ... but because he tries to filch the novelist's worldly prestige, an importantly different commodity'.[37]

In a bizarre twist, when the book was published Roth brought the controversy about the relationship between autobiography and fiction out of his work itself and into the extra-textual sphere by claiming, in an article published on the prime site of the *New York Times Book Review's* front page, that all the events described in the novel actually happened.[38] Roth expanded on this in subsequent interviews: although the novel ends with a traditional disclaimer, for instance, he explained that this was inserted at the insistence of an Israeli secret service operative.[39] ('Philip Roth' ends the novel as an agent for Mossad, helping to track down Jews giving money to the PLO.) Assuming that the extraordinary events related in *Operation Shylock* are not true – and there is no evidence for them other than that presented in the novel – Roth's strategy here is puzzling, and a complete turnaround from his insistence in all his previous interviews that his writing and his life should be kept strictly separate. There might be a suspicion that this was merely a strategy aimed at publicizing his novel if Roth had not proved so fiercely dismissive of book promotion in the past, usually contriving to be out of the country as each new novel appeared.

These textual and extra-textual games have left many readers and critics impatient with Roth's insistence that his work should be treated with impersonal academic rigour. Despite achieving critical acclaim for his more recent works – including the National Book Award and the Pulitzer Prize – he is not an author to whom the media generally warms. As one *Boston Globe* reporter says: 'Roth has been the target of more venom than even Norman Mailer. He has been described as a self-hating Jewish pornographer. A malicious destroyer of women. An obsessive anti-Semite whose greatest obsession is himself'.[40] This received wisdom about the author, which is disseminated by both journalists and literary critics well-versed in the 'intentional fallacy', is implicitly based on an assumption of correspondence between the writer's life and his work. The popular view of Roth spilled over from the books pages into the news sections in 1996, when he became the subject of an unflattering portrait in a book, *Leaving A Doll's House*, written by his ex-wife, Claire Bloom, which was widely seen as 'revenge' for the fictional portrait of a marriage in *Deception*. Roth's novel *I Married a Communist* reignited the controversy in 1998, many critics and journalists assuming that Roth was 'getting his own back' for Bloom's account. (In this book, set in McCarthy-era America, the lead character, Ira Ringold, is betrayed by his scheming actress wife, Eve Frame, who publishes a confessional, untruthful book denouncing him as a Russian spy.) This desire to interpret literary works as simply a way of settling personal scores, in order to recycle them as gossip column fodder, has eerie similarities with the fame achieved by *Portnoy's Complaint* almost 30 years previously. In fact, this debasement of the public sphere, as represented by the appetite for Eve's 'true confessions', is one of the novel's principal themes. As one of its narrators says, the McCarthy era inaugurated

> the postwar triumph of gossip as the unifying credo of the world's oldest democratic republic. In Gossip We Trust. Gossip as gospel, the national faith. McCarthyism as the beginning not just of serious politics but of serious everything as entertainment to amuse the mass audience … He took us back to our origins, back to the seventeenth century and the stocks. That's how the country began: moral disgrace as public entertainment.[41]

At the same time, it would be naive not to recognize that the unsettling combination of apparently naked self-revelation and still greater obfuscation and textual playfulness in Roth's more recent work – even if this originates in his attempt to work through and transcend autobiographical readings of his work – cannot help but make these connections between life and art easier to make. Many critics have suggested that Roth implicitly buys into the logic of celebrity, by producing what one of them calls 'peekaboo narratives' which invite speculation, gossip and rumour.[42] John Updike has referred wearily to the 'self-on-self grapple' of Roth's later work, suggesting that 'this cultivation of hypothetical selves has become an endgame'.[43] Others have accused Roth of protesting too much: Joseph Epstein has dismissed Roth's complaint about readers getting a 'voyeuristic kick' out of his later novels, suggesting that 'if a writer doesn't wish to supply such kicks, perhaps he would do better not to undress before windows opening onto thoroughfares'.[44]

Although this last comment seems harsh, dismissing Roth's experiments in autobiography as mere authorial narcissism, his post-*Portnoy* work does raise questions about the complex interrelationship between autobiography and fiction which are not always answered by his attempts to shut up shop in interviews. While interviewing Roth, for example, Ian Hamilton suggests to the author that it is hard not to read his works as partly confessional, and Roth replies: 'It's very easy to read it this way. This is the easiest possible way to read. It makes it just like reading the evening paper. I only get annoyed because it isn't the evening paper I've written'. Hamilton goes on: 'Surely the journalistic approach is inescapable – unless the reader forgets everything he knows or has read about you, Philip Roth'.[45] Hamilton is right: reading Roth's novels 'autobiographically' may be regrettable but is often unavoidable, even if this is accompanied by all kinds of other, more sophisticated readings. This is equally true for academic critics, generally discouraged from reading biographicist assumptions into texts since the rise of the New Criticism and its theoretical successors, but probably expunging a lot of their average readerly curiosity in more 'objective' interpretations. As Bourdieu puts it, one of the defining characteristics of the 'popular' as opposed to the 'bourgeois' or 'high-culture' aesthetic is

> the affirmation of the continuity between art and life, which implies the subordination of form to function, or, one might say, on a refusal of the refusal which is the starting point of the high aesthetic, i.e., the clear-cut separation of ordinary dispositions from the specifically aesthetic disposition.[46]

In other words, human interest, and a sense of connection between the text and something concrete in the 'real' world, are what many readers look for in books. Failure to recognize this is to condemn out of hand a large number of reading practices, and to dismiss *any* interest in Roth's personal investment in his work as naive and prurient. It also conflates different kinds of celebrity together, equating all 'autobiographical' readings with the post-Portnoy demonization of Roth as a sex maniac. The strength of Roth's fictionalizations of celebrity – as opposed to his public comments – is that they do not do this, presenting literary celebrity instead as an awkward amalgam of authorial assertiveness and readerly misunderstanding.

It is clear that Roth's explorations into the nature of fame and his resulting experiments with conjectural autobiography, although they may have provided him with a way of writing about and coming to terms with his celebrity, have ultimately only reproduced that celebrity. It is hardly surprising, then, given the particular form of celebrity that he has received, that much of Roth's public response to fame is conducted from a level of intellectual detachment and high cultural disdain. If anything, the enormous discrepancy between these two different ways of reading – Roth's deadly earnestness and gravitas and celebrity's love of gossip and low farce – has only widened since the publication of *Portnoy's Complaint*. In his work, however, no other contemporary author has so insistently explored the competing impulses behind literary celebrity and its convoluted workings on the authorial self.

7
Silence, Exile, Cunning, and So On: Don DeLillo

Don DeLillo's celebrity has accrued gradually: although he published his first novel in 1971, it took him over a dozen years and seven novels to cross over from a minority readership, with healthy but modest book sales and generally respectful reviews, into bestsellerdom, media attention and critical acclaim. Before he became more broadly famous, however, DeLillo was clearly wary about the effects of even minor celebrity. The dustjackets of his early novels contained the briefest of bio-blurbs – a list of publications and his place of residence (New York) – and he did not give an interview until the late 1970s. (When this interviewer, Tom LeClair, tracked him down to Athens, DeLillo handed him a calling card on which was written: 'I don't want to talk about it'.[1]) In the mid-1980s, Philip Stevick wrote of him admiringly as an author who had managed to escape the celebrity baggage of the contemporary author, suggesting that this had also contributed to the lack of attention he had received: 'No public drunk, no junkie, no talk show exhibit, no vagabond in search of America, he seems to spend a lot of time at the typewriter. The culture has a hard time knowing quite what to do with him'.[2] Stevick's comments, however, coincided with a stepping up of DeLillo's celebrity after the critical and commercial success of *White Noise*, which also won the National Book Award in 1985. At about the same time, his backlist was reprinted by Gary Fisketjon at Random House as a series of distinctive quality paperbacks, in a kind of trial run for Fisketjon's innovative *Vintage Contemporaries*. DeLillo was thus a major beneficiary of the efforts of publishing houses in the 1980s to exploit the potential of serious, intellectually complex fiction as a consumer product, which helped, among other factors, to turn him into a national celebrity.

DeLillo, though, is still perhaps the most publicly anonymous of all the authors discussed in this part of the book, and maintains a view that writers should resist any easy assimilation into their culture. He argues that artists should be

> independent of affiliation and independent of influence ... There are so many temptations for American writers to become part of the system ... that now, more than ever, we have to resist. American writers ought to stand and live in the margins, and be more dangerous.[3]

In the only television programme he has participated in – a documentary for the BBC – DeLillo similarly deplores the way that writers have recently become 'part of the background noise – part of the buzz of celebrity and consumerism'.[4] In fact, DeLillo's own career points to the ways in which even the most avowedly non-commercial and eremetic of contemporary American authors have been drawn into self-publicity, but also shows that authors can use a limited public persona skilfully in order to maintain their privacy and ways of working.

This chapter discusses the ways in which DeLillo has used his work to interrogate the phenomenon of celebrity – and specifically his own celebrity – in contemporary America. Although his novels are very far from being crypto-autobiography, I want to suggest that DeLillo uses some of them – and particularly his 1991 book, *Mao II* – as a way of making sense of and dealing with some of the issues raised by the trajectory of his own career as he came to terms with major-league fame. DeLillo provides a link between literary celebrity and contemporary debates about postmodernism and postmodernity, by relating notions of authorship to anxieties about the rise of what Fredric Jameson calls 'a new depthlessness' in society and culture created by the replacement of the 'real' with surface image.[5] These anxieties are used as a way into a number of issues concerning the future of serious writing, authorship and the self in consumer culture: the notion of fame as entrapment; the relationship between celebrities and their audiences; the media's obsession with escapees from celebrity; and the self-romanticization of the reclusive artist.

Celebrities and Fans

These issues are first introduced extensively in DeLillo's third novel, *Great Jones Street* (1973), narrated by a 26-year-old rock star, Bucky Wunderlick, who tires of fame and adulation in the middle of a national tour and hides himself in a seedy bedsitter in Manhattan. Bucky's wholly mercenary manager, Globke, fearing that the valuable commodity of Bucky's celebrity will be squandered, tries to persuade the star to release his mysterious 'mountain tapes' in order to fill the silence, before eventually stealing them at the end of the novel, and telling Bucky:

> You were failing to deliver product. Product is something that matters deeply. You owed us product. Contracts in our files specified what product you owed, when it was due, how it was to be presented. This was not a question of a few thousand dollars gurgling down the drain. We're a parent corporation. We've got subsidiaries and affiliates all over the place. Do you know what they're constantly doing? They're yowling for their food. Feed me, feed me. Enormous sums of money were involved in your disappearing act.[6]

Predictably, Bucky's fame is more complicated than this – his disappearance from public view is followed by a clamour of interest from fans and news media, and becomes a commercial proposition in itself. As an ABC reporter who visits Bucky in Great Jones Street says to him: 'Your power is growing ... The more time you spend in isolation, the more demands are made on the various media to communicate some relevant words and pictures ... The less you say, the more you are'.[7]

The novel, however, is about more than simply the ability of the media to reverse the terms of celebrity and transform the cultural capital of artistic 'integrity' into commercial advantage. Even as he shows real disdain for the trappings of fame, Bucky is still an intelligent commentator on its dangerous pleasures and an astute manipulator of his own self-image, as his opening comments in the novel reveal:

> Fame requires every kind of excess. I mean true fame, a devouring neon ... Fame, this special kind, feeds itself on outrage, on what the counselors of lesser men would consider bad publicity – hysteria in limousines, knife fights in the audience, bizarre litigation, treachery, pandemonium and drugs. Perhaps the only natural law attaching to true fame is that the famous man is compelled, eventually, to commit suicide.[8]

Bucky's friends and associates convince him that he must indeed take his silence to its logical extreme by committing suicide and supplying his fans with 'a gorgeous death' – preferably in a foreign city, so that doubts remain and the tantalizing possibility of his survival can generate further rumours. In the end, Bucky fakes his suicide and, sure enough, the stories accumulate of him being kidnapped or murdered, or 'living among beggars and syphilitics,

performing good works'.[9] Both the first and second stages of Bucky's disappearance – his retreat to Great Jones Street and his phony suicide – are thus
inspired by a combination of astute careerism and more idealistic motives.

Mark Osteen has suggested that this novel 'amounts to self-criticism, a
critique of DeLillo's own withdrawal from the public eye; to resist fame is
only to allow it to escape one's own management, to allow facsimiles to
replace the "true" self'.[10] It is true that by centring on the fame not of a
wholly manufactured celebrity but of a creative artist in *Great Jones Street* –
and dealing with a period (the late 1960s and early 1970s) when the rock
singer-songwriter was beginning to be valued as a serious cultural figure –
DeLillo is able to point to the subtly corrupting nature of contemporary
fame. But he also introduces here a rather schematic characterization of
audiences and crowds in celebrity culture which becomes a consistent
element in his work: Bucky's actions in *Great Jones Street* are partly determined by obsessional fans desperate for 'answers', who commit arson,
vandalism and rape at his concerts – 'murderous in their love of me' – and
for whom his disappearance at the beginning of the novel is not quite
complete enough. Bohack, the member of a clandestine organization
known as the Happy Valley Farm Commune which is devoted to restor-
ing the idea of privacy to American life and which makes a pilgrimage to
Bucky's house in Great Jones Street, voices the demand of the star's fans for
his suicide: 'It's the final inward plunge. It's what you owe us. It really is.
We patterned our whole lives after your example ... it's what everyone
expects of you, right down to the littlest scribbler of fan mail'.[11]

DeLillo offers further speculations on the deadly nature of fan culture in
Libra (1988), his fictionalized account of the conspiracy leading to the
Kennedy assassination. Kennedy throughout is described as the ultimate
celebrity to a needy nation – 'the object of a thousand longings ... he floats
over the landscape at night, entering dreams and fantasies, entering the
act of love between husbands and wives. He floats through television
screens into bedrooms at night'.[12] This luminous glamour, however,
creates an explosive mixture of hero-worship and disaffection amongst
his public. Most significantly, the character at the centre of the narrative,
Lee Harvey Oswald, appears to be motivated not so much by his confused
revolutionary politics as by a kind of psychic need to destroy the distance
between Kennedy's fame and his own anonymity through the use of
violence. 'His life had a single clear subject now, called Lee Harvey Oswald',
he thinks in his prison cell after the assassination. 'He and Kennedy were
partners. The figure of the gunman in the window was inextricable from
the victim and his history ... It gave him what he needed to live'. These
feelings of resentment and exclusion are shared by the misfits and loners,

the loose affiliation of anti-Castro Cuban exiles and disgruntled ex-CIA men, who organize the conspiracy around Oswald – another character's rage at Kennedy is described as 'partly a reaction to public life itself, to men who glow in the lens barrel of a camera'.[13] Celebrity is thus seen as a deeply unhealthy symptom of a diseased society, a kind of opium for the masses which attempts to channel their feelings of exclusion but actually leaves them feeling even more alienated.

The Endgame of Reclusiveness

These issues are brought together most fully in DeLillo's 1991 novel, *Mao II*, where they are linked to a particular concern which is even closer to home for him – the apparently paradoxical fascination with author-recluses in celebrity culture. This novel's central character is Bill Gray, the celebrated author of two slim works of fiction who has neither published nor appeared in public for over 20 years, and who lives a hermitical existence in an unidentified rural hideout, supported by two assistants, Scott Martineau and Karen Janney. The plot of the novel begins as this situation is about to alter, and is divided roughly into two parts. In the first part, Gray emerges falteringly from his seclusion by agreeing to have his picture taken by a New York photographer, Brita Nilsson, as a possible precursor to his publishing a novel which he has been working on for years and knows to be a failure. In the second part, Gray embarks on a more emphatic attempt to go public when he becomes involved, partly as a result of contacts made through Brita, with the campaign to free a poet and UN worker, Jean-Claude Julien, who is being held hostage in Beirut. DeLillo has praised reclusive authors for 'refusing to become part of the all-incorporating treadmill of consumption and disposal', in spite of the 'automatic mechanism' of the media which tries 'to absorb certain such reluctant entities into the weave'.[14] *Mao II* is about what happens when this absorption takes place, and whether or not this wholly devalues the author's own strategies of silence and renunciation.

Bill Gray's initial decision to have his photograph taken allows DeLillo to provide a series of variations on a recurrent theme in his work – the reproduction and circulation of media images as exchangeable commodities. As Gray puts it during his photo session with Brita:

> There's the life and there's the consumer event ... Nothing happens until it's consumed ... Nature has given way to aura. A man cuts himself shaving and someone is signed up to write the biography of the cut. All the material in every life is channeled into the glow.[15]

The frequent references to the life and work of Andy Warhol (the novel takes its title from Warhol's line drawing, *Mao II*, held in New York's Museum of Modern Art) allow this theme to be developed and expanded on throughout the narrative. The purposely flattened style of Warhol's silkscreen prints of celebrities such as Marilyn Monroe, Elvis Presley, Elizabeth Taylor and even Mao himself, aptly demonstrates, as one reviewer of *Mao II* put it, 'how fame is transformed into a death mask, how a portrait can freeze the mind behind the face'.[16] Aside from this, there is Warhol's own consciously achieved shallowness as a public figure and cultural icon – when Karen tries to summon up a mental image of who he is, all she can remember is that 'he was famous, he was dead, he had a white mask of face and glowing white hair' (62). (Warhol, of course, neatly encapsulated the notion of contemporary celebrity as superficial and valueless by predicting that 'in the future, everyone will be world famous for 15 minutes'.)

Gray's agreement to sit for Brita is curious because his theory of photographs seems to be summed up in Fredric Jameson's comment on Warhol's work, that there is 'no way to complete the hermeneutic gesture'.[17] When Brita has left the house with the negatives after the photo session, Bill thinks of himself as used and discarded: 'Got what she came for, didn't she? I'm a picture now, flat as birdshit on a Buick' (54). Brita also points out that, once Bill's photograph has appeared, he will be expected to resemble it and that people will 'absolutely question your right to look different from your picture' (43). These comments connect with what DeLillo has said was his original inspiration for *Mao II* – the photograph of J.D. Salinger appearing on the front page of the *New York Post* in 1988 (discussed already in Chapter 3). DeLillo referred to this

> startling picture of an elderly man – he looked frightened and angry ... For the editor to send these two men to New Hampshire was a little like ordering an execution. And when you look at the face of the man being photographed, it's not a great leap of imagination to think he's just been shot.[18]

Susan Sontag has similarly pointed to the implicitly violent nature of photography, inscribed in its very vocabulary – 'loading' a film, 'aiming' the camera, 'shooting' a picture, and so on:

> There is something predatory in the act of taking a picture. To photograph people is to violate them, by seeing them as they never see themselves, by having knowledge of them that they can never have; it turns people into objects that can be symbolically possessed. Just as the

camera is a sublimation of the gun, to photograph someone is a sublimated murder – a soft murder, appropriate to a sad, frightened time.[19]

Mao II provides an extended discussion of these metaphors of the photographer as marksman, and the photographic image as an effacement of the self. Gray describes picture-taking as 'like a wake', and says of his fans that there is 'barely a glimmer of difference' between 'the camera-toters and the gun-wavers' (42, 197).

The phenomenon of celebrity is also heavily dependent on both the perpetual replication of images and the elision of public and private spheres which photography helps to produce. The collapse of this distinction between public and private could be said to be consistent with two particular characteristics of advanced capitalism: the ever-expanding search for new markets, and the exploitation of the self as a sellable commodity. The telephoto lenses of newspaper and magazine photographers – who, according to Scott, have sought out Gray's house in order to take long-range pictures of the author (30) – are a specific example of this commodification of the 'private' self, created in the pursuit of an exclusive image which will boost circulation and, therefore, profits. The commercial potential of celebrity, linked to the co-optation of literature into the 'culture industry', is signalled at the very beginning of *Mao II* as Scott browses around a New York bookstore, checking out the photographs of authors on the wall and stepping over piles of garishly marketed books all seeming to shriek '*Buy me*' (19). It is further embodied in the likeable but vacuous figure of the editor Charlie Everson – a mirror image of Globke in *Great Jones Street* in his ingenious attempts to mask corporate motives behind a spurious concern for his client – who wants to publish Gray's eagerly awaited masterpiece and sell it with modern massmarketing techniques. As Gray puts it, Charlie's emphasis is on the promotional potential of the product rather than the work itself: 'The more books they publish, the weaker we become. The secret force that drives the industry is a compulsion to make writers harmless' (47). The built-in obsolescence of celebrity culture thus turns the authors themselves into alienated, spectral figures, separated from the creative elements of their labour. As DeLillo states elsewhere:

> The fame-making apparatus confers celebrity on an individual in a conflagration so intense that he or she can't possibly survive ... this is how the larger cultural drama of white-hot consumption and instant waste is performed in individualized terms, with actors playing themselves.[20]

Mao II suggests that contemporary culture abhors a vacuum, and that the insatiability of publicity allows it to consume even its fiercest recusants in the end. Gray consents to Brita's request for a photo session partly because he realizes he is powerless to avoid the media's unremitting attention, and hopes that this compromise will provide him with some kind of breathing space. He needs the pictures 'to break down the monolith I've built', the elaborate operation to maintain his privacy which has entailed 'a state of constant religious observance' (44). James Knowlson provides a real-life parallel in his biography of Samuel Beckett, Gray's role model in his unbending adherence to silence and abnegation. (Beckett claimed that his plays should ideally be performed to empty theatres and spoke of his 'dream of an art unresentful of its insuperable indigence and too proud for the farce of giving and receiving'.[21]) Knowlson describes Beckett's efforts to deal with the 'catastrophe' of his Nobel Prize success in 1969, as dozens of journalists swarmed around the lobby of his Paris hotel and thwarted his attempts to go into hiding. The author's French publisher, Jérôme Lindon, flew to Paris and brokered a gentlemen's agreement with the press allowing them to take pictures for a few minutes, as long as Beckett did not speak:

> Three days after the award, then, Beckett made an appearance ... smoking a cigar, with his hair cut very short ... he sat down, looking ill at ease, said nothing, and puffed away at his cigar. The cameras whirred, and, before the cigar even had time to burn down a single centimetre, he was whisked away and back to his room.[22]

Beckett understood reluctantly, as Gray does, that even reclusive authors cannot prevent both the commercial exploitation of their life and work and the development of new technologies which allow for the constant proliferation and circulation of news and information.

But celebrity in DeLillo's novel is more than merely the effect of capitalistic overproduction. For the notion that author-recluses achieve fame primarily as a product of capitalism's appropriation of previously uncommodified spheres does not explain why they are viewed so differently from other celebrities. There is, after all, another reason why Gray finally allows himself to be photographed: he is aware that his disappearance from public life has itself become an inverted form of self-promotion. Just as Bucky Wunderlick's disappearance only increases the media speculation about him, there have been thousands of pages of print devoted to Gray's reclusiveness and unpublished work-in-progress, and rumours circulating feverishly that he has committed suicide, changed identity or exiled himself in Canada. As Gray puts it: 'When a writer doesn't show his face, he becomes a local symptom of God's famous reluctance to appear ... The image world is corrupt, here is a man who hides his face' (36). Despite Gray's notion of photography as flattening the subject and destroying his or her uniqueness, the pictures of him also seem to add to this sense of mystery, testifying to what Roland Barthes calls photography's *punctum* – its ability to disturb the looker with more than simply its surface appearance, 'a kind of subtle *beyond* ... as if the image launched desire beyond what it permits us to see'.[23] Although Scott is initially opposed to Bill's decision to have his photograph taken, he also believes that 'a great man's face shows the beauty of his work', and when Brita's negatives arrive through the post at the end of the novel, he thinks that she has 'established rhythms and themes, catching a signal, tracking some small business in Bill's face and working to enlarge it or explain it, make it true, make it him' (60–1, 221).

Scott's unusual relationship to Bill's writing and legend points to the ambiguity of the author-recluse as a cultural signifier. His obsessive and eventually successful attempt to penetrate Gray's inner sanctum (which even involves finding work as a mail sorter in order to find out the author's address), and his concern with the auratic origins of Gray's writing – the painstaking filing and cataloguing of the diaries, letters and manuscripts, and pride in 'being part of this epic preservation, the neatly amassed evidence of driven art' (32) – seem to represent an effort to get beyond Gray's image as a writer and reach the 'real' artist underneath. Scott believes that Bill should not publish his long-awaited novel, using his silence to demonstrate that, in a culture of simulation and the hyperreal, 'the withheld work of art is the only eloquence left' (67). However, this concern with purity and essence also seems to stem from an anxiety that Gray may diminish his stock of cultural capital by undermining its rarity value. As Scott says: 'Bill gained celebrity by doing nothing ... [He] gets bigger as his distance from the scene deepens' (52). With the help of a monthly check debited directly from Gray's account, Scott also proves a careful custodian of the author's reputation after his disappearance at the end of the novel, releasing some of the pictures but leaving the manuscript where it is, 'collecting aura and force, deepening old Bill's legend, undyingly' (224). Although his aims are not narrowly mercenary, Scott is keen to exploit the less tangible benefits of Gray's anti-celebrity – as though, as Stuart Ewen puts it in a similar context, 'the critique has been turned on its head, packaged, and used against itself ... skinned and transmuted into a consumable style'.[24] There is a suspicion here that an all-consuming culture of publicity has simply packaged and marketed the author-recluse for consumption like other kinds of celebrity.

Authors and the Masses

DeLillo further develops some of these ideas when Gray comes out of hiding in the second part of the novel at the suggestion of Charlie Everson, flying to London to speak at a reading aimed at raising awareness of the Beirut hostage's plight. The reading, however, is interrupted by a terrorist bomb, a botched attempt to capture Gray and release Jean-Claude Julien simultaneously. Then, at the suggestion of an intermediary, George Haddad – and apparently exasperated at the ways in which his celebrity name has been used to give publicity to both the campaign for the Swiss poet's release and the terrorists themselves – Gray makes his way to Lebanon to negotiate with Julien's captors in person. This extraordinary move is a product of his frustration at being turned into a cultural commodity in spite of his best efforts to prevent it, and his subsequent conclusion that his failure as a writer to be 'dangerous' means that his life has been 'a kind of simulation' (97). Gray's efforts to find a more active social and political role for the author are thus part of his belief that writers have become 'famous effigies as our books lose the power to shape and influence' – only terrorists can now 'alter the inner life of the culture', he laments, because writers have all been 'incorporated' (41).

Gray's plan to bring about the hostage's release ends in anticlimactic failure – he dies on a ferry on the way to Lebanon (from internal injuries sustained during an earlier car accident), his passport and identification stolen by a cleaner to sell to a Beirut militia – but in a way which overturns this earlier idea of terrorists as unco-opted and promotes Gray's view of the writer as the last, fading hope of humanity. The terrorists depicted in the novel's epilogue have emphatically become part of a mediatized world, wearing an image of their leader, Abu Rashid, on their T-shirts, looking at videos of themselves taking part in the war, and apparently aiming to kill Bill, photograph the corpse and release the picture to the world's media whenever it will have most impact. In an age when 'news of disaster is the only narrative people need' (42), terrorists who exploit the impact of news as 'new' – wrenched from its context and mined simply for narrative and dramatic effect – are the new power-brokers, and individuals like Gray cannot hope to survive, because the narcotic effect of television has destroyed the writer's ability to function as the critical intelligence of a culture. In fact, Brita describes herself at the beginning of the novel as undertaking a 'species count' of writers (26), and the suggestion that they are a hunted, dying breed replaced by this newly influential group is reinforced at the end of the novel when she gives up her project to begin photographing terrorists instead. However, DeLillo's characterization of the broader social world which Gray fleetingly embraces suggests that the latter's inability to survive in this world is partly because of his admirable refusal to compromise, and that there is some deep, essential self which cannot be extinguished in the figure of 'the secluded writer, the arch individualist, living outside the glut of the image world'.[25]

The central connection between writers and terrorists in *Mao II* seems to pivot around their rival relationship to 'crowds'. The novel, according to DeLillo, is about

> different sorts of crowds. My book ... is asking who is speaking to these people. Is it the writer who traditionally thought he could influence the imagination of his contemporaries or is it rather the totalitarian leader, the military man, the terrorist, those who are twisted by power and who seem capable of imposing their vision on the world, reducing the earth to a place of danger and anger.[26]

DeLillo has been criticized for failing to complicate his notion of the 'terrorist', disconnecting this figure from any broader geopolitical context and presenting him simply as a violent, dangerously charismatic individual.[27] My own view is that terrorists are a secondary concern in *Mao II*, and that the representation of them in the novel derives from a sense that the relationship between the writer and his audience has tragically deteriorated, allowing the terrorist to take the writer's place in the social sphere. In fact, DeLillo's notions of the 'writer' and the 'crowd' are not closely interrogated either – he universalizes the white, male American author into the symbolic figure of the 'writer', and presents crowds as essentially all alike.

DeLillo has referred in an interview to the 'implicit panic' suggested by all crowds: 'There's something menacing and violent about a mass of people which makes us think of the end of individuality, whether they are gathered around a military leader or a holy man'.[28] It is possible to draw parallels between DeLillo's comments here and influential turn-of-the-century writings on the psychology of the collective mind by figures such as Gustave Le Bon, Scipio Sighele and Gabriel Tarde. This group of writings – an elitist attempt to make sense of the rise of mass, democratic, urban, industrialized society – characterizes crowds as emotional, irrational and possessing a dangerous and growing power. Indeed, the prediction at the end of *Mao II*'s prologue, which describes the mass moonie wedding of thousands of couples at Yankee Stadium at which Karen is present, that 'the future belongs to crowds' (16) closely parallels Le Bon's assertion that 'the power of the crowd is the only force that nothing menaces ... The age we are about to enter will in truth be the ERA OF CROWDS'.[29]

Mao II contains several descriptions of crowds taken from the news events of 1989, when the novel is set, as well as actual images from the Hillsborough football stadium tragedy, the Ayatollah Khomeini's funeral and the Tiananmen Square massacre – all in grainy black and white, so that individual faces cannot be picked out and they merge into a homogeneous mass. The passage which describes Karen's television viewing of the deaths of the Liverpool supporters at the Hillsborough disaster is particularly revealing in this context. She seems to observe the crushed bodies dispassionately as she fastens on a news report by chance while zapping through the channels with the sound turned down, believing that 'you could make up the news as you went along by sticking to picture only' (32). The novel's indirect interior monologue – which partly transposes Karen's thoughts here but which also seems to float between the characters, having a similar style and tone throughout the novel – describes the scene as 'a crowded twisted vision of a rush to death as only a master of the age could paint it' (34), representing the crowd itself as both a spectacle to be viewed voyeuristically and as somehow responsible for its own demise. Even as the novel portrays its characters' cultural amnesia about such events, it seems to homologize quite specific contexts and present all crowds as faceless and faintly menacing – different crowds are described throughout the narrative as 'fuelled by credulousness', 'swarming', 'straining and heaving', 'anguished' and 'frenzied' (7, 32, 33, 188).

It is worth noting that P. David Marshall has linked the rise of celebrity as a pervasive cultural phenomenon in this century to these earlier characterizations of the crowd as herd-like and susceptible to emotional appeals, and to subsequent efforts by different institutions to deal with the perceived threat from the mass. He argues that celebrity functions as a means by which the affective is sublimated and controlled in an increasingly organized and bureaucratized society which normally suppresses this aspect of people's personalities. It thus represents a 'rationalization of the irrational ... positioning these undisciplined areas of human life within a coherent and prevalent worldview'.[30] The persistent belief in the madness of crowds may explain the frequent attempt to characterize followers of celebrities as unreflectively fanatical,[31] even in work by theorists such as Theodor Adorno and Max Horkheimer which has shown how the culture industry discursively constructs this hierarchical division between individual and mass. In fact, Joli Jenson has suggested that this negative representation of fans typically takes one of two related forms: the hysterical crowd or the maladjusted loner[32] – the latter epitomized by such phenomena as celebrity stalkers and celebrity-fixated assassins or would-be assassins like Chapman and Hinckley.

Both these types of fan appear in *Mao II*, either directly or as imagined by the subject of their devotion, Gray himself. Gray argues that 'people' find the reclusive author fascinating but also

> resent him and mock him and want to dirty him up and watch his face distort in shock and fear when the concealed photographer leaps out of the trees ... In our world we sleep and eat the image and pray to it and wear it too. The writer who doesn't show his face is encroaching on holy turf. He's playing God's own trick (36–7).

In this sense, the fanatical crowd is seen as being wholly complicit with the mass media in their hounding of unwilling celebrities. The sociopathic loner is also present in the narrative at least in displaced form, as Gray lives in constant fear that someone might walk out of the shadows and harm him, believing that his deep seclusion 'made it possible that some lonely young man might see a mission here' (197). He seems to have some grounds for this anxiety – according to Scott, a deranged fan once sent him a severed finger by post.

There is no doubt that such deluded individuals exist, and they may be partly an effect of a manufactured culture of intimacy which presents celebrities as simultaneously extraordinary and familiar. Salinger, for instance, has been frequently harassed by monomaniacal fans – one man dressed himself up in fake wounds and lay moaning and writhing outside the author's house in Cornish in an effort to lure him out, and he also took a fan to court in 1982 who had both publicly impersonated and constructed an elaborate imaginary friendship with him.[33] In setting up an apparent binary opposition between the 'individual' (represented by the figure of the author) and the 'crowd', however, DeLillo's novel seems to point to the typicality of these pathological cases, suggesting that they are somehow indicative of the nature of fandom in contemporary culture.

In particular, by reproducing the idea of an automated mass being instilled with 'good' or 'bad' influence ('who is speaking to these people?'), *Mao II* seems to endorse Gray's inability to find a role for the author in the broader social world and his retreat again into silence. By most criteria Gray is a failure: he is making endless, painful revisions to a work which he knows to be misconceived, drowning in a 'shitpile of hopeless prose' (122) and keeping his own mental and physical collapse uneasily at bay with depressants, anti-depressants, sedatives and steroid ointments. But there is a double edge to his creative and personal decline, partly because the relationship with his public is so thoroughly dysfunctional anyway. When Gray's modernist notion of art as negation coexists with a sense of the postmodern death of art in the age of mass media, the only available move seems to be towards an aesthetics of silence. But such an aesthetics is undermined by the fact that, as Susan Sontag claims, 'the artist's activity is cursed with mediacy':

> As long as art is understood and valued as an 'absolute' activity, it will be a separatist, elitist one. Elites presuppose masses. So far as the best art defines itself by essentially priestly aims, it presupposes and confirms the existence of a relatively passive, never fully initiated, voyeuristic laity that is regularly convoked to watch, listen, read, or hear – and then sent away.[34]

What qualifies silence, then, is not simply that postmodern culture seeks to absorb it, but that silence itself presumes an audience. The effect is to foreground the figure of the author as romantic individualist while precluding any meaningful social role for him, and the novel's conclusion underlines this when Gray dies an undignified death in pursuit of such a role. For in what sense can the novel be (as Gray originally hopes) a 'democratic shout', and the novelist aim to 'increase the flow of meaning, be a reply to power' (159, 200), if his work remains unfinished, unpublished and unread? Gray's unsuccessful foray into the corrupted public sphere thus only reaffirms and vindicates his initial decision to withdraw from it. Although DeLillo is clearly aware of the complexities and nuances of celebrity culture, his novel seems to reproduce here the image of the author-recluse which Gray himself is trapped inside – that of a charismatic figure separated from the rest of society by the transcendent qualities of his work and personality. *Mao II* is grounded ultimately in a certain blindness about the cultural capital invested in the author's withholding of himself and his work – the way in which the choice of silence 'imparts retroactively an added power and authority to what was broken off – disavowal of the work becoming a new source of its validity, a certificate of unchallengeable seriousness'.[35]

DeLillo and the Publicity Machine

DeLillo's own celebrity and adroit manipulation of his public image, in fact, represents a much more dialogic and productive model of contemporary American authorship. For an author who, like Gray, professes a Joycean creed of 'silence, exile, cunning, and so on',[36] it is surprising how much space he has given recently to discussing his work. Since the publication of *Libra* in 1988, DeLillo has reluctantly undertaken interviews, book signings and other appearances organized around publicity tours, at least one result of which has been a series of strikingly photogenic photographs to accompany magazine and newspaper articles – whatever DeLillo thinks of the camera as a murderous instrument, the camera seems to love him. He has also written dustjacket blurbs for other authors' novels, helped to produce a documentary for BBC television on his work to coincide with the publication of *Mao II*, and co-authored a pamphlet (with Paul Auster, another author who has written about reclusiveness in his *New York Trilogy*) in support of Salman Rushdie. Although this hardly qualifies DeLillo as a self-publicist, it still represents a significant contrast to both his earlier career as a public figure, and *Mao II*'s implacably hostile attitude towards the publicity machine, the public sphere and even the public itself.

It is worth restating, of course, that Bill Gray is not DeLillo's surrogate self, although it is sometimes easy to confuse DeLillo's views with those of his characters because of the nature of the publicity opportunities he pursues and his avoidance of the usual 'at-home' celebrity profiles. DeLillo partly uses his novels to wrestle with ideas about contemporary culture, and then purposely deals with particular publicity outlets which do not intrude into his personal life and allow him to explore similar ideas freely in interviews. Literary journals such as *Paris Review*, which interviewed DeLillo in 1993, even allow interviewees to edit their transcripts, over a period of several months, so that the process of self-presentation in these interviews becomes difficult to distinguish from literary composition. Perhaps because of this practice, DeLillo can sound a little like his characters in print – often using similar or even the same wording and sentence structures – and there is a temptation to conflate the two.

It is better to think of Bill Gray, though, as a means by which DeLillo has interrogated issues raised by his own celebrity, by creating a hypothetical situation with only superficial similarities to his own. This strategy may be particularly valuable to DeLillo within a climate in which many of his extra-literary activities are circumscribed by the marketplace – his semi-conversion to public life in the 1980s and 1990s is clearly, in part, a product of the growing pressure placed on authors to market their work by con-glomerate-owned publishers. This has involved both the increasing exploitation of subsidiary rights – DeLillo's most recent novel, *Underworld*, was published by Scribner's, released in audiobook form by Simon and Schuster and optioned by Paramount, all sibling companies owned by the media giant Viacom – and extensive marketing campaigns for authors involving publicity tours.

When asked about his attitude to this promotional game in an inter-view, DeLillo replied:

I keep the greatest psychological distance I can maintain from all of this. I'm not part of it except in the sense that you and I are having this conversation. It's there. Writers write, publishers sell. That's probably a very old-fashioned conviction but I do maintain it.[37]

Mao II, of course, is partly about the difficulty of maintaining this distinction in celebrity culture, but DeLillo has generally proved more adept at this than his characters. His cautious move into the public eye may be part of his awareness that authors who are perceived as labouring the point of their reclusiveness can become, as Bill Gray does, 'trapped in [their] own massive stillness' (45). DeLillo's approach has been successful in that most interviews and profiles are able to discuss his work intelligently without delving into his private life, and he has not been celebritized as a hermit – although America's *Entertainment Weekly* did recently rate him seven out of ten on a writers' 'reclusiveness scale', claiming also that he 'frequently uses his characters to dis the whole celebrity thing'.[38] What DeLillo has been trying to avoid, I think, is Gray's problem of having to fall back on a romantically alienated persona which he knows to be outmoded, so that his silence itself becomes a kind of reflex statement of an oppositional aesthetic. But Bill Gray is more than a satirical figure – he is a character through which DeLillo both romanticizes and critiques the role of author-recluses in contemporary culture, by pointing to both the unavoidable involvement of such authors in the commodification of culture and the admirably unyielding nature of their rearguard action. The fact that DeLillo has himself rejected this approach suggests that he is aware that it may be laudable but is ultimately unsustainable.

8

A Star of Bohemia: Kathy Acker

Kathy Acker's celebrity is the most unusual of all the authors discussed in the second half of this book – a challenging and difficult author, her fame is partly dependent on the increasing diversity of the American cultural marketplace. She emerged out of a thriving avant-garde subculture located in the Lower East Side of New York ('downtown') in the 1970s, her influences being a whole range of transgressive authors traditionally ignored by the mainstream: Genet, Rimbaud, Sade, Baudelaire, Bataille, Burroughs and Ballard. Her early work was either self-published or appeared with underground publishers and small presses, and she was often forced to sell her own books to New York bookstores. Acker formed a grouping of avant-garde authors, including Lynne Tillman and Constance DeJong, who performed in SoHo bookshops and venues like The Kitchen, The Mudd Club and CBGBs (the punk club which discovered Patti Smith, Blondie and Talking Heads) and whose work was published in magazines like *Bomb*, *Evergreen*, *Benzene* and *Between C&D*.[1]

From the mid-1980s onwards, however, Acker emerged from this subculture to become a mainstream star. Her major breakthrough came with the British publication of *Blood and Guts in High School* in 1984 by Picador, after which she had a *South Bank Show* special devoted to her work. She became a well-known figure in London, where she lived for most of the decade, writing for the *New Statesman* and frequently appearing on British TV, and on her return to the US in the late 1980s also achieved considerable celebrity there. After William Burroughs, as Elizabeth Young and Graham Caveney point out, Acker was 'the only real inheritor of th[e] bohemian tradition to cross over fully into the big-time publishing world'.[2] But Acker's crossover to mainstream media has not been complete – she usually occupies a more limited sphere of Internet sites, newsgroups and fanzines, literary events and, most importantly, discussion of her work within the academy. Her celebrity is the product of a difficult mediation between bohemian and mass culture, and this chapter aims to explore some of the tensions inherent in this kind of trade-off.

Despite publishing an appreciative interview with the Spice Girls in the *Guardian* towards the end of her life,[3] Acker's relationship with American celebrity culture – a culture in which, as she puts it, 'we know what every mole looks like on the arm of every movie star, the tattoos on the cocks of every rock'n'roll star'[4] – is usually implacably hostile. Martina Sciolino makes a link between the emphasis in Acker's work on capitalism's construction and entrapment of the individual subject and her own commoditization as public figure:

> Just as the Acker protagonist is typically enmeshed in and frustrated by the throwaway discourses of a consumer culture, so too Acker's own canon to date is a study of the ways in which capitalism informs publishing to the extent that a writer who 'blasphemes' against every conventional value imaginable can be safely incorporated into consumer culture.[5]

Although Acker's work may not always be optimistic about the ability of her characters to step outside their own culture, however, her acceptance of her own participation in celebrity culture is more questionable: her statements in interviews about her transformation into a cultural icon are often fiercely antagonistic and uncompromising. This uncompromising stance obscures – indeed, to some extent contributes to – her inescapable involvement in the creation of her celebrity persona. In particular, Acker formulates a notion of authorship which has become a mainstay of celebrity culture, that of the uniquely inspired creative genius occupying a privileged position outside the sphere of exchange, in opposition to the 'hack' writer and the tawdry world of literary professionalism.

Mass Culture and the Bohemian

Elizabeth Wilson's work on the development of the idea of the 'bohemian' in Europe and the US, from its origins in the 1830s to the present day, shows how literary celebrity has historically been produced by this problematic intersection between the avant-garde and the popular. Wilson suggests that the bohemian identity aimed 'to dramatize the role of artist as rebel and outcast' by contrasting the authenticity of bohemian life with the superficiality of mass culture and bourgeois society, and viewing artistic 'failure' as a sign of genius.[6] (Bourdieu, similarly, defines the bohemian sphere as the 'purest' element of the artistic field, one in which the doctrine of 'art for art's sake' is most widely accepted.[7]) According to Wilson, however, this separatist discourse was permanently undermined by the continual fascination in bourgeois society with the transgressive aesthetic of the bohemians, which produced ever-shifting boundaries of taste and acceptability. As Klaus Mann wrote in 1942: 'Unending and involved is the flux of attraction and repulsion between those two opposite characters, bohemian and bourgeois, constantly irritating and enchanting, missing and desiring each other ... Eros floats between them, disguised as envy or scorn or admiration'.[8]

Beginning with the newspaper articles of Henry Murger in the 1840s, popular media have enthusiastically sought 'bohemian copy', recycling the lives of avant-garde artists in newspapers, magazines, popular novels and films for vicarious consumption by a mass audience.[9] (This is perhaps best exemplified in America by the massmarketing of the Beat writers, from Lawrence Lipton's bestselling *The Holy Barbarians* (1960) through to David Cronenberg's 1991 film of *The Naked Lunch*.[10]) More generally, the bohemian lifestyle was progressively embraced in both mass culture and society as a whole, a gradual acceptance of sexual freedom, expressiveness and spontaneity replacing the traditional values of self-control and family duty.[11] This has meant that, from the beginning, bohemians have feared that they were always already corrupted, and have looked back nostalgically to a period when their art was uncommodified and consumer culture was not always appropriating their innovations and rendering them harmless.[12]

I want to argue that Acker's celebrity is partly an effect of mass culture's ongoing preoccupation with the bohemian, while much of her stated opposition to that fame is an attempt to shore up the boundaries of bohemia against the encroachments of mass culture. The issue is a pressing one because these borrowings have become more insistent in recent years. The *New York Times* recently ran a feature on the new commercial potential of 'transgressive fiction', which it defines as 'books pitched to young adults, written by authors descended from William Burroughs and the Marquis de Sade, that explore aberrant sexual practices, urban violence, drug use and dysfunctional families in graphic detail'. It suggests that the readership for this fiction, exemplified by authors like Dennis Cooper, William T. Vollman and Acker herself (and, in the UK, authors like Irvine Welsh and Will Self), is made up of 'young, semi-intellectuals looking for something hip but relatively esoteric; essentially college-educated 20-somethings'.[13] The *New York Times*'s notion of 'transgressive fiction' is itself a convenient label, and one might question the grouping together of these very different authors, but it is true that Acker's celebrity is partly a product of the diversification of literary culture which has pushed cult authors into the mainstream, and her success thus points to literary celebrity's continuing flirtation with the offbeat and anti-commercial.

As publishers have begun to exploit these niche markets (and new publishing technologies and changing demographics make their exploitation easier), this has inevitably led to anxieties that the subversive potential of such fiction will be dissipated by its entry into the marketplace. In a recent survey of 'cult fiction', for example, the authors lament: 'What was the counterculture is now over-the-counter culture, the deviant behaviour at the core of cult fiction has reached the middle of the marketplace, and there is nothing anyone can do about it.'[14] These anxieties about recuperation and co-optation were, of course, continually expressed in connection with punk music, the movement with which Acker was closely associated in the 1970s – a subculture made up of the disenfranchised of society and based fundamentally on opposition and negation was accused of filtering all too readily into mainstream pop – but it is increasingly true of other cultural forms like art and literature. Istvan Csicsery-Ronay has argued that the big question for artists is now 'whether any authentic countercultural forms of art can exist for long without being transformed into self-annihilating simulations of themselves for mass consumption, furthering central cultural aims'.[15] This is a central preoccupation of the contemporary avant-garde, and a crucial question when discussing the celebrity of figures like Acker.

It is clear that the graphic descriptions of sado-masochism, incest and rape in Acker's work – which have led to her books being banned or withdrawn from publication in some countries – account at least partly for some of the wider attention she has received. In the words of one critic, Acker in the 1980s came to be seen as 'a symbol, a shocking Statuette of Libertinism',[16] particularly in the UK where she first rose to prominence. Ellen Friedman suggests that what made Acker a media figure in Britain was that she was

> called upon to represent the interesting or evil, but definitively crazy fringe, the extreme by which the public measures its distance from the edge. Thus defined as the products of the devil or madness, or at least eccentricity, her books – as far as the public is concerned – have no authority and are thus disarmed.[17]

Acker's frequently unfavourable reviews – *Publishers' Weekly* dismissed her work as 'repulsive and impenetrable', while *Library Journal* called her 'infantile, lacking even the skill to be shocking ... despite the author's underground reputation, this puerile fiction does not deserve print'[18] – also functioned as powerful negative publicity, reinforcing this popular stereotype of her as 'the beat mistress of outrage',[19] deliberately out to cause offence.

Acker was certainly concerned about the way in which her work and personality were being marketed and publicized, complaining that 'the media invented someone named Kathy Acker', and that the 'fetishization' of her public image as a primarily sexual one was a misrepresentation which amounted to 'slander'.[20] Her friend and lover, Charles Shaar Murray, reinforced this point after her death, when he wrote in response to the many newspaper obituaries of her which reproduced this image:

> The tattoos, piercings, muscles and motorcycles were simply private pursuits and public window-dressing. They were not what she was 'about', either as an artist or a human being. In both capacities ... she was far more sophisticated, and far more complex, than the standard reductionist 'underground sex queen' clichés with which she seems to be saddled as firmly in death as in life.[21]

Can these elements of Acker's image be dismissed so readily as 'public window-dressing', as Murray suggests? Other critics have accused her of knowingly exploiting the shocking elements of her work and persona. Danny Karlin, in a review of *Empire of the Senseless* (1988), suggests that Acker subscribes to a cult of 'antinomian chic'. Referring to Picador's dustjacket blurb for the book, which boasts that it is 'at least an extraordinary achievement, at best an ultimate act of outrage', he writes that Acker

> makes the mistake of taking herself seriously ... as though 'ultimate outrage' were not a commodity being peddled by her agents and publishers as assiduously as 'towering genius', 'warm humanity' or 'delightful touches of wit' ... The shock-value of such writing is diffused by the context of its literary production; readers who buy this book have already read it, or, to put it another way, it can't reach them in the way it intends. The medium is like a lightning rod which conducts Acker's fierce bolt and domesticates it into a thrill.[22]

Karlin's comments seem a little unfair, ascribing to Acker a control over the promotion of her books which she may not have had, although it is true that she often drew attention to the controversies surrounding the 'pornographic' nature of her work in interviews and occasionally in her work itself – at the back of *Hannibal Lecter, My Father* (1991), for example, she reprints a judgment by the Federal Inspection Office for Publications

Harmful to Minors in Germany, setting out its reasons for banning *Blood and Guts in High School*.[23] Karlin does point to the central difficulty in contemporary literary culture of separating out the work and public persona of an author from the way she is produced and marketed. The issue is complicated in Acker's case by the fact that avant-garde culture has often had what Wilson calls a 'lifestyle dimension', an element of public performance which led to perpetual accusations of hypocrisy and play-acting from mainstream culture. As Wilson says, the new urban identity of the bohemian was

> one in which the dramatization of poverty combined with romantic masquerade and living on one's wits to become a performance in its own right, a demonstration of the will to shock ... Whether genius or a mountebank, the bohemian was a rebel, heroically rejecting middle-class safety and comfort for a life of poverty, risk and transgression.[24]

Other critics have gone further in suggesting that the avant-garde artist was more concerned with fashioning a particular artistic identity than with creating art itself, becoming the 'representative figure of a society unable to set clear limits for the identities and activities of its members', her task being to challenge 'the limits of individual and social existence' by examining 'marginal states of being and consciousness'.[25]

In fact, Acker always protested that her art rather than her life was central, and that the image she may have presented was an act, a mere textual representation; numerous friends and acquaintances, meanwhile, have testified that Acker in person was very different from her various public or literary personae. But it is true that Acker's celebrity has largely focused on a particular look (leather or PVC, close-cropped dyed hair, thick lipstick, stiletto heels, tattoos, dark glasses, Yamaha motorcycle, and so on) which she cultivated carefully. From her first publicity photograph onwards (taken by Robert Mapplethorpe, perhaps the only other figure to move from New York's *demi-monde* into major celebrity), the distinctiveness of this image was exploited by her book publishers and the media in general. Even in an era when dustjacket photographs are an omnipresent marketing tool, Acker's image is unusually prominent, adorning the front covers of virtually all Grove's editions of her books and circulating widely to accompany interviews and profiles. This image is attractive to celebrity culture precisely because it represents a mildly transgressive but also readily assimilable aspect of underground art – sartorial codes have relaxed along with moral ones in recent years, and tattooing, leather and other kinds of fetish-wear, previously linked only with sado-masochism and other sexual 'perversions', have now become acceptable mainstream fashion statements.[26]

The Avant-garde and Celebrity

Acker's complicated relationship to literary celebrity stemmed partly from the political ambitions she had for her work – she wanted her books to have a broad impact in society without sacrificing her radical ideals to big business and 'the literary industry'.[27] She often spoke of her fierce opposition to the tyranny of the major American publishing houses and book chains and the conservative literary conventions – the emphasis on 'a good read' and hostility to 'experimental' work – which they enforce with access to corporatized media and huge publicity budgets. She argued that the power of the major publishers and media had produced a highly selective 'pantheon of great living American writers', made up almost exclusively of white male authors such as Norman Mailer, Philip Roth, John Cheever and Saul Bellow who 'criticized United States society as it needed to be criticized in cultured tones'. Acker lamented that, in Anglo-Saxon culture,

> art is increasingly confined to a world of whimsy, an amusing stock market for the rich. There isn't one American artist who has managed to become a spokesperson for even a segment of his culture, whose radical imagination and perceptions haven't been chewed into bits of baby food by the fame factory.[28]

This fame machine is supported by a critical apparatus which is wholly at ease with the marketplace and which dices culture up into conveniently straightforward units and meanings, denying the ambiguity in works of art 'so that the buyers know what to buy. So that the culture-mongers know what culture to eat. Those who deal in commerce do not want to, cannot afford to live in chaos'.[29] At the same time as she attacked the dominant institutions of literary capitalism, however, Acker was also worried that avant-garde authors might limit their influence by acquiescing in their own invisibility: 'By internalizing these definitions and expectations, by accepting literary and personal marginalization, the non-commercial writer denies the political realities surrounding and underlying his or her literary choices'.[30] If Acker was concerned that the ways she was sold as a literary commodity might blunt the more uncomfortable political aspects of her work, then, she also wanted it to be read and noticed – which may explain why she broke with the independent house, Grove, to publish with the conglomerate-owned Pantheon Books (a division of Random House) in the early 1990s.

It is also worth stressing that Acker's celebrity is not merely an effect of mass culture's infiltration of the marginal, but that marginalized cultures also generate their own hierarchical structures, their celebrities and their fans. In fact, Bourdieu suggests that, since financial gain can never be a criterion for success within the restricted field, this puts an added emphasis on the acquisition of celebrity (albeit of a necessarily limited kind) since 'the only legitimate accumulation ... consists in making a name for oneself, a name that is known and recognized, the capital of consecration'.[31] This may well be true, but I would suggest that Acker's avant-garde fame relied primarily on the fostering of a sense of dialogue and community between artist and audience which initially thrived within the concentrated atmosphere of New York's punk art scene in the late 1970s. As with many other avant-garde groupings, the feelings of marginality and difference from the mainstream created the need for a network of like-minded souls who could provide mutual support and encouragement. As David Robbins, one of the artists who emerged out of the same avant-garde art scene, explains, this kind of collective subculture emerged in opposition to a star system:

> Above all, we are reasonable, and consequently are suspicious of artistic practices that promote the neo-divinity of artists. The star search mechanism of the art world is unusable because if we've learned anything from a lifetime steeped in the public fictions of television, movies, magazines, and advertising, it's that people become stars so that their public image may better jump through the hoop of commerce. And for them to jump, someone else must be holding the hoop.[32]

Acker's background in collaborative work, performance art and avant-garde 'happenings', though, also helped to engender a sense that her work was usefully supplemented by her presence, helping to make her a recognized figure in her own right. Throughout her career, in fact, she explored many different possibilities for public performance – appearing with bands like Tribe 8 and the Mekons and creating a CD with the latter group to accompany her last novel, making art films, writing plays and opera libretti, and, most important, appearing and speaking at conferences and literary events, particularly on college campuses. Acker's relationship with universities cemented her fame, providing an important link between avant-garde culture and society as a whole. Acker frequently spoke of her disdain for the academy for its depoliticization of the radical energies of the poststructuralist critical theory which emerged out of France in the late 1960s, and for its creation of a self-interested, professional machinery,[33] but she also seems to have recognized that it represented the best hope of creating a pocket of resistance, a solid institutional basis for an alternative art and culture. As well as giving frequent readings at universities, she was often employed as a writer-in-residence and then launched her own writing department at the San Francisco Art Institute in 1990, as well as being interviewed many times in academic and quasi-academic journals. Acker's willingness to discuss and read her work within this sizeable (but not massmarket) milieu has produced a fan base of great loyalty and also put into place a critical machinery of academics and graduate students eager to write about her.

'What Matter Who's Speaking?'

In her work itself, Acker explores issues around her own celebrity both directly and indirectly. An important feature of her work is the use of literary parody, assumed identities, self-confessed plagiarism and pseudonymous writing as a way of questioning the notion that individual authors are always the authoritative producers of texts. At the beginning of her career, this extended to the design and marketing of the books themselves – Acker named 'the Black Tarantula' as the author of *The Childlike Life of the Black Tarantula* (1975), for example, even listing herself as such in the Manhattan telephone directory, and librarians and booksellers often catalogue the book (and other Acker works 'by' Pier Paolo Pasolini and Toulouse Lautrec) under its pseudonym. Acker also routinely plagiarizes or reworks plots, themes and sometimes verbatim passages from canonical literature (*Wuthering Heights, Great Expectations, The Scarlet Letter, Don Quixote*) and, more controversially, books by contemporary authors such as Harold Robbins and William Gibson, often without formal attribution. (This has sometimes got Acker into trouble: Robbins's publisher threatened to sue after she used two thousands words of a sex scene from his novel, *Pirate*, in *The Adult Life of Toulouse-Lautrec* (1975), and she was forced by her own publisher, Pandora, to issue a public apology.) Acker, though, makes no secret of her plagiaristic tendencies – the back cover of Semiotext(e)'s edition of *Hannibal Lecter, My Father* says: 'This writing is all fake (copied from other writing) so you should go away and not read any of it'.

In many cases, Acker is appropriating the works of classic male authors – and their predominantly male characters – in order to subvert the patriarchal assumptions of the Western canon. More usually, though, her plagiarism is an end in itself, designed to challenge one of the fundamental premises of literary celebrity – the romantic notion of literature as the product of the original genius of an 'author'. Acker attributes this notion to an 'ideology of creativity' dating back to capitalism's invention of copyright law: 'We are living and working, whether we like it or not, in a bourgeois-industrialist, in a capitalist society, a society based on owner-ship. One needs to own in order to survive, in fact in order to be'.[34] Acker also seeks to historicize American and Western culture's promotion of the individual author by pointing to other traditions and contexts, like Arab culture, in which the concept of originality is less valued, where 'they write new stories paint new pictures et cetera only by embellishing old stories pictures ... by cutting chunks out of all-ready written texts and in other ways defacing traditions'.[35] Her aim seems to be to draw attention to the question raised by Foucault (after Beckett) in his essay on the role of the author in Western culture: 'What Matter Who's Speaking?'[36]

One wonders, though, how subversive this strategy is within the con-text in which Acker's work is published and sold, at least since she became a celebrity. The dustjacket copy, design and marketing of her books make it apparent that they are 'by' her, so it is unclear whether these plagiaristic and pseudonymous strategies really dispense with the author or whether they privilege her own inventiveness and creativity in bringing together so many disparate elements – a question which might also be raised about other postmodern texts which stress the intertextual nature of all cultural material. Acker produces what Leslie Dick calls 'new narrative ... equal parts gossip, kinky sex and high theory'[37] – a heady mix of serious literature, critical discourse (Lacan, Bataille, Deleuze and Guattari) and popular cul-ture texts like the Japanese 'Godzilla' movies, film noir, detective fiction, cyberpunk and pornography. Acker's experiments with the notion of novelistic character also create an appealing mix of different, recognizable personalities in her work, which frequently intersperses figures from literature (Hester Prynne, Don Quixote, Heathcliff) with writers (Jean Genet, Arthur Rimbaud, the Brontë sisters, Maya Angelou), politicians (Newt Gingrich, Jimmy Carter, Richard Nixon, George Bush) and popular culture icons (Janis Joplin, James Dean).

This is not to say that Acker's works are deliberately 'popular', and she would certainly have baulked at the leftist critique of postmodernism as destroying the radical impetus of the avant-garde with its uncritical blur-ring of the divisions between high art and mass culture. No one could accuse Acker's work of being easy to assimilate: she rejects almost all the conventional means by which readers can orient themselves through a text, including narrative structure, plot, everyday logic and the discrete identity of individual characters, who are often not named or transform themselves into other characters. Above all, Acker's radical questioning of the notion of identity in her work – and the way that individual subjectivities are constructed by discourse – precludes any of the conventional satisfactions of narrative.

The Body and Identity

In fact, though, I want to suggest that Acker puts forward two contrasting views of identity – one textual and one essentialist – both of which are capable of being appropriated and reinvented by celebrity culture. This is perhaps most clearly shown in her writings and reflections on the female body, which have been strongly influenced by the connections made between language and desire in French feminist theory. As Toril Moi and others have pointed out, French feminist critics like Luce Irigaray and Hélène Cixous combine a Derridean-influenced notion of textuality and the self with an essentialist emphasis on the female body as the location of *écriture feminine*.[38] Acker, similarly, seems to present the body as both an unstable site of textual play and as the one absolute, unarguable reality in an age of uncertainty. The disguising or embellishing of her body with conscious signs of artifice – make-up, piercing, body-building and tattooing – became a significant part of her public image, a way of asserting a position of radical difference. Acker called tattooing, for example, 'a sign of the outcast ... [of] people who are beginning to take their own sign-making into their own hands'.[39] This emphasis is continued in Acker's work, notably *Empire of the Senseless*, which is dedicated to 'my tattooist', and which includes a quite detailed cultural history of the phenomenon which stresses that it is the mark of society's pariahs: 'In decadent phases, the tattoo became associated with the criminal – literally the outlaw – and the power of the tattoo became intertwined with the power of those who chose to live beyond the norms of society'.[40]

This celebration of the surface of the body as a way of remaking the self, however, is accompanied by a conviction that 'the body does not lie ... the body is real'.[41] As Arthur F. Redding points out, Acker's enjoyment of deliberately artificial bodily transformations existed in tandem with a fierce opposition to other ways of remodelling and reshaping the body, such as dieting and plastic surgery, which seek to disguise their artificiality in an effort to produce the 'perfect' body image idealized by consumer society.[42] This extended to medical interventions: when Acker was diagnosed as having breast cancer in 1996, she made public and wrote about her refusal to submit to chemotherapy and her reliance on 'natural' remedies, declaring: 'I will make myself well or at least I will die in control of my own body'.[43] Acker's decision led to an angry exchange of letters and articles in the *Guardian* after her death in November 1997, about the rights and wrongs of her rejection of conventional forms of treatment.[44]

In an interview with Larry McCaffery, Acker characterizes the materiality of the body as a kind of anchor amid the surface gloss of postmodern culture, a way of escaping 'Baudrillard's black hole':

> The Western attitude towards the body in the twentieth century has to do with the fact that when reality ... is up for grabs the body becomes the only thing you can return to ... when you get to something called the actual *act* of sexuality, or the actual act of disease, there is a kind of undeniable materiality which *isn't* up for grabs.[45]

These comments mirror Terry Eagleton's more critical account of what he sees as 'the new somatics', the fetishization of the body in postmodern culture in everything from High Theory to the High Street. According to Eagleton,

> there is a glamorous kind of materialism about body talk, which compensates for certain more classical strains of materialism now in dire trouble. As a stubbornly local phenomenon, the body fits well enough with postmodern suspicions of grand narratives, as well as with pragmatism's love affair with the concrete ... the body provides us with a little sensuous certitude in a progressively abstract world.[46]

For Acker, certainly, the body offers the opportunity for self-display and performance while also pointing to an incontrovertible reality which transcends this.

More generally, Acker's work can be seen as both a sustained critique and an inevitable restating of Western notions of identity. Acker's questioning of the idea of the free, autonomous individual stems from her belief that this figure perpetuates capitalist, patriarchal society by invisibly privileging the white, male, Western subject. In this sense, her work responds to French feminist theory's espousal of an *écriture feminine*, a variety of textual strategies aimed at subverting traditionally 'phallocentric' writing and its emphasis on fixed, coherent subjectivities, and revealing women's identities as contradictory and multifaceted. Identities, particularly sexual identities, are rarely fixed in Acker's work: narrators and characters exchange names, sexes and time periods at will, underlining Airplane's comment in *In Memoriam to Identity* (1990) that 'identities are holes'.[47] Acker clearly aims to subvert the conventional narrative techniques of much feminist writing of the 1970s and 1980s, with its emphasis on an autobiographical narrative of redemption – as Noel King puts it, she 'has no time for social-realist stories of the I-used-to-be-trapped-in-anuclear-hetero-marriage-but-now-I-have-found-my-true-self-in-lesbian-ism-kind'.[48] Acker has openly criticized the tendency for autobiographical self-expression among many feminist authors, suggesting that this form of writing mistakenly supposes that subjectivities can float free of their social and economic conditions: 'Writing which says all the time "here I am, and I want, I want ..." presents a Hobbist universe which suits Reagan and Thatcher fine. Autobiography really is selfish.'[49]

Acker's works, then, are clearly not 'autobiographical' in any conventional sense – at the same time, they do have a recognizable Acker protagonist, sometimes even called 'Kathy', who shares at least some biographical correspondences with her author and who participates in what Glenn Harper calls 'a primal narrative',[50] a common thread running through many of her books. With numerous variations, this narrative tells the story of a girl from a middle-class family, with a mother who commits suicide and a sadistic father or stepfather who rapes and abuses her, who escapes from home to enter a world of prostitution, crime and poverty, before eventually becoming a writer. More rarely, this material is explicitly to do with the experience of literary fame – as in *My Mother: Demonology* (1993), in which a celebrated, motorcycling author, Laure, participates reluctantly in a publicity tour of Germany, touted by the promoters as a 'representative of America and of "new American writing"'. Laure, like Acker, is uncomfortable with the compromises of fame, finding that her Berlin audience are 'interested only in glamour. They seemed to be eager to transform problematic political questions into those discourses and opinions that comfort'.[51] Acker's experiments with speculative autobiography – particularly through sexually explicit, violent material often perceived as 'confessional' – have inevitably contributed to a certain public interest in the author, as they have in the case of supposedly 'confessional' works by other writers Acker admires, such as Bataille and Burroughs. This persona is particularly appealing to celebrity culture, I want to argue, because it suggests that the self can be reinvented at the same time as it points to the existence of an innate, deep-seated identity.

In one sense, Acker's writing is informed by a deep scepticism that the enforced identities of patriarchal society will ever be overcome, simply because, as she puts it, 'you can't get to a place, to a society, that isn't constructed according to the phallus'.[52] Indeed, Acker's work has been attacked by some feminist critics as pornographic – as actually reproducing rather than challenging existing patriarchal power structures – precisely because her female characters are often trapped in dysfunctional, heterosexual relationships from which they seem powerless to escape. As Ellen Friedman says about this aspect of her work: 'Acker's questers' searches for identity and a new healing myth lead to silence, death, nothingness, or reentry into the sadomasochism of patriarchal culture'.[53]

On the other hand, and particularly in Acker's later novels, there is a more idealistic impulse, a belief that the self can be recreated as a way of escaping the confining identities of our culture. 'There's no more need to deconstruct ... to reveal the fraud on which our society's living', she argues in a brief essay on her work. 'We now have to find somewhere to go, a belief, a myth'.[54] At the end of *In Memoriam to Identity*, for example, Airplane escapes from a series of abusive sado-masochistic relationships by remaking her life as fiction:

> By returning to a reality which no longer mattered or existed for her ... she was actually building a new life. Not in terms of content, but form. Fiction. Realized that fiction, only as reality, must work: life begins in nothingness.[55]

In *The Childlike Life of the Black Tarantula*, similarly, 'Kathy' tries to escape her traumatic childhood by creating a new identity for herself, one whose artifice is all too apparent: 'I want to be a tough motorcycle hood silver leather on a BMW I take shit from nobody ... I'm the shyest black leather freak in the world'.[56] In fact, in this novel, the effort at self-invention is related explicitly to the desire to become famous:

> I'm trying to become other people because this is what I find interesting. I was interested in 'fame' as one end: (1) people whose work I want to find out about would talk to me, (2) I would somehow be able to pay for food rent etc. doing something connected, (3) artists I fall in love with would fuck me: these desires are fucking over my work (and me). So I say the desires out loud.[57]

Writing in Fever

Alongside this idea of reinventing her identity as textual surface, however, Acker employs a much more grounded notion of the self. Together with one of her main influences, Georges Bataille, Acker's work is not simply destructive, but seems to be reaching towards a reality which is 'pure' and unmediated – the sexual and other kinds of excess depicted in her work are a way not only of disrupting and subverting the conventional identities imposed by capitalist, patriarchal society, but also of returning to a 'purer', natural state which lies beyond exchange value – what Bataille calls the 'sacred', which he defines as 'a privileged moment of communal unity, a moment of the convulsive communication of what is ordinarily stifled'.[58] In this sense, again, Acker's work recalls French feminist theory's aim of casting off enforced identities and returning to the repressed, pre-Oedipal, pre-linguistic period – Cixous, for example, calls for 'the invention of a *new insurgent* writing' that 'will return to the body', that 'will tear away from the superegoized structure in which [woman] has always occupied the place reserved for the guilty ... Her flesh speaks true. She lays herself bare'.[59] This utopian element in Acker's work could be said to be part of the classic avant-garde project of breaking down the conventional division between art and everyday life and using art to create identities which have been suppressed by the structures and limitations of bourgeois society. As Acker herself puts it: 'My strongest desire (it's beyond desire, it's a need) is to make it possible for people like me to be in society.'[60]

This aspect of Acker's work seems to go hand-in-hand with a romantic idea of writing as transparently revealing its author's thoughts and feelings. Acker's (female) Don Quixote posits a view that literature should ideally be produced in a frenzy of creative inspiration: 'I wasn't sent to Oxford or anywhere, so what I do to write is cut crosses into the insides of my wrists. I write in fever.'[61] This faith in *furor poeticus* is echoed in Acker's non-fictional writings, in which she praises writers like Sade and Burroughs for 'present[ing] the human heart naked so that our world, for a second, explodes into flames'.[62] Karlin points to this tension in Acker's work between its obvious questioning of the 'natural' and its passionate embracing of 'the Gothic, the Romantic conjunction of imaginative and sexual excess'.[63] In *Empire of the Senseless* (1988), Acker makes explicit the connection between her avant-garde project and a more classically romantic sensibility when one of her characters rejects the Enlightenment investment in 'reason':

> Reason which always homogenizes and reduces, represses and unifies phenomena or actuality into what can be perceived and so controlled. The subjects, us, are now stable and socializable. Reason is always in the service of the political and economic masters. It is here that literature strikes, at this base, where the concepts and actings of order impose themselves. Literature is that which denounces and slashes apart the repressing machine at the level of the signified. Well before Bataille, Kleist, Hoffman etc., made trial of Hegelian idealism, of the cloturing dialectic of recognition: the German Romantics sung brazenly brassily in brass of spending and waste. They cut through conservative narcissism with bloody razor blades. They tore the subject away from her subjugation to her self, the proper; dislocated you the puppet; cut the threads of meaning; spit at all mirrors which control.[64]

Despite the radical nature of her textual strategies, many critics seem to praise Acker for precisely this kind of quality: an ability to cut through posture and hypocrisy with a highly personalized, distinctive 'voice' – 'a voice not often heard from the suburbanized media of American culture, one that is full of pain, rage, and lacerating barbs of social commentary'.[65] Young and Caveney similarly suggest that Acker's work forms part of a tradition of 'grittily authentic postrealism' in 'downtown' writing, a tradition sharply at odds with texts by other contemporary authors like John Barth, Donald Barthelme and Robert Coover whose work is 'so deeply involved in irony, pastiche, plays on fictional traditions and author games that, ultimately, it becomes mired in what has been termed "post-modern paralysis"'. Postpunk or 'downtown' authors like Acker, by contrast, are 'reporting from within a lived reality, not dissecting its constituents from the academic perimeters'.[66] This partly accounts for Acker's broader popularity – the difficulty of her work does not seem to be a mere intellectual 'game' but the product of an urgent engagement with and an attempt to transcend consumer culture's appropriation of the self.

There are thus two overlapping notions of identity in Acker's work – one which emphasizes the constructedness of the self and another which seeks to break through to the personal, spontaneous and experiential. It is these two notions, I would argue, which make Acker's life and work so readily appropriable by celebrity culture. In pointing to the infinitely improvisational character of the self, and the idea of individual identity as fluid and unstable, Acker arguably reproduces the conventions of a media and publishing world which seeks to promote the author as marketable 'pseudo-event'. In the other three authors discussed in the second half of this book, antipathy towards celebrity manifests itself, to varying degrees, in a nostalgia for the 'true' authorial self. Acker, although in some ways more vociferously anti-fame than these three authors, does not necessarily assume a recoverable self prior to her public one. In fact, the 'autobiographical' character in many of her books invents a public self as a way of escaping from a much-damaged private one, and this public self becomes a form of salvation.

In another sense, though, Acker's life and work is constructed around a rhetoric of authenticity, a belief that the constraints of conventional society can be stripped away to reveal the 'real' self. This is accompanied by a romanticized view of the author as rebel and seer, touched with divine madness and aloof from ordinary mortals – what Bourdieu calls 'the Christlike mystique of the *artiste maudit*' which pervades in the restricted field[67] – as in her mythologizing of writers like Rimbaud and Genet as outlaws and outcasts. The fictionalized lives of these authors, in novels like *Blood and*

Guts in High School and *In Memoriam to Identity*, are similar to those of the 'autobiographical' female characters presented throughout Acker's work – they are portrayed as disturbed, persecuted youths with unhappy childhoods who sink into poverty and the sexual underworld, only to rescue themselves through art. Acker herself has always foregrounded her role as artistic outsider, in opposition to the philistinism of the capitalist middle class, describing the avant-garde art scene in New York in the 1970s as 'resembl[ing] an angel miraculously living amid the greed and zombielike behaviors of those outside the art world, the faceless business-suits who crowded into Wall Street every morning'.[68]

In Acker's admirable unwillingness to compromise her radical edge, she perhaps loses sight of the kinds of cultural capital at stake in this alternative culture and the ways in which consumer culture can mine this capital for its own ends. Acker's rhetoric of rebellious autonomy is both a genuine response to her actual situation within literary culture and a reformulation of the romantic aestheticism, with its foregrounding of authorial subjectivity, which has proved such a fertile source of literary fame for over two hundred years. But this is not to say that her adversarial approach is completely devalued by celebrity culture's on-off love affair with its bohemian antithesis. Above all, Acker's success – as with that of all the other authors examined here – shows that the changing nature of the literary marketplace has not led to the straightforward triumph of profit over art and the sidelining of resistant cultures. Instead, it points to the ways in which literary celebrity is continually adapting and transforming itself on the intersection of culture and commerce.

9
Conclusion: A 'Meet the Author' Culture

Literary celebrity, as I have sought to argue, works as much through the sphere of textual representation as it does through the material processes of cultural production and consumption. The celebrity authors discussed in the second half of this book do more than simply 'reflect' or 'react' to their celebrity in their work; these texts form part of literary celebrity itself, precisely because it is created symbolically through literary and cultural texts. Taken as a whole, these four authors show that celebrity cuts across a wide variety of constituencies and affects authors in complex and diverse ways. The quality which they all share is a kind of passionate ambivalence about the experience, which veers between hostility and acceptance, and blindness and insight about their own relationship to their fame. This ambivalence seems to rest ultimately on an acceptance that, whatever its merits or demerits, celebrity is an obdurate fact of the literary and cultural landscape which is here to stay, precisely because it is so capacious and adaptable. In these concluding pages, I want to point to some of the wider contexts of the phenomena I have been examining by looking briefly at literary celebrity outside the US and at a related form of fame: academic stardom.

The American Future

As this book has aimed to show, celebrity is becoming an increasingly significant part of literary culture, and its impact is progressively found not only in the US, but elsewhere. Discussion about the general phenomenon of celebrity in Britain, for example, is often couched in terms of concerns about American 'cultural imperialism', because it is viewed as the product of primarily American economic and cultural forces – a highly commercialized culture industry, technological changes in the mass media, the Hollywood star system and so on. These concerns have also been raised in literary culture, connecting with anxieties about what John Sutherland calls 'the American future of British fiction'.[1] The identification of the United States with the triumph of the marketplace over cultural distinction – a feature of British cultural life from Matthew Arnold's *Culture and Anarchy* onwards – has resurfaced as a way of voicing the fear that a climate of bestsellerdom and promotion is replacing any considered critical appraisal of books and authors.

These anxieties were heightened in the 1980s and 1990s as the literary marketplace became internationalized and independent UK houses such as Jonathan Cape, The Bodley Head and Chatto and Windus were swallowed up by American corporations. It is true that this process has been two-sided – shifts in the international balance of trade and the value of the dollar encouraged foreign conglomerates like Pearson, Bertelsmann, Holtzbrinck and News Corporation to begin to compete very successfully in the US market in the last decade or so. The initial battleground for this transnationalization, however, was the American domestic market, which has pioneered the new kinds of publicity techniques which promote certain books and authors vigorously. As Jason Cowley puts it, the European conglomerates

are not buying into the American market as an act of cultural imperialism, but precisely because the cultural hegemony of America is so intensely lucrative. These are global investments, the springboard from which to dive into an ocean of potential profit.[2]

One of the effects of these changes in publishing has been to make US books and authors culturally dominant throughout the English-speaking world, with foreign-rights sales of American books increasing more than twentyfold in the course of the 1990s.[3] (Only in the last decade have American publishers begun to realize the full potential of the international market as an extra source of revenue, particularly the highly profitable English language market of the UK and Commonwealth, which amounts to about a quarter of the world's population.) All the American literary celebrities mentioned in this book, for example, are also celebrities in Britain: it is American authors who are guaranteed to pack out the Barbican Centre, the Institute of Contemporary Arts or the major bookshops when they tour Britain, who receive disproportionate review coverage in the newspapers and who are heavily discussed on arts programmes like the *South Bank Show* and *Late Review*.

More significantly, the British book market has been steadily Americanized. Many of the most important developments in British publishing in recent years – the use of increasingly aggressive forms of book marketing, the growing size of advances for a small number of big-name authors, the new importance of literary agents who can broker huge deals for their clients, the vigorous attempts to sell British authors in other English-language markets – originated in America and are largely an effect of the more commercial instincts of the large, conglomerate-owned publishers. This has produced the same kinds of anxieties evident in the US about the new significance of the 'bottom line' and the importation of elements of showbusiness into publishing. The ICA recently held a seminar on 'Publishing, Principles and Style', the programme for which pointed to the possibility that 'youth, beauty and white teeth' might now be the main qualities publishers looked for in writers.[4] Robert McCrum, in similar vein, suggests that we live in 'a culture that seems ... to have become oppressed by a few, distinctly mediocre, literary brand names for which the seemingly all-powerful conglomerates pay lottery-style advances and then usually, a few years later, telephone number-style losses'.[5]

These anxieties came together in 1995 in what became known as 'the Amis affair'. In January of that year, Martin Amis dispensed with the services of his British agent and employed Andrew Wylie, a New Yorker nicknamed 'The Jackal' because of his alleged ruthlessness, to negotiate a £500,000 advance with HarperCollins for his new novel, *The Information*. (Controversies over large advances are common symptoms of broader concerns about developments in publishing: the news in 1997 that a performance poet, Murray Lachlan Young, had signed a million-pound deal with EMI for his first two albums, and was to receive a similar sum for appearing in a TV commercial for Virgin Atlantic, also inspired a great deal of media interest and complaints from impecunious authors.) The subsequent controversy about Amis, while conducted within the pages of the broadsheet (and, occasionally, tabloid) press, was also partly manipulated by HarperCollins, who 'rush-released' the book in March 1995, two months ahead of schedule, to exploit the publicity surrounding it. Although much of the Amis affair fed on gossip about the author's personal life, for many British authors and critics, most publicly A.S. Byatt (who dismissed this search for large advances as 'a kind of male turkey-cocking which is extremely bad for the industry and makes life hard for young authors'[6]), it primarily provided an opportunity to criticize what they saw as the baleful consequences of the Americanization of British book publishing.

Ironically, Amis actually contemplates the relationship between authorship and celebrity in *The Information*, the central characters of which,

Richard Tull and Gwyn Barry, are both authors, friends and fierce rivals. As the novel opens, Tull's literary career, once full of promise, is on the wane – he is reviewing biographies of minor English authors for *The Little Magazine* and composing long, turgid, unpublishable novels. Barry, who followed his undistinguished university career with a long period writing O-level crib notes for sale in supermarkets, now lives in palatial splendour in Holland Park having written a lavishly praised bestseller, *Amelior*, which Tull despises for 'its cuteness, blandness ... its tinkertoy symmetries'. The plot of *The Information* revolves around Richard's failed attempts to 'fuck Gwyn up'[7] by nobbling book reviewers, scuppering his chances of winning a distinguished American literary prize and accusing him of plagiarism.

The Information is about the rivalries inspired by prizes, plaudits, bestsellerdom and celebrity, and leaves the reader in no doubt about the origins of these new pressures on authors – its third and central section consists of a publicity tour to the United States made by both Barry and Tull, during which the latter reflects that he 'knew what America was capable of doing to British writers. Timid rubes who cross the Atlantic, timidly blinking, were immediately swept up in the indigenous panic of make-or-break'.[8] Standing in for Barry on a radio talk show, he refuses to play along with the publicity game by responding to the host's question about what his novel 'says', and reflects:

> The contemporary idea seemed to be that the first thing you did, as a communicator, was come up with some kind of slogan, and either you put it on a coffee mug or a T-shirt or a bumper sticker – or else you wrote a novel about it ... And now that writers spent as much time telling everyone what they were doing as they spent actually doing it, then they would start doing it that way round too, eventually.[9]

As Gerald Howard puts it, then, *The Information* is 'a prime postmodern instance in the dizzying circularity with which the book's whole publication saga mirrored its themes of venality and authenticity'.[10] The Amis affair demonstrated one of the most common characteristics of the transformation of the author into media celebrity, namely the assumption of a close relationship between the writer and his work – what Amis himself, in his account of the affair, terms 'literalism'.[11] Even before the book was published, the media discussion fed on the notion of *The Information* as *roman à clef* – Richard and Gwyn were supposedly modelled on Amis himself and Julian Barnes, a friend who fell out with Amis when the latter broke with his agent, Pat Kavanagh, (Barnes's wife) in search of a higher advance.

Amis offers a deliberately caricatured, *New Grub Street* view of literary celebrity in *The Information* in which authors are either penniless, neglected 'artists' or rich and successful hacks. (This is a recurrent element in Amis's work – the rivalry between Tull and Barry, for example, recalls the ego clash between the bestselling author, Mark Asprey, and the unsuccessful Samson Young in *London Fields* (1989).) In fact, as in the US, the transformation of British literary culture that Amis writes about has not so much produced the triumph of the marketplace as a mutually interdependent relationship between culture and commerce. In the bookseller Tim Waterstone's succinct judgment of the Thatcher era in Britain, 'it was a philistine decade which saw the restoration of the book'.[12] The phenomenon of the literary prize, which forms the centrepiece of *The Information*, is one example of this. It is true that prizes like the Booker are hugely significant (more so than in the US, in fact) in generating further promotion and book sales, and that publishers are becoming increasingly astute at manufacturing press coverage and bookshop displays for shortlisted and winning authors. But the fact that all the major prizes are awarded for 'literary' fiction, and that publishing houses select which of their authors should be considered, means that the real danger is that they give publishers' hype a veneer of cultural authority. The annual arguments in the broadsheets about the shortlists, which have occasionally involved judges resigning in protest, show what is at stake: these prizes help to create a kind of premier league of bankable literary names, contributing to a process of what Richard Todd, in his study of literary prize culture, calls 'contemporary literary canon-formation'.[13] This process of canon formation is supported by the media, not only in the publicity given to the prizes and the controversies surrounding them, but its relentless process of whittling the huge number of books published each year (roughly 100,000) into manageable chunks, through the features in which celebrity authors and critics pick their summer and winter reading and 'best books' of the year, the paperback roundups, the critics' choices and so on.

The same coalescence of culture and the marketplace is evident in the continuing growth of the bookstore chains. The new ascendancy of firms like Waterstone's and Books Etc. – and their opening of huge, American-style, Espresso-barred bookstores in the big metropolitan centres – as well as the spreading of American chains like Borders and Barnes and Noble to Britain, has led to fears that these stores will also help to squeeze out literary fiction by energetically promoting surefire successes like self-help books, television tie-ins and celebrity biographies. These fears were exacerbated by the collapse of the Net Book Agreement, which was finally killed off in September 1995 by the defection of three large transatlantic publishers – Random House, HarperCollins and Penguin – and pressure from the book chains, and which was portrayed by its opponents in the UK as a triumph for the American tradition of 'hard sell'. Any visit to a bookshop, though, will show that the effects of the success of the chains are more subtle and far-reaching. These stores are also involved in their own process of canon formation: they have instigated 'Books [and Authors] of the Month', in-house magazines, themed guides directing people to reading around a particular topic or genre, and, perhaps most significantly, book events – reading groups, signings and readings – all of which subtly influence our own habits of buying and consuming literature.

As Todd says, we now live in 'a "meet the author" culture'.[14] Apart from these bookshop appearances for authors, recent years have seen the growth of a whole circuit of literary festivals at Hay-on-Wye, Cheltenham, Dartington and elsewhere, at which readers can see authors in the flesh, listen to them reading their work and ask them questions. The largest of these, the Hay Festival, is now attended by about 50,000 people and several hundred authors each year: in fact, few commercially successful, 'literary' authors do not attend these events. As well as themselves being a product of the star system, the festivals generate their own hierarchies which perpetuate and reinforce it – the 'stars' among the participants perform in the biggest venues, can charge more expensive ticket prices and attract bigger audiences.

For the publishers, such festivals are clearly an attempt to stimulate book sales by getting authors to read from their work and sell signed copies, and they push as many kinds of authors as possible: cookery authors, academics, comedians, biographers and popular science writers as well as novelists. But there is more to them than this. There is no doubt that people come to see the 'literary' authors: the elder statesmen like Muriel Spark, Doris Lessing and Toni Morrison or the younger stars like Jeanette Winterson, Hanif Kureishi and Jay McInerney. In addition, the festivals are often in genteel, rural settings and the festivalgoers are perhaps the same people who tour around Wordsworth's Dove Cottage in the Lake District or the Brontë parsonage at Haworth, in search of 'culture'. The festivals thus form part of the literary and cultural tourist industry – increasingly a major growth area within tourism as a whole, and a highly lucrative one, given that its participants are disproportionately middle-class, middle-aged professionals.[15] These events are an example of the ways in which the commercialization of book publishing has combined with older historical survivals and other kinds of cultural phenomena like tourism and heritage. This is precisely why literary celebrity is so powerful: it is a promiscuous phenomenon, able to attach itself to all kinds of other activities and aspirations, including the genuine desire of readers to get close to authors and books.

The Pervasiveness of Celebrity

What I have been describing so far is celebrity as a pervasive phenomenon which cuts across cultural boundaries. In theory, then, it has the potential to infiltrate itself into all sorts of spheres not normally associated with celebrity: classical music, jazz, opera, art and other forms of writing such as journalism and cultural criticism (although in all these areas there are also histories of fame which could be uncovered). Examining celebrity in all these spheres is beyond the scope of this book, but I want to conclude by looking briefly at another form of celebrity associated with writing and publishing of which I have some direct experience: academic stardom. By this I do not so much mean intellectuals like Camille Paglia or Germaine Greer who become famous outside academia, but the emergence of a kind of self-contained star system within universities, which has been much debated within the academy.

Recent critiques of this star system have tended to focus on the celebrities themselves and the kinds of intellectual work they produce. In a mirroring of debates about the use of the confessional mode among celebrity authors, for example, several critics have examined the so-called 'autobiographical turn' in literary and cultural criticism in relation to the academic stars who are often associated with this form of criticism. Richard Burt, in an article about celebrity intellectuals, argues that 'the practice of marking one's subjectivity is troubled by the academic context in which it emerges. Personal criticism turns out to be cool. Too cool, in fact'. He suggests that

> reflexive critique inevitably becomes dysfunctional: a critic's institutional motivation to conduct a critique of the institution of criticism overrides the marks of gender, sexual orientation, and the race of a given critic; precisely because that motivation will invariably be pathologized, a given critic's subjective markings are insignificant and irrelevant.

Burt thus describes autobiographical criticism as 'an always failed drive away from the perceived bad effects of the institutionalization of criticism'.[16]

Burt points to a paradox that the emergence of big names in literary and cultural studies runs counter to this field's scepticism about conventional forms of academic authority and hierarchization, as well as its anxiety about the more recent changes in universities – the concern that the humanities have become 'operationalised', in Steven Connor's term,[17] determined increasingly by the logic of the marketplace. The use of autobiographical criticism, in fact, is part of this resistance to traditional notions of the academic as an impersonal scholarly dispenser of professional expertise. Nancy Miller, for example, has described autobiographical forms of cultural criticism, in the particular context of feminist theory, as connecting with a broader 'crisis of representativity' – the belief that it is better to 'speak as a' rather than to 'speak for', to situate oneself within a frame of reference rather than presume to speak for everybody in the constructed language of the 'academic sublime'.[18] However, there is a risk, as Laurie Langbauer points out, that this challenging of academic hierarchies with autobiographical writing will only succeed in reproducing them in a different form, by underlining the assumptions of the 'celebrity economy' of the academy.[19] Miller herself has expressed concern that this kind of writing can at least give the impression of being the preserve of 'networked, privileged selves, who get to call each other (and themselves) by their first names in print'.[20] The danger is that serious engagement with intellectual ideas and debates will give way to celebrity gossip – or worse, perhaps, that the two will become so interconnected as to be indistinguishable from each other.

This critique is often part of a wider belief that academic stars have imported some of the practices and conventions of popular culture celebrity into the academic field. Burt refers to the 'celebritization' and 'tabloidization' of cultural criticism,[21] for example, while David Shumway's discussion of stars in literary studies traces the historical development of celebrity from the mid-nineteenth century onwards, linking it to the growing ubiquity of images in contemporary culture and the subsequent emphasis on mere 'visibility' and 'knownness' as a source of fame. Shumway thus suggests that 'the importance in contemporary America of celebrity in its many forms, including stardom, helps account for the rise of the academic star system'.[22] Undoubtedly, there are parallels between academic and other forms of celebrity: the interviews, profiles and features about academic stars in the American magazine, *Lingua Franca*, founded in June 1990, for example, have partly thrived on this gossipy, glamorous strain in celebrity academia. The magazine's founding editor has described the purpose of the magazine in these terms:

> The fact is, just as jocks sometimes think serious thoughts, academics are riven with human frailties and human desires, both the good ones and the seven sins – you know, lust and all the rest ... And it's interesting to see how the corporeal factors of a scholar get mixed up with the more cerebral and abstract stuff.[23]

In Britain, this venal element also thrives: the *Guardian* recently ran a series on its education pages entitled 'Celebrity Scholars: A Cut-Out-and-

Keep Guide to the Academics Whose Phones are Always Ringing'. The academics were judged under various headings, including 'co-star verdict', 'credits', 'best notice', 'catchphrases', 'appearance', 'publications' and 'performing strengths and weaknesses'. Star academics can also be used for publicity purposes by the institutions which employ them, and publish or otherwise disseminate their work – as Michael Gorra says, 'we live in a culture of stardom, in which even academic publishers want to promote their authors as personalities'.[24] Scholarly publishers, both those recently purchased by large commercial conglomerates (Prentice-Hall, Harvester, Macmillan) and established university presses are increasingly driven by an emphasis on marketability and publicity, making them less willing, for example, to publish research monographs by unknown scholars.[25] (This new, profit-driven mentality was aptly demonstrated by Oxford University Press's decision in November 1998 to dispense with its poetry list, which provoked letters of protest to newspapers and demonstrations outside its offices by poets and critics.) Dustjacket photographs and extensive bio-blurbs and capsule summaries, once anathema to scholarly publishing, now appear routinely on the covers of books by academic stars; conference organizers, meanwhile, announce 'plenary' and 'keynote' speakers in bold letters on their publicity material, academic euphemisms for above-the-title billing. This in turn reinforces the star system: Andrew Wernick notes that academic celebrity tends to accumulate exponentially as 'professional credits' are joined by their 'promotionally amplified effects'. The biggest stars at the top of the academic hierarchy are used to promote the institution, book or conference with which they are associated, which in turn feeds back into their own celebrity.[26]

However, the suggestion that autobiographical criticism is a mere effect of academic stardom fails to recognize, first, that the star system within universities is not peculiar to this kind of criticism; and second, that mainstream celebrity has not simply absorbed academia, because elites within universities largely regulate the formation of stars. It is not a matter of criticizing particular academics for 'showing off', then, but of recognizing that autobiographical criticism may unavoidably be complicated by a context in which 'the adoption of a promotional mode has become indispensable to academic survival'.[27] As with other forms of celebrity, the phenomenon of academic stardom is structural, and the product of a complicated relationship between universities and the marketplace. The emergence of an academic star system is closely related to the development, in advanced capitalist societies, of the business-oriented, entrepreneurial university in which employees are increasingly viewed as 'human capital' – as repositories for skills which can help boost research rankings and gain more resources or, alternatively, drain away resources through their non-productivity. The new managerialist emphasis in higher education has led inevitably to greater disparities in the allocation of money and prestige among academics both within and between institutions. Sande Cohen refers to a 'spiralling of sign-value' in universities as one cause of academic stardom, which has meant that a person 'is deemed "hirable" only if signifiers are present that enhance the status and/or exchange value of the department or relevant academic sector'.[28] After the introduction of the HEFCE Research Assessment Exercise in the UK in 1986, for example, university departments began explicitly to discuss buying in 'star' names, in football-style transfers, to improve their overall grade, and individuals and institutions have had to become more astute in promoting themselves and their work.

As with literary celebrity, however, the impingement of market values on universities involves a highly complex relationship with the existing hierarchies of the academic 'field'. The relatively self-contained nature of this field means that economic imperatives function in complicated, displaced ways within it. As Bourdieu argues, the academic field (like the restricted field of cultural production) is based around 'the *autonomous* principle of hierarchization', producing '*degree specific consecration* ... the degree of recognition accorded by those who recognize no other criterion of legitimacy than recognition by those whom they recognize'.[29] In fact, he suggests that the academic field (like the field of cultural production as a whole) has developed around two opposing hierarchies: an internal social hierarchy of powerful people within the universities, and a more fluid, innovative cultural hierarchy with external links with newspaper and magazine journalism. However, the real power and influence within the academy is held by the former group, and the 'celeritas' of those who want to 'cut corners' by attempting to use capital gained in other fields is almost always successfully countered by people whose interests lie in reinforcing the autonomy of the academic field.[30] The growth of a star system within universities has thus emerged within an already hierarchical professional context, an intricate system which determines the means by which academics ascend (or fail to ascend) the career ladder by disseminating their work through publications, conference appearances and the like.[31] This hierarchical context, while ostensibly facilitating a rise through the ranks for the deserving, actually gives a disproportionate share of power and prestige to the already powerful. Prestigious institutions, for example, tend to have more resources to invest in research, allowing them to gain research points which in turn provide them with more resources to invest in research, and so on.

Since academic stars are partly a product of these differences in prestige and resources between institutions (they tend to be headhunted by older and more prestigious institutions, who have the money and status to be able to attract them), academic celebrity similarly represents a complex negotiation between cultural and economic capital. The effect of all this is to create a growing divide between what James Sosnoski refers to as the 'token professionals' and the 'master critics' – the large number of academics who survive with heavy teaching loads and little research money (not to mention the many PhD students failing to get full-time teaching posts), and the much smaller number of their illustrious counterparts in the top-ranking universities who receive a disproportionate share of resources, prestige and critical attention.[32] It is significant that it was a graduate student, Alexandra Chasin, who complained from the floor at the 1990 Illinois conference, 'Cultural Studies Now and in the Future', (by common consent a star-studded event) that the majority of conference delegates were being defined as passive 'fans' of the celebrities on the podium, to the extent that only known and named people could participate, and questions from the floor were being discreetly vetted.[33]

As with literary celebrity, much of the existing discussion around a star system within universities seems to turn on a view of America as the principal site of academic celebrity.[34] It is understandable that the US should be seen as a special case in this context, because it has been at the centre of the growing professionalization and promotionalization of universities and is still dominant in the academic world market even though its overall economic position has been increasingly challenged.[35] However, the growth of academic stardom, as with other forms of stardom, is a consequence of powerful economic and cultural forces which are not confined to one country. As Wernick argues, the rise of a promotional culture within academia is evident in differing degrees in all advanced capitalist societies, while other developments have a 'teleological typicality' because they are North American.[36]

Moreover, the internationalization of the academic marketplace also means that scholars need to be well-known across several countries to be recognized as 'stars'. International (particularly transatlantic) renown is often employed as a signifier of academic excellence – the Research Assessment Exercise in the UK, for example, awards the highest grades of 5 and 5A only to work of 'international significance'. An important factor in the internationalization of the academic star system has been the improved global communication between scholars caused by such factors as the increasing sophistication of electronic media and the growth of the global conference circuit. David Lodge satirizes this latter situation in his novel,

Small World, in which a few of the same big names scuttle around the world on Boeing 747s to international conferences, meeting up in student halls and hotel rooms to have affairs and exchange academic gossip. The novel, significantly, culminates with the most glittering event in the conference calendar, the MLA convention, where its hero, Persse McGarrigle, a young, unknown and not particularly career-minded lecturer from Limerick, incurs the wrath of the theoretical stars on the podium by daring to ask a question without an identification badge.[37]

Just as the phenomenon of literary celebrity cannot simply be attributed to the vanities and ambitions of its brightest stars, academic stardom cannot simply be blamed on a small subsection of the scholarly community, because the stars themselves are only a symptom of overall developments within universities. Starmaking within academia functions as a system, within which specific individuals and institutions are subordinate to a field of production in which positions between agents arise at least semi-automatically and obscure figures play a significant role as well as stars – a system in which 'no one is to blame yet everyone is implicated'.[38] Although I am only a tiny cog in the academic star system, then, I am still unavoidably a part of it. I had various personal reasons for wanting to write this book, of course, but it would be naive not to recognize that it has also been completed under the constraints of this system – the individualistic drive for tenure, promotion and scholarly reputation affects all academics, and has led me to realize that I am ultimately enmeshed in the cultural processes and mechanisms I have been describing in this book.

These structural determinants apply to literary celebrity as well: obscure, marginal figures are as implicated in any 'star system' as the stars themselves. Anyone who has attended the kinds of author events I have been describing – book signings, readings, literary festivals – will know that the audiences are disproportionately sprinkled with literary wannabes, aspirant literary talents hoping that, by coming into contact with the real thing, they will be helped on the way to attaining that magical status of 'author'. The *New York Times* recently visited the North Carolina Literary Festival at Chapel Hill, at which John Grisham was the star attraction, and the reporter met several of these wannabes, including an engineer, Gregory K. Norris, who had paid 350 dollars for a booth to display and sell his self-published novel, *Zon*. Norris tells the reporter: 'To tell you the truth, the guy [Grisham] gives me hope. He began selling books from the trunk of his car, and so am I.' As the reporter comments: 'Every writer these days is a combination marketer-littérateur who feels he's one *Oprah* call away from hitting the jackpot.'[39] The veritable industry created around residential courses in creative writing, and self-help and how-to manuals with titles like *You Can Write a Novel, Getting Your Book Published* and *Freeing the Writer Within*, is testament to this widely held belief.

This dream remains so appealing precisely because it still becomes reality for an albeit tiny number of people – although book publishing is becoming increasingly commercialized, rationalized and closed off to all but a favoured few, it is still more hit-and-miss than other areas of the mass media, ever-reliant on 'buzz' and the unearthing of new talent. As Ken Worpole writes:

> The publishing industry has become one of the brightest jewels in the otherwise rather tarnished crown of entrepreneurial capitalism. It remains one of the few industries where fortunes can still be made overnight, and consequently the press and other media have become obsessed with the rags-to-riches stories of unknown authors who have become millionaires in a very short space of time.[40]

The appeal of literary celebrity partly depends on this ingredient of wish-fulfilment, which conveniently glosses over the in-built factors which make this ascension highly unlikely – those factors which I have attempted to examine in this book. Perhaps this lies at the heart of celebrity's solemnizing of authorship as an individualistic activity: the belief that, when we finally finish that great masterpiece which has been gathering dust in the cupboard under the stairs, then we too will be a star.

Notes

1 Introduction: The Charismatic Illusion

1 See George Plimpton, 'Spotting the Literati in Their City Lairs: A Guide', *New York Times*, 16 September 1994, and '*Esquire's* Guide to the Literary Universe', *Esquire*, August 1987, pp. 51–9.
2 Richard Schickel, *Intimate Strangers: The Culture of Celebrity* (New York: Fromm International, 1986), p. 286.
3 Joshua Gamson, *Claims to Fame: Celebrity in Contemporary America* (Berkeley, CA: University of California Press, 1994), p. 191.
4 Daniel Boorstin, *The Image: A Guide to Pseudo-Events in America* (New York: Vintage, 1992), pp. 57–8, 162.
5 Ibid., p. 61.
6 Jean Strouse, 'Updike in the Lion's Den', *Newsweek*, 18 October 1982, p. 67.
7 John Cawelti, 'The Writer as a Celebrity: Some Aspects of American Literature as Popular Culture', *Studies in American Fiction*, vol. 5, no. 1 (Spring 1977): 164.
8 Alan Spiegel, *James Agee and the Legend of Himself: A Critical Study* (Columbia, MO: University of Missouri Press, 1998), p. 2.
9 See, for example, James Monaco, 'Introduction', in idem (ed.), *Celebrity* (New York: Delta, 1978), pp. 5–6, and Christopher Lasch, *The Culture of Narcissism: American Life in an Age of Diminishing Expectations* (New York: Norton, 1991), pp. 59–63.
10 Pierre Bourdieu, 'Intellectual Field and Creative Project', in Michael F. D. Young (ed.), *Knowledge and Control: New Directions in the Sociology of Education* (London: Collier-Macmillan, 1971), p. 163.
11 Pierre Bourdieu, *The Field of Cultural Production: Essays on Art and Literature*, ed. Randal Johnson (New York: Columbia University Press, 1993), p. 137.
12 Pierre Bourdieu, *The Rules of Art: Genesis and Structure of the Literary Field*, tr. Susan Emanuel (Cambridge: Polity Press, 1996), p. 319.
13 Bourdieu, *The Field of Cultural Production*, p. 76.
14 Leo Braudy, *The Frenzy of Renown: Fame and Its History* (New York: Oxford University Press, 1986), pp. 351, 363.
15 Bourdieu, *The Field of Cultural Production*, pp. 115, 125.
16 Ibid., p. 30.
17 Bourdieu, *The Rules of Art*, p. 224.
18 Pierre Bourdieu, *Distinction: A Social Critique of the Judgement of Taste*, tr. Richard Nice (London: Routledge, 1984), p. 7.
19 Merv Griffin quoted in Marshall Blonsky, *American Mythologies* (New York: Oxford University Press, 1992), p. 270; Schickel, *Intimate Strangers*, p. 354.
20 Charles Newman, *The Post-Modern Aura* (Evanston, IL: Northwestern University Press, 1985), p. 168.
21 See Gamson, *Claims to Fame*, pp. 17–19, and P. David Marshall, *Celebrity and Power: Fame in Contemporary Culture* (Minneapolis, MN: University of Minnesota Press, 1997), pp. 4–9.
22 See, for example, Joan Shelley Rubin, *The Making of Middlebrow Culture* (Chapel Hill, NC: University of North Carolina Press, 1992), and Janice A. Radway, *A*

Feeling for Books: The Book-of-the-Month Club, Literary Taste and Middle-Class Desire (Chapel Hill, NC: University of North Carolina Press, 1997). Although his subject matter and approach are slightly different, Lawrence Levine's *Highbrow/Lowbrow: The Emergence of Cultural Hierarchy in America* (Cambridge, MA: Harvard University Press, 1988) also provides some useful insights into the historicity of divisions between high and low culture and the importance of the market in constructing hierarchies of culture in late nineteenth-century America.

23 Ken Worpole, *Reading By Numbers: Contemporary Publishing and Popular Fiction* (London: Comedia, 1984), p. 15.

24 Braudy, *The Frenzy of Renown*, pp. 351, 363, 371, 9n, 4.

25 Roland Barthes, 'The Writer on Holiday', in idem, *Mythologies*, tr. Annette Lavers (London: Jonathan Cape, 1972), p. 30.

26 Gamson, *Claims to Fame*, p. 132.

27 Terry Eagleton, *Literary Theory: An Introduction* (Oxford: Basil Blackwell, 1983), p. 19.

28 Walter Benjamin, *Charles Baudelaire: A Lyric Poet in the Era of High Capitalism*, tr. Harry Zohn (London: New Left Books, 1973), p. 71.

29 Bourdieu, *The Field of Cultural Production*, pp. 76, 29.

30 Roland Barthes, 'La vedette, enquetes d'audience?', *Communications* 2 (1963), p. 213, cited in Richard deCordova, *Picture Personalities: The Emergence of a Star System in America* (Urbana, IL: University of Illinois Press, 1990), p. 9 (his translation).

31 John Updike, *Bech: A Book* (London: André Deutsch, 1970), p. vi.

32 Duncan Webster, *Looka Yonder! The Imaginary America of Populist Culture* (London: Comedia/Routledge, 1988), p. 180.

2   Mark Twain Absurdity: Literature and Publicity in America

1 Jennifer Wicke, *Advertising Fictions: Literature, Advertisement and Social Reading* (New York: Columbia University Press, 1988), p. 1.

2 Gamson, *Claims to Fame*, pp. 19–20.

3 Philip Collins, 'Introduction', in idem (ed.), *Charles Dickens: The Public Readings* (Oxford: Clarendon Press, 1975), p. lii.

4 *Saunders's News-Letter*, August 1858, cited in ibid., p. lii.

5 David R. Shumway, *Creating American Civilization: A Genealogy of American Literature as an Academic Discipline* (Minneapolis, MN: University of Minnesota Press, 1994), p. 226.

6 Cawelti, 'The Writer as a Celebrity', p. 166.

7 Louis J. Budd, *Our Mark Twain: The Making of His Public Personality* (Philadelphia, PA: University of Pennsylvania Press, 1983), p. 24.

8 Carl Bode, *The American Lyceum: Town Meeting of the Mind* (Carbondale and Edwardsville, IL: Southern Illinois University Press, 1968), p. 201.

9 Philip Collins, '"Agglomerating Dollars with Prodigious Rapidity": British Pioneers on the American Lecture Circuit', in James Russell Kincaid and Albert J. Kuhn (eds), *Victorian Literature and Society: Essays Presented to Richard D. Altick* (Columbus, OH: Ohio State University Press, 1984), p. 9.

10 Aaron Fogel, 'Talk Shows: On Reading Television', in Stephen Donadio, Stephen Railton and Ormond Seavey (eds), *Emerson and His Legacy: Essays in*

Honour of Quentin Anderson (Carbondale and Edwardsville, IL: Southern Illinois University Press, 1986), p. 151.

11 Budd, *Our Mark Twain*, p. 57.

12 Mary Kupiec Cayton, 'The Making of an American Prophet: Emerson, His Audiences and the Rise of the Culture Industry in Nineteenth-Century America', *American Historical Review*, vol. 92, no. 3 (June 1987): 601, 616.

13 James L.W. West III, *American Authors and the Literary Marketplace Since 1900* (Philadelphia, PA: University of Pennsylvania Press, 1988), p. 43.

14 Cited in Budd, *Our Mark Twain*, p. 58.

15 Fred Kaplan, *Dickens: A Biography* (London: Hodder and Stoughton, 1988), p. 126, citing the eyewitness account of the Boston publisher, James T. Fields.

16 Linda Haverty Rugg, *Picturing Ourselves: Photography and Autobiography* (Chicago, IL: University of Chicago Press, 1998), p. 42.

17 John Ellis, *Visible Fictions: Cinema, Television, Radio* (London: Routledge and Kegan Paul, 1982), p. 91.

18 Cayton, 'The Making of an American Prophet', p. 617.

19 Donald M. Scott, 'The Popular Lecture and the Creation of a Public in Mid-Nineteenth Century America', *Journal of American History*, vol. 66, no. 4 (March 1980): 809.

20 Van Wyck Brooks, *The Ordeal of Mark Twain* (New York: E.P. Dutton, 1920), p. 15.

21 Bruce Michelson, *Mark Twain on the Loose: A Comic Writer and the American Self* (Amherst, MA: University of Massachusetts Press, 1995), p. 2.

22 Merle Curti, *The Growth of American Thought* (New Brunswick, NJ: Transaction Press, 3rd edn 1982), p. 346.

23 Radway, *A Feeling for Books*, pp. 247–8; see also Rubin, *The Making of Middlebrow Culture*.

24 Justin Kaplan, *Mr Clemens and Mark Twain: A Biography* (London: Jonathan Cape, 1967), p. 30.

25 Alexis de Tocqueville, *Democracy in America*, tr. Henry Reeve (New York: Modern Library, 1981), p. 354.

26 Paul Fatout, *Mark Twain on the Lecture Circuit: A Grand Torchlight Procession* (Carbondale and Edwardsville, IL: Southern Illinois University Press, 1969), p. 142; Bode, *The American Lyceum*, p. 201.

27 Quoted in Susan Gillman, *Dark Twins: Imposture and Identity in Mark Twain's America* (Chicago, IL: University of Chicago Press, 1989), p. 30.

28 Dwight Macdonald, 'Mark Twain', in idem, *Against the American Grain* (New York: Random House, 1962), p. 111; Theodor Adorno and Max Horkheimer, 'The Culture Industry: Enlightenment as Mass Deception', in idem, *Dialectic of Enlightenment*, tr. John Cumming (London: Verso, 1986), p. 142.

29 Quoted in Gillman, *Dark Twins*, p. 24.

30 Ibid., pp. 29, 16.

31 Mary Poovey, *Uneven Developments: The Ideological Work of Gender in Mid-Victorian England* (London: Virago, 1989), pp. 106, 108.

32 Paul Zweig, *Walt Whitman: The Making of the Poet* (New York: Basic Books, 1984), p. 266.

33 Budd, *Our Mark Twain*, p. 216.

34 Gillman, *Dark Twins*, p. 6.

35 Jeffrey Steinbrink, *Getting to Be Mark Twain* (Berkeley, CA: University of California Press, 1991), p. 16.
36 John Raeburn, *Fame Became of Him: Hemingway as Public Writer* (Bloomington, IN: Indiana University Press, 1984), pp. 130, 132.
37 W.A. Swanberg, *Luce and His Empire* (New York: Charles Scribner's Sons, 1972), pp. 454–5.
38 Schickel, *Intimate Strangers*, pp. 41, 75–6.
39 Raeburn, *Fame Became of Him*, pp. 106, 130.
40 Malcolm Cowley, *The Faulkner-Cowley File* (London: Chatto and Windus, 1966), pp. 123, 125.
41 'All Stories End ...', *Time*, 18 October 1937, pp. 80–1; 'An American Storyteller', *Time*, 13 December 1954, pp. 42–3.
42 M. Thomas Inge, 'Faulknerian Folklore: Public Fictions, Private Jokes, and Outright Lies', in Doreen Fowler and Ann J. Abadie (eds), *Faulkner and Popular Culture* (Jackson, MS: University Press of Mississippi, 1990), p. 24.
43 John Cheever, *The Journals*, ed. Benjamin Cheever (London: Jonathan Cape, 1991), p. ix.
44 Cited in Swanberg, *Luce and His Empire*, p. 181.
45 Cited in Marshall W. Fishwick, *Seven Pillars of Popular Culture* (Westport, CT: Greenwood Press, 1985), p. 120.
46 Robert Coover, *The Public Burning* (New York: Viking, 1977), p. 319.
47 'An Obliging Man', *Time*, 12 January 1953, p. 44; 'Private Historian', *Time*, 10 August 1936, p. 53.
48 Cited in James Steel Smith, '*Life* Looks at Literature', in Peter Davison, Rolf Meyersohn and Edward Shils (eds), *Literary Taste, Culture and Mass Communication, Volume 12: Bookselling, Reviewing and Reading* (Cambridge, MA: Chadwyck-Healey/Teaneck, NJ: Somerset House, 1978), pp. 151, 148–9.
49 'Ovid in Ossining', *Time*, 27 March 1964, p. 52; 'Spruce Street Boy', *Time*, 7 March 1949, p. 46.
50 Cleveland Amory (ed.), *International Celebrity Register: US Edition* (New York: Harper and Row, 1959), p. 338, cited in Raeburn, *Fame Became of Him*, p. 54.
51 Raeburn, *Fame Became of Him*, p. 165.
52 Jane Howard, 'Whiskey and Ink, Whiskey and Ink', *Life*, 21 July 1967, p. 67.
53 'The Second Chance', *Time*, 2 June 1967, pp. 68, 67.
54 Barry Farrell, 'The Guru Comes to Kansas', *Life*, 24 May 1966, p. 84.
55 Rubin, *The Making of Middlebrow Culture*, pp. xi, xviii.
56 Quoted in John Kobler, *Luce: His Time, Life and Fortune* (London: Macdonald, 1968), p. 46.
57 Malcolm Cowley, 'Limousines on Grub Street: How Writers Earned Their Livings, 1940–1946', in idem, *The Flower and the Leaf: A Contemporary Record of American Writing Since 1941*, ed. Donald W. Faulkner (New York: Viking, 1985), p. 89.
58 Cited in Marshall McLuhan, *The Mechanical Bride: Folklore of Industrial Man* (London: Routledge and Kegan Paul, 1967), p. 10.
59 Cited in Dan Greenburg and James Ransom, 'A Snob's Guide to Status Magazines', in William Hammell (ed.), *The Popular Arts in America* (New York: Harcourt Brace Jovanovich, 2nd edn 1977), p. 463.
60 Cited in Janice Radway, 'The Scandal of the Middlebrow: The Book of the Month Club, Class Fracture, and Cultural Authority', *South Atlantic Quarterly*, vol. 89, no. 4 (Fall 1990): 704, 715.

61   Irving Howe, 'The New York Intellectuals: A Chronicle and a Critique', *Commentary*, vol. 46, no. 4 (October 1968): 35.

62   William Phillips, *A Partisan View: Five Decades of the Literary Life* (New York: Stein and Day, 1983), pp. 96–7.

63   Clement Greenberg, 'Avant-Garde and Kitsch', in idem, *Art and Culture* (London: Thames and Hudson, 1973), p. 10.

64   George Cotkin, 'The Tragic Predicament: Post-War American Intellectuals, Acceptance and Mass Culture', in Jeremy Jennings and Anthony Kemp-Welch (eds), *Intellectuals in Politics: From the Dreyfus Affair to Salman Rushdie* (London: Routledge, 1997), p. 249.

65   Norman Podhoretz, *Making It* (London: Jonathan Cape, 1968), pp. 117–18.

66   Elizabeth Hardwick, 'The Decline of Book Reviewing', *Harper's*, October 1959, p. 138.

67   Norman Podhoretz, 'Book Reviewing and Everyone I Know', in idem, *Doings and Undoings: The Fifties and After in American Writing* (New York: Farrar, Straus and Co., 1964), p. 261.

68   Dwight Macdonald, 'Masscult and Midcult', in idem, *Against the American Grain*, p. 37.

69   Ibid., pp. 21, 27.

70   Ibid., p. 73.

71   Ibid., p. 5.

72   Bourdieu, *Distinction*, pp. 56–7.

73   Quoted in Peter Manso, *Mailer: His Life and Times* (New York: Viking, 1985), p. 269.

74   Podhoretz, *Making It*, p. xviii.

75   Howe, 'The New York Intellectuals', p. 51; Tom Wolfe, *Radical Chic and Mau-Mauing the Flak Catchers* (London: Michael Joseph, 1971), p. 85.

76   Quoted in Norman Podhoretz, *Breaking Ranks: A Political Memoir* (New York: Harper and Row, 1979), p. 270.

77   Neil Postman, *Amusing Ourselves to Death: Public Discourse in the Age of Showbusiness* (New York: Viking, 1985), pp. 45–64 passim.

3 The Reign of Hype: The Contemporary Star System

1   Thomas Whiteside, *The Blockbuster Complex: Conglomerates, Show Business and Book Publishing* (Middletown, CT: Wesleyan University Press, 1981), p. 192.

2   Lewis A. Coser, Charles Kadushin and Walter Powell, *Books: The Culture and Commerce of Book Publishing* (New York: Basic Books, 1982), pp. 202–5.

3   M.P. Levin, 'The Marketing of Books – A National Priority for the Eighties', *Library Trends*, vol. 33, no. 2 (1984): 199.

4   West, *American Authors and the Literary Marketplace*, p. 17.

5   Quoted in Ted Solataroff, 'The Literary-Industrial Complex', *New Republic*, 8 June 1987, p. 28.

6   Coser et al., *Books*, pp. 206, 158.

7   C. Anthony, 'Beating the Drum for Books', *Publishers' Weekly*, 30 November 1992, p. 27.

8   Whiteside, *The Blockbuster Complex*, p. 34.

9   Random House's court battle with Joan Collins in February 1996, in which the publishers unsuccessfully sued Collins for the return of $1.2 million as part of

a two-book contract after receiving manuscripts which they deemed unpublishable, was portrayed in the press as a blow for the celebrity novel but actually illustrated the ways in which big-name authors are treated differently by publishers. The contract had only stipulated the submission of two 'complete' novel manuscripts, with no caveat about the quality of the work received, an unusual arrangement which would not have been signed with a non-celebrity.

10 Edwin McDowell, 'Coaches Help Authors to Talk Well to Sell Well', *New York Times*, 2 March 1988.
11 Richard Schickel, *His Picture in the Papers: A Speculation on Celebrity in America, Based on the Life of Douglas Fairbanks, Sr.* (New York: Charterhouse, 1973), p. 27; see also deCordova, *Picture Personalities*, p. 46.
12 Michael Norman, 'A Book in Search of a Buzz: The Marketing of a First Novel', *New York Times Book Review*, 30 January 1994.
13 Whiteside, *The Blockbuster Complex*, p. 198.
14 James B. Twitchell, *Carnival Culture: The Trashing of Taste in America* (New York: Columbia University Press, 1992), p. 100.
15 Joseph Turow, 'The Organizational Underpinnings of Contemporary Media Conglomerates', *Communication Research*, vol. 19, no. 6 (1992): 688, 683.
16 See, for example, Richard Ohmann, *Politics of Letters* (Middletown, CT: Wesleyan University Press, 1987), pp. 72, 75; Richard Kostelanetz, *The End of Intelligent Writing: Literary Politics in America* (New York: Sheed and Ward, 1974), p. 64.
17 Joanna Coles, '$$$$$$$$$$$ That's Publishing!', *Guardian*, 30 April 1993.
18 Michael Norman, 'Reader by Reader and Town by Town, a New Novelist Builds a Following', *New York Times Book Review*, 6 February 1994.
19 Kostelanetz, *The End of Intelligent Writing*, p. 91.
20 Frank Rich, 'Star of the Month Club', *New York Times*, 23 March 1997.
21 Doreen Carvajal, 'Book Chains' New Role: Soothsayers for Publishers', *New York Times*, 12 August 1997.
22 Richard Dyer, *Stars* (London: BFI, 2nd edn 1998), pp. 60–1.
23 George Garrett, '"Once More Unto the Breach, Dear Friends, Once More": The Publishing Scene and American Literary Art', *Review of Contemporary Fiction*, vol. 8, no. 3 (Fall 1988): 15.
24 Andrew Wernick, *Promotional Culture: Advertising, Ideology and Symbolic Expression* (London: Sage, 1991), p. 106.
25 Bourdieu, *The Rules of Art*, p. 147.
26 Ibid., pp. 367, 343–7.
27 Quoted in James Surowiecki, 'The Publisher's Curse', *New York Times Magazine*, 31 May 1998.
28 Worpole, *Reading By Numbers*, p. 16.
29 Stephanie Girard, '"Standing at the Corner of Walk and Don't Walk": Vintage Contemporaries, *Bright Lights, Big City*, and the Problems of Betweenness', *American Literature*, vol. 68, no. 1 (March 1996): 161.
30 Norman, 'A Book in Search of a Buzz'.
31 David Wyatt, *Out of the Sixties: Storytelling and the Vietnam Generation* (Cambridge: Cambridge University Press, 1993), p. 51.
32 Peter Applebome, 'Festivals Booming Amid Publishing Gloom', *New York Times*, 7 April 1998.

33   Philip Fisher, 'Introduction: The New American Studies', in idem (ed.), *The New American Studies: Essays from Representations* (Berkeley, CA: University of California Press, 1991), p. ix.

34   Maureen Howard, 'Can Writing Be Taught at Iowa?', *New York Times Magazine*, 25 May 1986.

35   For example, Paglia posed for *Vanity Fair* in 1992, in her own words, 'in full vamp drag, with fake red nails and my arms around the bulging biceps of two black bodyguards'. See Camille Paglia, 'Downfall of a Glittering Star', *Observer*, 12 July 1998.

36   bell hooks, *Outlaw Culture: Resisting Representations* (New York: Routledge, 1994), pp. 83, 92, 88. For other negative critiques of Paglia, see Sandra M. Gilbert, 'Freaked Out: Camille Paglia's *Sexual Personae*', *Kenyon Review*, vol. 14, no. 1 (1992): 158–64, and Jennifer Wicke, 'Celebrity Material: Materialist Feminism and the Culture of Celebrity', *South Atlantic Quarterly*, vol. 93, no. 4 (Fall 1994): 754–6.

37   See Camille Paglia, 'Junk Bonds and Corporate Raiders: Academe in the Hour of the Wolf', in idem, *Sex, Art, and American Culture: Essays* (New York: Vintage, 1992), pp. 170–248, and 'The M.I.T. Lecture: Crisis in the American Universities', in ibid., pp. 249–98.

38   Pierre Bourdieu, *On Television and Journalism*, tr. Priscilla Parkhurst Ferguson (London: Pluto Press, 1996), p. 93.

39   Godfrey Hodgson, 'A Backsliding, Backscratching Elite', *British Journalism Review*, vol. 9, no. 2 (1998): 71.

40   Régis Debray, *Teachers, Writers, Celebrities: The Intellectuals of Modern France*, tr. David Macey (London: New Left Books, 1981), p. 1.

41   Benda himself had bitter experience of the corruptions of literary politics: he was deprived of the Prix Goncourt, France's most prestigious literary prize, in 1912 because of his vocal support for Dreyfus.

42   Debray, *Teachers, Writers, Celebrities*, pp. 165, 81.

43   Bourdieu, *On Television*, pp. 29, 59.

44   Bourdieu, *Distinction*, pp. 323–26.

45   David Swartz, *Culture and Power: The Sociology of Pierre Bourdieu* (Chicago, IL: University of Chicago Press, 1997), p. 222.

46   Ohmann, *Politics of Letters*, pp. 75, 71.

47   Donald Morton and Mas'ud Zavarzadeh, 'The Cultural Politics of the Fiction Workshop', *Cultural Critique*, vol. 11 (Winter 1988–89): 169.

48   Newman, *The Post-Modern Aura*, p. 131.

49   John W. Aldridge, *Talents and Technicians: Literary Chic and the New Assembly-Line Fiction* (New York: Charles Scribner's Sons, 1992), pp. xii, 7, 9, 15, 28.

50   Ibid., pp. 28–9.

51   R.M. Shusterman, *Pragmatic Aesthetics* (Oxford: Blackwell, 1992), p. 172, cited in Bridget Fowler, *Pierre Bourdieu and Cultural Theory: Critical Investigations* (London: Sage, 1997), p. 152.

52   Cited in Jason Cowley, 'Writing is My Work, But Not My Job', *The Times*, 5 May 1998.

53   See Edwin McDowell, 'Black Writers Gain Audiences and Visibility in Publishing', *New York Times*, 12 February 1991.

54   Cowley, 'Writing is My Work'.

55   Toni Morrison, *Playing in the Dark: Whiteness and the Literary Imagination* (Cambridge, MA: Harvard University Press, 1992), p. xii; see also Toni Morrison,

'The Official Story: Dead Man Golfing', in Toni Morrison and Claudia Brodsky Lacour (eds), *Birth of a Nation'hood: Gaze, Script, and Spectacle in the O.J. Simpson Case* (London: Vintage, 1997), pp. vii–xxviii.

56 Andrew Wernick, 'Authorship and the Supplement of Promotion', in Maurice Biriotti and Nicola Miller (eds), *What is an Author?* (Manchester: Manchester University Press, 1993), pp. 92–6.

57 Wernick, *Promotional Culture*, pp. 109, 121.

58 deCordova, *Picture Personalities*, p. 11.

59 See, for example, Jane M. Gaines, *Contested Culture: The Image, The Voice, and The Law* (London: BFI, 1992), Rosemary J. Coombe, 'The Celebrity Image and Cultural Identity: Publicity Rights and the Subaltern Politics of Gender', *Discourse*, vol. 14, no. 3 (1992): 59–87, and George M. Armstrong, Jr, 'The Reification of Celebrity: Persona as Property', *Louisiana Law Review*, vol. 51, no. 3 (1991): 443–68.

60 Marshall, *Celebrity and Power*, p. x.

61 Bourdieu, *Distinction*, p. 122.

62 Bourdieu, *The Field of Cultural Production*, p. 78.

63 Bourdieu, *The Rules of Art*, pp. 383, 256.

64 Philip Stevick, 'The World and the Writer: A Speculation on Fame', *South Atlantic Quarterly*, vol. 85, no. 3 (1986): 251.

65 James Wood, 'Literary Calculations', *Guardian*, 29 January 1996.

66 Quoted in Michael Arditti, 'A Stylist in Search of a Style', *Independent*, 18 December 1998.

67 'Obituary: Harold Brodkey', *The Times*, 29 January 1996.

68 Julian Loose, 'The Great, Brave Journey: Harold Brodkey', *Sunday Times*, 27 March 1994.

69 Ron Rosenbaum, 'The Man in the Glass House', *Independent on Sunday*, 7 September 1997.

70 Walter Benjamin, 'The Work of Art in the Age of Mechanical Reproduction', in idem, *Illuminations*, ed. Hannah Arendt, tr. Harry Zohn (London: Fontana, 1973), pp. 226–7.

71 Bourdieu, *The Rules of Art*, pp. 216–17.

72 Wicke, 'Celebrity Material', 757.

73 Pierre Bourdieu, *Outline of a Theory of Practice*, tr. Richard Nice (Cambridge: Cambridge University Press, 1977), p. 197.

4 Disembodied Images: Authors, Authorship and Celebrity

1 W.K. Wimsatt, Jr and Monroe C. Beardsley, 'The Intentional Fallacy', in W.K. Wimsatt, Jr, *The Verbal Icon: Studies in the Meaning of Poetry* (Lexington, KY: University of Kentucky Press, 1954), p. 5.

2 Malcolm Bradbury, 'The Telling Life: Thoughts on Literary Biography', in idem, *No, Not Bloomsbury* (London, André Deutsch, 1987), p. 311.

3 Peter Washington, *Fraud: Literary Theory and the End of English* (London: Fontana, 1989), p. 50.

4 Roland Barthes, 'The Death of the Author', in idem, *Image/Music/Text*, ed. and tr. Stephen Heath (London: Fontana, 1977), p. 143.

5 Barthes, 'The Writer on Holiday', p. 29.

6 Michel Foucault, 'What is an Author?', in *Language, Counter-Memory, Practice: Selected Essays and Interviews*, ed. Donald F. Bouchard, tr. Donald F. Bouchard and Sherry Simon (Ithaca, NY: Cornell University Press, 1977), pp. 124–6. Raymond Williams also stresses the clear relationship 'between the idea of an author and the idea of "literary property," notably in the organization of authors to protect their work, by copyright and similar means, within a bourgeois market'. See Raymond Williams, *Marxism and Literature* (Oxford: Oxford University Press, 1977), p. 192.

7 Adorno and Horkheimer, 'The Culture Industry', pp. 154, 161.

8 Walter Benjamin, 'The Work of Art in the Age of Mechanical Reproduction', p. 233.

9 Gaines, *Contested Culture*, p. 212.

10 Celia Lury, *Cultural Rights: Technology, Legality and Personality* (London: Routledge, 1993), pp. 62, 51. See also the essays collected in Martha Woodmansee and Peter Jaszi (eds), *The Construction of Authorship: Textual Appropriation in Law and Literature* (Durham, NC: Duke University Press, 1994) for the ways in which copyright law has been affected by the development of new technologies.

11 Braudy, *The Frenzy of Renown*, p. 8.

12 Stuart Ewen, *All-Consuming Images: Style in Contemporary Culture* (New York: Basic Books, 1988), p. 101.

13 Lasch, *The Culture of Narcissism*, p. 231; see also Schickel, *Intimate Strangers*, p. ix.

14 Gamson, *Claims to Fame*, p. 31.

15 Richard Dyer, *Heavenly Bodies: Film Stars and Society* (New York: St. Martin's Press, 1986), pp. 11, 17.

16 Gamson, *Claims to Fame*, pp. 139, 141.

17 See, for example, Jeffrey Meyers, *Hemingway: A Biography* (New York: Harper and Row, 1985), and Kenneth S. Lynn, *Hemingway* (London: Simon and Schuster, 1987).

18 Gordon Burn, 'Deterioration of the Middle-Aged Businessman', *London Review of Books*, 9 January 1992, p. 18. See also Cheever, *The Journals*; John Cheever, *The Letters*, ed. Benjamin Cheever (London: Jonathan Cape, 1989); Susan Cheever, *Home Before Dark* (London: Weidenfeld and Nicolson, 1984); and Benjamin Cheever, *The Plagiarist* (London: Hamish Hamilton, 1992).

19 Jean Baudrillard, 'The Ecstasy of Communication', in Hal Foster (ed.), *Postmodern Culture* (London: Pluto Press, 1985), p. 130.

20 Boorstin, *The Image*, pp. 254–5.

21 Jean Baudrillard, 'Simulacra and Simulations', in idem, *Selected Writings*, ed. Mark Poster (Cambridge: Polity Press, 1988), p. 171.

22 Ernest Havemann, 'The Search for the Mysterious J.D. Salinger: The Recluse in the Rye', *Life*, 3 November 1961, pp. 130, 135, 144.

23 'Catcher Caught', *New York Post*, 21 April 1988.

24 Joyce Maynard, *At Home in the World* (London: Picador, 1998).

25 Betty Eppes, 'What I Did Last Summer', *Paris Review*, vol. 80 (Summer 1981): 221–39.

26 Nancy Jo Sales, 'Pynchon's Coming Home', *Guardian*, 6 December 1996.

27 Julian Barnes, 'The Salinger Affair', *London Review Of Books*, 27 October 1988, p. 5; James Park (ed.), *Cultural Icons* (London: Bloomsbury, 1991), p. 380.

28 Ian Hamilton, *In Search of J.D. Salinger* (London: Heinemann, 1988), pp. 156, 22, 7.

29 Rosenbaum, 'The Man in the Glass House'.

30 Steffen Hantke, 'God Save Us from Bourgeois Adventure: The Figure of the Terrorist in Contemporary American Conspiracy Fiction', *Studies in the Novel*, vol. 28, no. 2 (Summer 1996): 235.

31 Albert Camus, 'The Enigma', in idem, *Selected Essays and Notebooks*, ed. and tr. Philip Thody (Harmondsworth: Penguin, 1970), p. 144.

32 Wernick, 'Authorship and the Supplement', pp. 87, 101, 89.

33 Wernick, *Promotional Culture*, p. 193.

34 Wernick, 'Authorship and the Supplement', p. 87.

35 Pierre Bourdieu, *In Other Words: Essays Towards a Reflexive Sociology*, tr. Matthew Adamson (Cambridge: Polity Press, 1990), p. 14.

36 Ibid., p. 62; Bourdieu, *The Field of Cultural Production*, p. 59.

37 Cheever, *The Journals*, p. 330.

38 Bourdieu, 'Intellectual Field and Creative Project', p. 161.

39 Camus, 'The Enigma', p. 142.

40 Quoted in Gerald Clarke, *Capote: A Biography* (London: Hamish Hamilton, 1988), p. 499.

41 Lasch, *The Culture of Narcissism*, p. 17.

42 James Atlas, 'Confessing for Voyeurs: The Age of the Literary Memoir is Now', *New York Times Magazine*, 12 May 1996.

43 Lasch, *The Culture of Narcissism*, p. 18.

44 Norman Mailer, *Advertisements for Myself* (New York: G.P. Putnam's Sons, 1959), pp. 93, 92.

45 Ibid., pp. 233, 93.

46 James Atlas, 'Life with Mailer', *New York Times Magazine*, 9 September 1979; Marvin Mudrick, 'The Talk of the Town: Interview with Norman Mailer', *New Yorker*, 23 October 1948, p. 25.

47 Mailer, *Advertisements*, p. 279; Norman Mailer, *The Armies of the Night: History as a Novel, the Novel as History* (London: Weidenfeld and Nicolson, 1968), p. 134.

48 Mailer, *The Armies of the Night*, p. 5.

49 Ibid., p. 4.

50 Ibid., p. 6.

51 Leo Braudy, 'Introduction: Norman Mailer: The Pride of Vulnerability', in idem (ed.), *Norman Mailer: A Collection of Critical Essays* (Englewood Cliffs, NJ: Prentice-Hall, 1972), p. 2.

52 Norman Mailer, 'Of a Small and Modest Malignancy', in idem, *Pieces* (Boston, MA: Little, Brown, 1982), p. 17.

53 Norman Mailer, *The Prisoner of Sex* (London: Weidenfeld and Nicolson, 1971), p. 8.

54 Mailer, *Advertisements*, p. 154.

55 Quoted in Manso, *Mailer*, p. 285.

56 Mailer, *Advertisements*, p. 464.

57 Mailer, *The Armies of the Night*, p. 45.

58 Nicholson Baker, *U and I: A True Story* (London: Granta Books, 1991), pp. 15, 28.

59 Ibid., p. 13.

60 Ibid., pp. 67, 153–4, 173.

61   Gerald Howard, 'Mistah Perkins – He Dead: Publishing Today', *American Scholar*, vol. 58, no. 3 (Summer 1989): 366.

62   Elizabeth Young and Graham Caveney, *Shopping in Space: Essays on American 'Blank Generation' Fiction* (London: Serpent's Tail, 1992), pp. 45–7.

63   Ibid., p. 73.

64   Jay McInerney, *Brightness Falls* (London: Bloomsbury, 1992), p. 73.

65   Ibid., pp. 240–1.

66   Ibid., pp. 378–9.

67   W.P. Kinsella, *Shoeless Joe* (New York: Ballantine Books, 1982), p. 27.

68   Ibid., p. 70.

69   Schickel, *Intimate Strangers*, p. 5.

70   Paul Auster, *The New York Trilogy* (London: Faber and Faber, 1987), pp. 213, 207.

71   Ibid., p. 231.

72   Ibid., pp. 247, 236.

73   Ibid., p. 247.

74   Ibid., p. 210.

5   The Scribe of Suburbia: John Updike

1   Frederick Crews, *The Critics Bear it Away: American Fiction and the Academy* (New York: Random House, 1992), p. 168.

2   Janice Radway, 'The Book of the Month Club and the General Reader: On the Use of "Serious" Fiction', *Critical Inquiry*, vol. 14, no. 3 (Spring 1988): 532.

3   John Updike, *Picked-Up Pieces* (London: André Deutsch, 1976), p. 386.

4   Hermione Lee, 'The Trouble with Harry', *New Republic*, 24 December 1990, p. 36.

5   Joseph Kanon, 'Satire and Sensibility', *Saturday Review*, 30 September 1972, p. 78.

6   D. Keith Mano, 'Doughy Middleness', *National Review*, 30 August 1974, p. 987.

7   Elizabeth Hardwick, 'Citizen Updike', *New York Review of Books*, 18 May 1989, pp. 3, 6.

8   John Updike, *Bech at Bay: A Quasi-Novel* (London: Hamish Hamilton, 1999), p. 5.

9   John Updike, *Hugging the Shore: Essays and Criticism* (London: André Deutsch, 1984), p. 874.

10   Mano, 'Doughy Middleness', p. 987.

11   John Updike, 'Midpoint', in idem, *Midpoint and Other Poems* (New York: Knopf, 1969), pp. 3, 10.

12   John Updike, 'Afterword', in idem, *Buchanan Dying* (London: André Deutsch, 1974), p. 252.

13   Curt Suplee, 'Women, God, Sorrow and John Updike', *Washington Post*, 27 September 1979.

14   Kate Muir, 'Bestsellers for Couch Potatoes', *The Times*, 2 July 1993; William Findlay, 'A Conversation with John Updike', *Cencrastus*, 15 (New Year 1984): 36.

15   John Updike, *Odd Jobs: Essays and Criticism* (London: André Deutsch, 1992), p. 122.

16 Updike, *Picked-Up Pieces*, p. 30; Updike, *Odd Jobs*, p. 140.
17 John Updike, *Assorted Prose* (New York: Knopf, 1965), p. 264.
18 John Updike, *Self-Consciousness: Memoirs* (New York: Knopf, 1989), p. 205. Subsequent references to this book are in parentheses next to the relevant quote in the text.
19 John Updike, 'Foreword', in idem, *Olinger Stories: A Selection* (New York: Vintage, 1964), p. vi.
20 John Updike, 'Flight', in idem, *Pigeon Feathers and Other Stories* (New York: Knopf, 1962), pp. 50, 49.
21 Sanford Schwartz, 'Top of the Class', *New York Review of Books*, 24 November 1983, p. 29.
22 Sanford Pinsker, 'John Updike and the Distractions of Henry Bech, Professional Writer', *Modern Fiction Studies*, vol. 37, no. 1 (Spring 1991): 99.
23 See Philip Stevick, 'The Full Range of Updike's Prose', in Stanley Trachtenberg (ed.), *New Essays on Rabbit, Run* (Cambridge: Cambridge University Press, 1993), pp. 31–52.
24 Updike, *Bech: A Book*, p. 49.
25 Ibid., p. 50.
26 John Aldridge, *Time to Murder and Create: The Contemporary Novel in Crisis* (Freeport, NY: Books for Libraries Press, 1966), pp. 67, 74.
27 Updike, *Bech: A Book*, p. 108.
28 John Updike, *Bech is Back* (London: André Deutsch, 1983), p. 17.
29 Ibid., p. 27.
30 Updike, *Bech: A Book*, pp. 160, 169.
31 Ibid., p. 118.
32 Robert Detweiler, *John Updike* (Boston, MA: Twayne, 2nd edn 1984), p. 118.
33 Updike, *Bech: A Book*, p. 134.
34 Updike, *Bech is Back*, p. 107.
35 Updike, *Bech at Bay*, p. 224.
36 Otto Rank, *Art and Artist: Creative Urge and Personality Development*, tr. Charles Francis Atkinson (New York: Norton, 1989), pp. 407–8.
37 John Haegart, 'Autobiography as Fiction: The Example of *Stop-Time*', *Modern Fiction Studies*, vol. 33, no. 4 (Winter 1987): 622.
38 Paul John Eakin, *Touching the World: Reference in Autobiography* (Princeton, NJ: Princeton University Press, 1992), p. 201.
39 John Updike, 'Minority Report', in idem, *Midpoint*, p. 76.
40 Bourdieu, *The Rules of Art*, p. 387.
41 Jane Howard, 'Can a Nice Novelist Finish First?', *Life*, 4 November 1966, p. 74.
42 James Atlas, 'John Updike Breaks Out of Suburbia', *New York Times Magazine*, 10 December 1978.
43 Paul Grey, 'Perennial Promises Kept', *Time*, 18 October 1982, p. 81.
44 Robert Winder, 'Such Sweet Swinging', *Independent on Sunday*, 4 May 1997.
45 Schwartz, 'Top of the Class', p. 26.
46 Grey, 'Perennial Promises', p. 73.
47 Philip Seib, 'A Lovely Way Through Life: An Interview with John Updike', *Southwest Review*, vol. 66, no. 4 (Autumn 1981): 348.

6   Reality Shift: Philip Roth

1 Albert Goldman, 'Portnoy's Complaint by Philip Roth Looms as a Wild Blue Shocker and the American Novel of the Sixties', Life, 7 February 1969, pp. 58, 61–4.
2 Philip Roth, Reading Myself and Others (New York: Penguin, 2nd edn 1985), pp. 271–2.
3 Ibid., p. 273.
4 Ibid., p. 115.
5 James Lull and Stephen Hinerman, 'The Search for Scandal', in idem (eds), Media Scandals (Cambridge: Polity Press, 1997), pp. 1–33.
6 Herman Gray, 'Anxiety, Desire, and Conflict in the American Racial Imagination', in Lull and Hinerman (eds), Media Scandals, p. 90.
7 Lull and Hinerman, 'The Search for Scandal', p. 21.
8 Philip Roth, The Facts: A Novelist's Autobiography (London: Jonathan Cape, 1989), p. 4.
9 Linda Matchan, 'Philip Roth Faces "The Facts"', in George J. Searles (ed.), Conversations with Philip Roth (Jackson, MS: University Press of Mississippi, 1992), p. 238.
10 Roth, Reading Myself, pp. 83, 77.
11 Ibid., pp. 111–12.
12 Ronald Hayman, 'Philip Roth: Should Sane Women Shy Away From Him at Parties?', Sunday Times Magazine, 22 March 1981.
13 Howard Junker, 'Will This Finally Be Philip Roth's Year?', in Searles (ed.), Conversations with Philip Roth, p. 15.
14 Irving Howe, 'Philip Roth Reconsidered', Commentary, vol. 54, no. 6 (December 1972): 73, 77.
15 Roth quoted on Arena: Philip Roth, BBC2, 19 March 1993.
16 Asher Z. Milbauer and Donald G. Watson, 'An Interview with Philip Roth', in Milbauer and Watson (eds), Reading Philip Roth (Basingstoke: Macmillan, 1988), p. 3.
17 Quoted in Clive Sinclair, 'The Son is Father to the Man', in Milbauer and Watson (eds), Reading Philip Roth, p. 168.
18 Roth, The Facts, p. 6.
19 Philip Roth, Zuckerman Bound: A Trilogy and Epilogue (New York: Farrar, Straus and Giroux, 1985), p. 56. Subsequent references to this book are in parentheses next to the relevant quote in the text.
20 Roth, Reading Myself, pp. 79–80.
21 Sara Davidson, 'Talk with Philip Roth', New York Times Book Review, 18 September 1977.
22 Philip Roth, The Breast (London: Jonathan Cape, 1973), p. 74.
23 Ewen, All-Consuming Images, pp. 92–6.
24 Schickel, Intimate Strangers, pp. 5, 2–3, 28–9.
25 Joli Jenson, 'Fandom as Pathology', in Lisa A. Lewis (ed.), The Adoring Audience: Fan Culture and Popular Media (New York: Routledge, 1992), pp. 24–5.
26 Michiko Kakutani, 'Roth's Complaint', San Francisco Chronicle, 7 June 1981.
27 Roth, Reading Myself, p. 146.
28 Philip Roth, My Life as a Man (London: Jonathan Cape, 1974), p. 1.
29 Roth, The Facts, p. 6.

30 Ibid., pp. 170–2.
31 Hillel Halkin, 'How to Read Philip Roth', *Commentary*, vol. 97, no. 2 (February 1994): 45.
32 Philip Roth, *The Counterlife* (London: Jonathan Cape, 1987), pp. 214, 231.
33 Ibid., p. 288.
34 Mervyn Rothstein, 'Philip Roth and the World of "What If?"', in Searles (ed.), *Conversations with Philip Roth*, p. 199.
35 Philip Roth, *Deception: A Novel* (London: Jonathan Cape, 1990), pp. 100, 190–1.
36 Philip Roth, *Operation Shylock: A Confession* (London: Jonathan Cape, 1993), p. 87.
37 Jonathan Raban, 'A Vanity Affair', *Independent on Sunday*, 21 March 1993.
38 Philip Roth, 'A Bit of Jewish Mischief', *New York Times Book Review*, 7 March 1993.
39 Esther B. Fein, 'Philip Roth Sees Double. And Maybe Triple, Too', *New York Times*, 9 March 1993.
40 Matchan, 'Philip Roth Faces "The Facts"', p. 237.
41 Philip Roth, *I Married a Communist* (London: Vintage, 1999), p. 284.
42 Brian D. Johnson, 'Intimate Affairs', in Searles (ed.), *Conversations with Philip Roth*, p. 256.
43 Updike, *Odd Jobs*, p. 367.
44 Joseph Epstein, 'What Does Philip Roth Want?', *Commentary*, vol. 77, no. 1 (January 1984): 64.
45 Roth, *Reading Myself*, p. 129.
46 Bourdieu, *Distinction*, p. 32.

7   Silence, Exile, Cunning, and So On: Don DeLillo

1   Tom LeClair, 'Don DeLillo', in Tom LeClair and Larry McCaffery (eds), *Anything Can Happen: Interviews with Contemporary American Novelists* (Urbana, IL: University of Illinois Press, 1983), p. 79.
2   Stevick, 'The World and the Writer', p. 250.
3   Quoted in Ann Arensberg, 'Seven Seconds', *Vogue*, August 1988, p. 390.
4   'The Word, The Image, and the Gun', BBC1, 27 September 1991.
5   Fredric Jameson, *Postmodernism, Or the Cultural Logic of Late Capitalism* (London: Verso, 1991), p. 6.
6   Don DeLillo, *Great Jones Street* (London: André Deutsch, 1974), p. 186.
7   Ibid., p. 128.
8   Ibid., p. 1.
9   Ibid., pp. 231, 265.
10 Mark Osteen, '"A Moral Form to Master Commerce": The Economics of *Great Jones Street*', *Critique: Studies in Contemporary Fiction*, vol. 35, no. 4 (1994): 169.
11 DeLillo, *Great Jones Street*, pp. 2, 243.
12 Don DeLillo, *Libra* (London: Viking, 1988), p. 324.
13 Ibid., pp. 433, 62.
14 Jonathan Bing, 'The Ascendance of Don DeLillo', *Publishers' Weekly*, 11 August 1997, pp. 261, 263.

15 Don DeLillo, *Mao II* (New York: Penguin, 1992), pp. 43–4. Subsequent references to this book are in parentheses next to the relevant quote in the text.

16 Lorrie Moore, 'Look for a Writer and Find a Terrorist', *New York Times Book Review*, 9 June 1991.

17 Jameson, *Postmodernism*, p. 8.

18 Quoted in William Leith, 'Terrorism and the Art of Fiction', *Independent on Sunday*, 18 August 1991.

19 Susan Sontag, *On Photography* (London: Allen Lane: 1978), pp. 14–15.

20 Don DeLillo, 'The Power of History', *New York Times Magazine*, 7 September 1997.

21 Beckett quoted in Susan Sontag, 'The Aesthetics of Silence', in idem, *Styles of Radical Will* (London: Vintage, 1994), p. 8.

22 James Knowlson, *Damned to Fame: The Life of Samuel Beckett* (London: Bloomsbury, 1996), pp. 570–1.

23 Roland Barthes, *Camera Lucida*, tr. Richard Howard (London: Vintage, 1993), p. 59.

24 Ewen, *All-Consuming Images*, p. 98.

25 DeLillo quoted in Adam Begley, 'The Art of Fiction CXXXV: Don DeLillo', *Paris Review*, 128 (1993): 296.

26 Maria Nadotti, 'An Interview with Don DeLillo', *Salmagundi*, 100 (Fall 1993): 87.

27 See, for instance, Peter Baker, 'The Terrorist as Interpreter: *Mao II* in Postmodern Context', *Postmodern Culture* (online journal), vol. 4, no. 2 (January 1994).

28 Nadotti, 'An Interview with Don DeLillo', p. 87.

29 Gustave Le Bon, *The Crowd* (London: Ernest Benn, 1952), p. 14.

30 Marshall, *Celebrity and Power*, pp. 37, 54.

31 Serge Moscovici, *The Age of the Crowd: A Historical Treatise on Mass Psychology* (Cambridge: Cambridge University Press, 1985), p. 72.

32 Jenson, 'Fandom as Pathology', p. 9.

33 Rosenbaum, 'The Man in the Glass House'; Christian Williams, 'J.D. Salinger's Day in Court', *Washington Post*, 6 November 1982.

34 Sontag, 'Aesthetics of Silence', pp. 5, 8.

35 Ibid., pp. 5–6.

36 LeClair, 'Don DeLillo', p. 80.

37 Bing, 'The Ascendance of Don DeLillo', p. 261.

38 *Entertainment Weekly*, 9 May 1997, p. 7, cited at http://haas.berkeley.edu/~gardner/ddoddsends.html. Accessed on 10 December 1997.

8   A Star of Bohemia: Kathy Acker

1 Noel King, 'Kathy Acker on the Loose', *Meanjin*, vol. 55, no. 2 (1996): 334.

2 Young and Caveney, *Shopping in Space*, p. 7.

3 Kathy Acker, 'All Girls Together', *Guardian*, 3 May 1997.

4 Kathy Acker, *My Mother: Demonology* (New York: Pantheon, 1993), p. 214.

5 Martina Sciolino, 'Confessions of a Kleptoparasite', *Review of Contemporary Fiction*, vol. 9, no. 3 (Fall 1989): 63–4.

6 Elizabeth Wilson, 'Bohemian Love', *Theory, Culture and Society*, vol. 15, nos. 3–4 (August–November 1998): 111; Elizabeth Wilson, 'The Bohemianization of Mass Culture', *International Journal of Cultural Studies*, vol. 2, no. 1 (April 1999): 12.

7   Bourdieu, *The Field of Cultural Production*, p. 169.

8   Klaus Mann, *The Turning Point: Thirty Five Years in This Century* (London: Oswald Wolff, 1984), cited in Wilson, 'The Bohemianization of Mass Culture', p. 11.

9   Wilson, 'The Bohemianization of Mass Culture', p. 17.

10   Ibid., pp. 16–19.

11   Wilson, 'Bohemian Love', p. 125.

12   Wilson, 'The Bohemianization of Mass Culture', p. 14.

13   Rene Chun, 'Naked Breakfast, Lunch and Dinner', *New York Times*, 23 April 1995.

14   Andrew Calcutt and Richard Shephard, *Cult Fiction: A Reader's Guide* (London: Prion, 1998), p. xvi.

15   Istvan Csicsery-Ronay, Jr, 'Cyberpunk and Neuromanticism', in Larry McCaffery (ed.), *Storming the Reality Studio: A Casebook of Cyberpunk and Postmodern Fiction* (Durham, NC: Duke University Press, 1991), p. 183.

16   Leslie Dick, 'Kathy Acker', in Harriet Gilbert (ed.), *The Sexual Imagination: From Acker to Zola: A Feminist Companion* (London: Jonathan Cape, 1993), p. 3.

17   Ellen G. Friedman, '"Now Eat Your Mind": An Introduction to the Works of Kathy Acker', *Review of Contemporary Fiction*, vol. 9, no. 3 (Fall 1989): 40.

18   Cited in Glenn Harper, 'The Subversive Power of Sexual Difference in the Work of Kathy Acker', *SubStance*, 16 (1987): 44–5.

19   Jessica Berens, 'Queen of the Pirates', *Guardian*, 26 March 1996.

20   'Ack! Ack!', *Gargoyle*, 37 (Winter 1990): 17–18; Kathy Acker, 'Devoured by Myths: An Interview with Sylvère Lotringer', in idem, *Hannibal Lecter, My Father* (New York: Semiotext(e), 1991), p. 20.

21   Charles Shaar Murray, 'Piercing Memories of Acker', *Guardian*, 3 December 1997.

22   Danny Karlin, 'Antinomian Chic', *London Review of Books*, 2 June 1988, pp. 9–10.

23   Acker, *Hannibal Lecter*, pp. 142–48.

24   Wilson, 'The Bohemianization of Mass Culture', p. 13.

25   Jerrold Siegel, *Bohemian Paris: Culture, Politics, and the Boundaries of Bourgeois Life, 1830–1890* (New York: Viking, 1986), pp. 389–90, cited in Wilson, 'The Bohemianization of Mass Culture', p. 13.

26   Wilson, 'The Bohemianization of Mass Culture', p. 22.

27   Kathy Acker, *Bodies of Work: Essays* (London: Serpent's Tail, 1997), p. 102.

28   Ibid., pp. 1, 41.

29   Ibid., p. 88.

30   Kathy Acker, speech for the Artist in Society conference, Chicago, October 1994, cited at http://www.duke.edu/~wmgau/text/acker.html. Accessed on 21 May 1999.

31   Bourdieu, *The Rules of Art*, p. 148.

32   Cited in Robert Siegle, *Suburban Ambush: Downtown Writing and the Fiction of Insurgency* (Baltimore, MD: Johns Hopkins University Press, 1989), pp. 11–12.

33   'Kathy Acker Interviewed by Rebecca Deaton', *Textual Practice*, vol. 6, no. 2 (Summer 1992): 272; Ellen Friedman, 'A Conversation with Kathy Acker', *Review of Contemporary Fiction*, vol. 9, no. 3 (Fall 1989): 20–1.

34   Kathy Acker, 'A Few Notes on Two of My Books', *Review of Contemporary Fiction*, vol. 9, no. 3 (Fall 1989): 33; Acker, *Bodies of Work*, p. 101.

35   Kathy Acker, *Don Quixote, Which Was a Dream* (London: Grafton, 1986), p. 25.

36 Foucault, 'What is an Author?', p. 138.
37 Dick, 'Kathy Acker', p. 3.
38 Toril Moi, *Sexual/Textual Politics: Feminist Literary Theory* (London: Methuen, 1985), p. 126.
39 Friedman, 'A Conversation with Kathy Acker', p. 18.
40 Kathy Acker, *Empire of the Senseless* (London: Picador, 1988), p. 140.
41 Acker, 'A Few Notes', p. 36.
42 Arthur F. Redding, 'Bruises, Roses: Masochism and the Writing of Kathy Acker', *Contemporary Literature*, vol. 35, no. 2 (Summer 1994): 289.
43 Quoted in Calcutt and Shephard, *Cult Fiction*, p. 1.
44 See, for example, Linda Grant, 'In Defiance of Reason', *Guardian*, 2 December 1997.
45 Larry McCaffery, 'An Interview with Kathy Acker', *Mississippi Review*, vol. 20, nos. 1–2 (1991): 93.
46 Terry Eagleton, *The Illusions of Postmodernism* (Oxford: Blackwell, 1996), p. 70.
47 Kathy Acker, *In Memoriam to Identity* (New York: Grove Weidenfeld, 1990), p. 115.
48 King, 'Acker on the Loose', p. 338.
49 Kathy Acker, 'A Radical American Abroad', *Drama*, 160 (1986): 17, cited in Richard Walsh, *Novel Arguments: Reading Innovative American Fiction* (Cambridge: Cambridge University Press, 1995), p. 148.
50 Harper, 'The Subversive Power of Sexual Difference', p. 44.
51 Acker, *My Mother: Demonology*, pp. 223, 236.
52 Friedman, 'A Conversation with Kathy Acker', p. 17.
53 Friedman, '"Now Eat Your Mind"', p. 44.
54 Acker, 'A Few Notes', p. 35.
55 Acker, *In Memoriam to Identity*, p. 244.
56 Kathy Acker, *Portait of an Eye: Three Novels* (New York: Pantheon, 1992), pp. 24, 69.
57 Ibid., p. 86.
58 Georges Bataille, 'The Sacred', in *Visions of Excess: Selected Writings, 1927–1939*, ed. Allan Stoekl, tr. Allan Stoekl, Carl R. Lovitt and Donald M. Leslie, Jr (Minneapolis, MN: University of Minnesota Press, 1985), p. 242.
59 Hélène Cixous, 'The Laugh of the Medusa', in Elaine Marks and Isabelle de Courtivron (eds), *New French Feminisms: An Anthology* (Hemel Hempstead: Harvester, 1981), pp. 250–1.
60 'Body Bildung: Laurence A. Rickels Talks with Kathy Acker', *Artforum*, vol. 32, no. 6 (February 1994): 103.
61 Acker, *Don Quixote*, p. 107.
62 Acker, 'A Few Notes', p. 31.
63 Karlin, 'Antinomian Chic', p. 9.
64 Acker, *The Empire of the Senseless*, p. 12.
65 Siegle, *Suburban Ambush*, p. 47.
66 Young and Caveney, *Shopping in Space*, pp. 10, 13–14.
67 Bourdieu, *The Field of Cultural Production*, p. 169.
68 Acker, *Bodies of Work*, p. 84.

9 Conclusion: A 'Meet the Author' Culture

1   John Sutherland, *Fiction and the Fiction Industry* (London: Athlone Press, 1978), p. 46.
2   Jason Cowley, 'Winners in the Title Fight', *Sunday Times*, 16 August 1998.
3   Ibid.
4   The Literator, 'Books: Cover Stories', *Guardian*, 29 August 1998.
5   Robert McCrum, 'McCrum on the End of Publishing', *Observer*, 19 October 1997.
6   'In the Pay of the Jackal', *Guardian*, 7 January 1995.
7   Martin Amis, *The Information* (London: Flamingo, 1995), pp. 43, 45.
8   Ibid., p. 335.
9   Ibid., pp. 339–40.
10 Gerald Howard, 'Slouching Towards Grubnet: The Author in the Age of Publicity', *Review of Contemporary Fiction*, vol. 16, no. 1 (Spring 1996): 45.
11 Quoted in Will Self, 'Something Amiss in Amis Country', *Esquire*, April 1995, p. 73.
12 Quoted in Robert McCrum, 'Lunatics and Suits', *Guardian*, 4 March 1995.
13 Richard Todd, *Consuming Fictions: The Booker Prize and Fiction in Britain Today* (London: Bloomsbury, 1996), p. 9.
14 Ibid., p. 100.
15 Heather Zeppel and C. Michael Hall, 'Selling Art and History: Cultural Heritage and Tourism', *Journal of Tourism Studies*, vol. 2, no. 1 (May 1991): 29, 32.
16 Richard Burt, 'Getting Off the Subject: Iconoclasm, Queer Sexuality, and the Celebrity Intellectual', *Performing Arts Journal*, vol. 17, nos. 2–3 (May–September 1995): 139, 149.
17 Steven Connor, *Postmodernist Culture: An Introduction to Theories of the Contemporary* (Oxford: Basil Blackwell, 1989), p. 17.
18 Nancy K. Miller, *Getting Personal: Feminist Occasions and Autobiographical Acts* (New York: Routledge, 1991), pp. x–xi.
19 Laurie Langbauer, 'The Celebrity Economy of Cultural Studies', *Victorian Studies*, vol. 36, no. 4 (Summer 1993): 472.
20 Miller, *Getting Personal*, p. 25.
21 Burt, 'Getting Off the Subject', p. 139.
22 David Shumway, 'The Star System in Literary Studies', *PMLA*, vol. 112, no. 1 (January 1997): 87–8.
23 Janny Scott, 'At Home with Jeffrey Kutay: Whipshawing the Groves of Academe', *New York Times*, 12 December 1996.
24 Michael Gorra, 'The Autobiographical Turn: Reading the New Academic Autobiography', *Transition*, vol. 5, no. 4 (Winter 1995): 152.
25 See, for example, Peter Applebome, 'Profit Squeeze for Publishers Makes Tenure More Elusive', *New York Times*, 18 November 1996.
26 Wernick, *Promotional Culture*, p. 171.
27 Ibid., p. 177.
28 Sande Cohen, *Academia and the Luster of Capital* (Minneapolis, MN: University of Minnesota Press, 1993), p. 42.
29 Bourdieu, *The Field of Cultural Production*, p. 38.
30 Pierre Bourdieu, *Homo Academicus*, tr. Peter Collier (Cambridge: Polity Press, 1988), p. 87.

31   Wernick, *Promotional Culture*, p. 169.
32   James Sosnoski, *Token Professionals and Master Critics: A Critique of Orthodoxy in Literary Studies* (Albany, NY: State University of New York Press, 1994).
33   See Lawrence Grossberg, Cary Nelson and Paula Treichler (eds), *Cultural Studies* (New York: Routledge, 1992), p. 293. For another account of the debate, see Joel Pfister, 'The Americanization of Cultural Studies', in John Storey (ed.), *What is Cultural Studies? A Reader* (London: Edward Arnold, 1996), p. 287.
34   See, for example, Stuart Hall, 'Cultural Studies and Its Theoretical Legacies', in Grossberg et al. (eds), *Cultural Studies*, p. 285.
35   Gary Rhoades and Sheila Slaughter, 'Academic Capitalism, Managed Professionals and Supply-Side Higher Education', *Social Text*, vol. 15, no. 2 (Summer 1997): 15.
36   Wernick, *Promotional Culture*, p. 158.
37   David Lodge, *Small World: An Academic Romance* (Harmondsworth: Penguin, 1985), p. 319.
38   Wernick, *Promotional Culture*, p. 177.
39   Applebome, 'Festivals Booming'.
40   Worpole, *Reading By Numbers*, p. 22.

Index